Urban Politics After Apartheid

Urban Politics After Apartheid presents an understanding of gendered urban politics in South Africa as an interactive process. Based on long-term fieldwork in the former townships 20 years after the end of apartheid, it provides an in-depth analysis of how activists and local politicians engage with each other.

Sandrine Gukelberger contributes to the ongoing debate on urban governance by adding a new historicising perspective as an entry point into the urban governance arena, based upon the political trajectories of ward councillors and activists. Integrating urban governance studies with new perspectives on policy and social movements provides insight on the everyday events in which people engender, negotiate, and contest concepts, policies, and institutions that have been introduced under the catch-all banner of democracy. By conceptualising these events as encounters at different knowledge interfaces, the book develops a locus for an anthropology of policy, highlighting everyday negotiations in urban politics.

Urban Politics After Apartheid dissects the social life of policies such as Desmond Tutu's rainbow nation metaphor beyond national symbolism, and academic and public discourse that largely portray participation in South Africa to be weak, local politicians to be absent, and social movements to be toothless tigers. Proving the inaccuracy of these portrayals, this book will be of interest to students and scholars of South African politics, urban studies, political anthropology and political sociology.

Sandrine Gukelberger is a postdoctoral research fellow in Sociology at the Ruhr-University Bochum and holds a PhD in Social Anthropology from Bielefeld University. At the end of 2018 she will take up a new position at Konstanz University to work on youth activism in Senegal.

Contemporary African Politics

Urban Politics After Apartheid

Sandrine Gukelberger

Routledge
Taylor & Francis Group

LONDON AND NEW YORK

First published 2018 by Routledge

2 Park Square, Milton Park, Abingdon, Oxfordshire OX14 4RN
52Vanderbilt Avenue, New York, NY 10017

Routledge is an imprint of the Taylor & Francis Group, an informa business

Firstissuedinpaperback2020

British Library Cataloguing in Publication Data
A catalogue record for this book is available from the British Library

Library of Congress Cataloging in Publication Data
Names: Gukelberger, Sandrine, author.
Title: Urban politics under apartheid : whose rainbow nation? / Sandrine
   Gukelberger.
Other titles: Contemporary African politics series ; 9.
Description: New York, NY : Routledge, 2018. | Series: Contemporary
   African politics series ; 9 | Based on the author's dissertation, Universitèat
   Bielefeld, 2013.
Identifiers: LCCN 2018002277| ISBN 9781472488954 (hardback) | ISBN
   9780429490828 (ebook) | ISBN 9780429956041 (mobipocket)
Subjects: LCSH: Municipal government–South Africa–Citizen
   participation. | Cape Town (South Africa)–Politics and government–21st
   century. | Democracy–South Africa. | Civil society–South Africa. | Cape
   Town (South Africa)–Race relations.
Classification: LCC JS7537.A15 G85 2018 | DDC 320.850968–dc23
LC record available at https://lccn.loc.gov/2018002277

ISBN: 978-1-4724-8895-4 (hbk)
ISBN: 978-0-367-59001-7 (pbk)

Typeset in Times New Roman
by Taylor & Francis Books

Contents

Acknowledgements

This book is the result of a long journey, and has been supported in its different stages by various people and institutions. First of all I would like to thank the people in Cape Town who played host to me so generously and who were willing to share their intimate knowledge on everyday politics to further my understandings of urban politics after apartheid. I also want to express my gratitude to the institutional and academic support of Bielefeld University, including both of my PhD supervisors Joanna Pfaff-Czarnecka and Gudrun Lachenmann. I am especially grateful to the critical feedback and companionship of Nadine Sieveking, Stefanie Strulik, Eva Gerharz, Friso Hecker, Raphael Susewind, and Sarah Potthoff. Without the financial support of the German Academic Exchange Service and the Bielefeld Graduate School of Sociology and History, crucial fieldwork and the completion of the PhD project that forms the basis for this book would not have been possible. I would like to thank Routledge's team and reviewers, and Tom Triglone for his thorough proofreading. Finally, I dedicate this book to my family, especially to Khanya, Lucienne, and Dieter.

Abbreviations

ABA	Area Based Approach
ACDP	African Christian Democratic Party
AEC	Anti-Eviction Campaign
ANC	African National Congress
ANCWL	African National Congress Women's League
APRM	African Peer Review Mechanism
ASALGP	Australia South Africa Local Governance Partnership
AU	African Union
BEE	Black Economic Empowerment
CBOs	Community Based Organisations
CDW	Community Development Worker
CDWP	Community Development Worker Programme
Comco	The Community Coalition
COSATU	Congress of South African Trade Unions
CPF	Community Police Forum
CRM	Concerned Residents Mitchells Plain
DA	Democratic Alliance
DP	Democratic Party
DPLG	Department Provincial and Local Partnership
ECCOC	Electoral Code of Conduct Observer Commission in the Western Cape
FBW	Free Basic Water
GEAR	Growth, Employment and Redistribution
GIZ	Deutsche Gesellschaft für Internationale Zusammenarbeit (German Agency for International Cooperation)
GTZ	Deutsche Gesellschaft für Technische Zusammenarbeit (German Agency for Technical Cooperation)
ID	Independent Democrats
IDP	Integrated Development Planning
ILRIG	International Labour Resource and Information Group
KfW	Kreditanstalt für Wiederaufbau (German government-owned development bank)
NEPAD	New Partnership for Africa's Development

NGM	National Machinery for Advancing Gender Equality
NP	National Party
NNP	New National Party
PDP	Peace and Development Project
RDP	Reconstruction and Development Programme
RSL	Rosa Luxemburg Foundation
SACP	South African Communist Party
Sanco	South African National Civic Organisation
SAP	South African Police
SAPS	South African Police Service
SPF	Sector Policing Forum
TRC	Truth and Reconciliation Report
UDF	United Democratic Front Movement
UR	Urban Renewal
URP	Urban Renewal Programme
UWO	United Women's Organisation
VPUU	Violence Programme through Urban Upgrading
WNC	Women National Coalition

Glossary of terms

amandla	power (isiXhosa and isiZulu)
awethu	to us (isiXhosa)
bambanani	helping hands (isiZulu)
batho Pele	people first (isiSotho)
bredie	breed (Afrikaans)
coconut	Black acting White (township slang)
dompas	passport (Afrikaans)
eie aan onself	own to ourselves (Afrikaans)
ikewezi	morning star (isiXhosa)
imbeleko	direct translation: the act of giving birth or to carry on; name of a ritual: a goat is slaughtered as a sign of paying respect to the ancestors (isiXhosa)
imbizo	direct translation: gathering; name of a political institution that sees senior officials from all spheres of government engaging with the general public (isiZulu)
kafir	derogative word for Black African (township slang)
lobola	wedding price (isiXhosa)
model C	Black African speaking fluent English (township slang)
ngawethu	to us (isiZulu)
sangoma	natural healer (isiXhosa)
shebeen	illegal liquor shop (township slang)
skollie	direct translation: scavenger; township slang: coloured gangster (Afrikaans)
skoothondjie	lap dog (Afrikaans)
tik tik	crystal meth or methamphetamine (township slang)
tuck shop	informal small shop in the backyard of a house (township slang)
tsotsi	Black African gangster (township slang)
ubuntu	reciprocity, respect for human dignity, community cohesion and solidarity (isiXhosa and isiZulu)
umkhonto we swizwe	speer of the nation (IsiZulu and isiXhosa)

umqombothi   name of a home-brewed beer made from maize (corn), maize malt, sorghum malt, yeast and water; name of a ritual: individuals beg the ancestors to bring luck to a person, with all drinking this beer out of a single bucket (isiXhosa)

volkekunde   Afrikaans-speaking section of social anthropology taught at universities during apartheid (Afrikaans)

1 Introducing urban politics after apartheid

The legal abolition of apartheid and the declaration of the Republic of South Africa in 1994 were heralded as the end of a system that was internationally condemned for racist segregation and dehumanisation. However, the legal abolition of apartheid has not put an end to the daily experiences of these forms of discrimination and disempowerment.

South Africa has a long history of violence and conflict, from colonial and civil wars, to political repressions and racial discrimination. Following the struggle for independence and the landmark democratic elections of 1994, hope burgeoned in South Africa as it began the transformation process into a new, self-assured democratic nation.

Given the huge inequalities in living conditions, and extreme poverty affecting the majority of the population during apartheid, people attached great expectations to the transition to democracy, which would bring with it equality in rights, social justice, and dignity, along with alleviation of poverty. In this sense, shared visions of democracy that induced ideas of peace, improvement, and reconciliation in people's lives were undisputed. Fulfilling these hopes and aspirations through policy means such as decentralisation and democratisation, however, is a different proposition, as Appadurai suggests (2007: 29):

> Democracy rests on a vision. And all visions require hope. But it is not clear whether there is any deep or inherent affinity between the politics of democracy and the politics of hope.

In the first two decades of democratisation in South Africa, "the politics of hope" became entangled with "the politics of democracy". The politics of hope built upon peoples' confidence and expectations of becoming a democratic nation and converted these into encouraging political slogans such as "The people shall govern". This slogan has its roots in the pursuit of independence by the liberation movement, which was outlawed by the apartheid state in the 1950s and thereafter forced to operate underground. The political project of the liberation movement, fighting for democratic principles and a better future, naturally required hope, yet at the same time its appeal to the people rested on the assumption that these goals were also achievable. Post-1994, when the process of formalising and institutionalising democracy began, the inherent affinity between the politics of democracy and the politics of hope did indeed become much more complicated than during the apartheid era. The politics of democracy lay the anchor of democratic values in the legal framework of the nation-building process. These were subsequently formalised in the constitution and white papers on the developmental nature of the (local) state, putting it in a role to influence policies on (good) governance, public participation, and leading the creation of an informed and engaged citizenry. In the same vein, the "rainbow nation" allegory, originally coined by the renowned anti-apartheid figure Archbishop Desmond Tutu, has been widely used in public discussions as a metaphor for sustaining a vision of unity and peace amid a society that is, in reality, segregated, divided, and fractured following decades of political, economic, and racial violence. The use of slogans such as "the people shall govern in the rainbow nation" aimed to channel the hopes of the citizenry post-1994 into a formally determined and legally sustained democratisation process. The will to and effort towards building an integrated society remain an unchanged narrative in politics and policies, which at the same time are being constantly challenged to attach the hope for a better South Africa to the concrete practices and institutions that aim to bring about social justice.

This book's interest lies in the politics at Cape Town's outskirts, focusing our lens on actors and their agency, in the context of the emergence of a contested post-apartheid political and social order. In contrast to existing approaches that discuss whether democracy has been achieved in post-colonial societies, this research concentrates on the processes of "negotiating order" (Strauss 1978: 5). Toward this end, the overarching purpose of this work is to outline how people at the urban periphery participate in political processes, contribute to the search for solutions to social and economic problems, as well as deliberate on the decisions that affect their lives.

Researching urban politics took place during 18 months of fieldwork (from 2005 to 2007) in two adjacent former townships in Cape Town, where some historical context is required in order to understand important racialised inscriptions of the places.[1] In Cape Town (now the capital of the Western Cape Province, located in the south west of South Africa), apartheid legislation forced classified non-White people out of central urban areas designated for Whites only, into the areas called the Cape Flats (Report of the Department of Social Welfare 1942 [1943]). The apartheid government originally built township settlements as dormitory suburbs for classified non-White, working class people who were additionally excluded from the dominant political system. Furthermore, beginning in the 1960s, non-White citizens were forcibly removed from urban centres to these peripheral suburban regions, being racially segregated into so-called Coloured and Black African settlements (Western 1996). During the apartheid era, these townships became racialised and evolved into violent hot spots. These peripheral areas also developed into arenas where people mobilised political organisations, formed movements, and developed practices in the fight for independence. This forming of oppositions in the townships was progressively outlawed by the apartheid state. Accordingly, opponents reacted by advocating revolution rather than reform, since the apartheid system did not allow for the accommodation of oppositional activism and blocked debate on potential changes. Protest actions were criminalised, and politics became polarised, turning the struggle from a multi-faceted one into, at its peak, a two-sided battle "for or against" the state. "*Amandla*" (power) represented a popular rallying cry used by the African National Congress (ANC) and its allies during the days of resistance against apartheid. The leader of a grouping would call out "*Amandla!*", with the crowd responding "*Awethu*" (in isiXhosa) or "*Ngawethu*" (in isiZulu), meaning "to us", the South African version of the rallying cry "Power", "[...] to the People!" This expression is still associated today with struggles against oppression, and is used in different political contexts.

In this book I conceptualise former townships as spaces where different social movements, coalitions, and configurations of actors and regimes of politics operate on different levels (i.e., local, municipal, regional, state, transnational, see Alvarez 2005: 254). In what follows, I describe townships as "formerly Coloured" or "formally Black African" only in reference to the way in which they were conceived of in the past, i.e. in the context of segregation politics during the apartheid era; I do not mean them as references to racial categories in the current context in South Africa. Nonetheless, the racialisation of townships as either Coloured or Black African remains relevant in everyday life and urban politics. Despite attempts to abolish the classification of people and places, the notion of townships embodies a historical legacy that is still remembered and relevant in people's everyday lives.

Therefore, the main task of this book is to heighten our understanding of differing and sometimes competing forms of activism, an activism that follows the traditions of the common force that laid the foundations for the constitution of a (to a great extent) non-racialised post-apartheid civil society. Meanwhile, in contrast, the development of local government in the Western Cape Province within the context of a specific history of segregation helps to explain the rise of racism as an indelible political issue. It is in this context that the legacy of apartheid-era racialised laws remains alive in people's social life-worlds. Women in particular started to assert themselves more forcefully and put voice to their concerns within the male-dominated liberation movement during the 1980s, the most important achievement of the women's movement at the time being, alongside the vision of a non-racialised democratic South Africa, that of a non-sexist one. This became manifest in the establishment of a "National Machinery for Advancing Gender Equality" (NGM) to foster a women's agenda and "gendered consciousness" within parliament, government, and civil society (Albertyn 1995: 12–13; Britton

2006: 71).[2] It is important to note that women's participation on the whole, in party and movement politics, and the sharing of power has been a complex and difficult process, due to the legacy of the colonial, patriarchal, and masculine nature of South Africa's state and societal order. Women's participation in South African politics, for example, has leaned towards political party initiatives to create women's movements with party affiliations or as part of the party structure. Moreover, South African politics were influenced by the introduction of quota policies in 1994, with the ANC being the first party to implement a 30 per cent-quota for female candidates, just before the national elections in 1994.[3]

Since the abolition of apartheid, both state and non-state actors, including international players, have re-structured local government and participated in the construction of civil society. Local government representatives, and activists of the former underground liberation movement, have become engaged in newly-emerged political spaces within and outside the urban governance system. The effects of state policies and participatory measures in and around the urban governance system have been little researched from an actor-oriented perspective. Most scholars have taken a more formal state-centred standpoint and categorise South Africa as a liberal democracy, i.e. a form of representative democracy, where elected representatives hold the decision-making power, based on a constitution emphasizing the protection of individual liberties and the rights of minorities in society (freedom of speech and assembly, freedom of religion, the right to private property, right to privacy, as well as equality before the law, etc.) (du Toit/Kotzé 2011; Misra-Dexter/February 2010; Muiu 2008). A common critique of South African democracy is that government tends to limit citizen participation to voting, leaving the actual governance to politicians, i.e. participatory governance is considered weak (Misra-Dexter/February 2010; Mathekga/Buccus 2006; Williams 2006; Mattes 2002). Despite having a constitution and formal institutions that supposedly enhance public participation, "it is in the functioning of institutions, in the interpretation of the constitution and in providing access to basic rights that democracy falls short" (Misra-Dexter/February 2010: vii). Critically examining this stance, my research develops a perspective from below and concentrates on local, national, and global dynamics, power structures, and appropriations of democratic and developmental reforms. Rather than concentrating upon the state and its failures, my main argument is that people have developed different forms of agency, thus challenging the oft-touted scholarly opinion of a total absence of public participation in council politics. The main contribution of my research to this debate is located in its actor-oriented approach, which examines local meanings, actions, and opinions circulating in different translocal and transnational social spaces, and changing forms of power and agency in the former townships of Cape Town.

1.1 National and global forces re-structuring local government after apartheid

Even in modern South Africa, a majority of those previously classified as non-Whites still live in Cape Town's outskirts, while the majority of inhabitants in the better-off suburbs are White. This fact is the legacy of apartheid local governments instituting spatial segregation of the classified non-White and White population groups (Stytler 2005; Cameron 1998; Meyer 1978; Cloete 1982; Evans 1969). Spatial segregation was linked with massive inequalities in the provision of basic services such as housing, sewage, and sanitation systems, and while classified White areas were provided with electricity and water, classified non-Whites received inferior or no such services (Cameron 1998: 76–80). During the apartheid era, local governments mainly functioned as the administrative arm of the highly centralised provincial and national governments, and were defined as the lowest tier in a strict government hierarchy. This book shows how the goal of the transformation of local government was to eradicate the racial origins of apartheid government. State actors and (international) policy makers expect post-apartheid local government to work as a vehicle for the equitable redistribution of resources and therefore the successful integration of previously disadvantaged townships into a fairer South Africa. The entrenchment of local government as a "fully-fledged sphere of government" (Stytler 2005: 184) in the 1996 constitution was fundamental to this undertaking. This shift was underlined by the expression of local government as a distinctive "sphere of government", alongside national and provincial governments. The term "sphere" reflected a deliberate modification of the category of "tier" used during apartheid, in an attempt to dismantle notions of hierarchy and instil importance to local self-government.[4]

Between 1993 and 1996, the transformation of metropolitan governance was marked by debate between the political parties concerning the exact nature of the governance system. The smaller opposition parties, including the National Party (NP), the former ruling party of the apartheid government, were against a model of a unified metropolitan system (so-called "unicity"), arguing that centralised governance would create distance between residents and their representatives (Stytler 2005: 190; Cameroon 1998; Parnell et al. 2002). Conversely, the ruling party, the ANC, was in favour of unicity, which became manifest in the White Paper of Local Government (1998). The immediate aim of the metropolitan government was to overcome the racialised divisions of the past by creating integrated cities where the surplus of the central tax base would be redistributed to the previously ignored townships (Wooldridge 2002: 128–129).

In order to avoid a centralised urban governance system, two internal devolutions of power were enacted in 1998[5] that invoked "the transfer of authority to locally instituted units of government" or to special purpose authorities (Crook/Manor 1998: 7).[6] The first delegation of powers was establishing ward committees in each municipal ward, with the geographical area electing a ward councillor. Second, several wards would constitute a metropolitan sub-council.

Both institutions are supposed to create effective channels of interaction with residents, in order to foster citizenship, and strengthen "community-state" relations. Integrating previously-excluded townships into the municipal system of Cape Town has proved to be a complex task for both local government and society. To this day, there are many informal settlements, both old and new, which remain unincorporated into the system and whose size and population are unknown.

These visions and imaginations of local self-government were the points of departure for conducting research into urban politics in the two adjacent former townships of Mitchells Plain and Khayelitsha. A set of key research questions were developed to uncover how participation works, and does not work, at the urban level. The key questions also proposed to look at relationships with people outside formal and elite political institutions, paying attention to gender relations that form important structuring dimensions of power relations at the local level. With reference to urban governance at Cape Town's outskirts, the guiding questions were: How do the institutions of ward councillor, ward committee, and sub-council perform in practice and give meaning to integration and public participation? How do women and men make use of the tools provided by local government for participation and representation? How do activists interact with local government and promote people's participation? Bearing these questions in mind, not only state actors and national policy makers, but also the international donor community had great expectations for the metropolitan governments, in terms of an agenda of urban redistribution, equity, and non-racialism.

Hearn (2000: 18) highlights that foreign aid to South Africa has been mainly directed towards democracy assistance, with the main aid programmes focusing on the political transition, the consolidation of democracy, and the idea of participatory development. International assistance and funding based on multilateral and bilateral agreements has been focused on decentralising power through enhancing community participation; principles that should contribute to the increased accountability, transparency, and efficiency of governance systems.

Since the 1990s, "participatory democracy" has developed as a byword in the context of development aid.[7] Before 1990, and especially during the era of powerful modernisation-driven aid politics from the late 1950s until the 1970s, state- and nation-building in the new post-colonial societies stood at the forefront of analysis, to the detriment of local government and inclusive urban planning (Parnell 2016). However, since the fall of the Berlin Wall and the dismantling of apartheid, rhetoric and conditionalities for cooperation between the North and the South have changed (Fuster 1998). Wickramasinghe (2005) points out that in the light of neoliberal thinking, efficient governance arrangements are supposed to include associational networks of private (market), civil society, and state actors. She situates the paradigmatic positioning of a Western historical idea of civil society as being linked with an upcoming idea of good governance (ibid.: 473). "Governance" stems etymologically from the Greek verb *"kybernan"* and Greek noun *"kybernetas"*, which can be translated as "to steer" and "pilot", respectively. Moreover, the author traces the first contemporary use of the notion of "good governance" back to a World Bank report on Sub-Saharan Africa, which argued that Africa's development problem is a crisis of governance (see also Fuster 1998). Wickramasinghe argues that in general the development community was eager to implement a western historical idea of civil society in countries of the Global South, where it

> [...] inhabits a social setting shared with other normative concepts, such as governance and partnership, forming a sort of matrix made of institutions and individual and collective advocates within a material infrastructure.
>
> (ibid.: 473)

Rahnema (2001) also sees the construction of these associated networks and partnerships as discursive narratives that stem from the ideas of participation and participatory development, the buzzwords of development theory and practice in the 1990s. Hence, in order to foster more inclusive and participatory development processes, guided by the *leitmotiv* of good governance, transnationally organised governance arrangements world-wide became increasingly institutionalised at the urban level. In South Africa, these arrangements included the ward committees, which were developed in 2000 by the South African Department of Provincial and Local Government (DPLG) with the transnational assistance of the formerly-named German Agency for Technical Cooperation[8] (GTZ), and the Australia-South Africa Local Governance Partnership (ASALPG). The African Peer Review Mechanism (APRM) in 2006, part of the New Partnership for Africa's Development is another example, albeit of a South-South initiative.[9] Normatively, good governance could be summarised as the relationship between a state and civil society, and the processes and structures derived from this relationship. Decentralisation processes in South Africa post-1994 with respect to this good governance rhetoric also foresaw the possibility to enhance women's participation, in politics in particular. It is worthwhile to note that politics worldwide since 1975 have been shaped to various extents by international conferences on women's rights and their position in society. According to Lachenmann (1999) and Sarr (2007), especially through processes that took place around the Fourth World Conference on Women in Beijing in 1995, international organisations became more aware of the marginalisation of women in formal politics and began to mainstream gender equality in their policies and related funding politics. From this point on, gender seemingly became mainstreamed, and found its way into the rhetoric of participatory development and good governance.

Interestingly, Parnell (2016) demonstrates how slowly urban knowledge, bottom-up urban planning, heterogeneity within urban societies, and the pernicious effects of past modernisation-driven development assistance have become acknowledged in participatory development theory and practice. Parnell traces first mentions of a sort of urban agenda within supra-national development institutions back to the first United Nations Conference on Human Settlements in Vancouver in 1976, known as Habitat I. The author highlights that Habitat I and II (1996) were practically the only development institutions focusing on cities, with a specific eye on how development could take place in cities, although they still ignored the role that cities play in development (ibid.: 532). Indeed, the role of cities in development has only recently become a topic in Habitat III, and manifest in the Sustainable Development Goals from 2015. On this subject I subscribe to the theories of Haferburg/Huchzmeyer (2015), who state that when taking into account the historical connections between neoliberalism and globalisation, the role that cities play in directing urban development is not an entirely new empirical phenomenon. The conceptual appearance of urban governance took place at the same time as South Africa's transformation into a post-apartheid society in the 1990s, and the ways of engaging with urban dynamics coincided with the second decade of post-apartheid development, to which this book makes reference. In this context, I put the emphasis upon my ethnographic observations of governance phenomena insofar as they provide a broader understanding of urban, institutional, as well as non-formalised arrangements.

1.2 The urban governance arena and parallel spaces

Employing a governance perspective enables the researcher to put their focus on structures, mechanisms, and effects in locating interdependencies between individual, collective, and corporative actors (Benz et al. 2007: 8; Benz et al. 2010). It provides heuristic tools to identify coordination configurations, and to interpret them in terms of negotiations, networks, competitions, and communities, in order to understand their interrelationships and interactions. Informed by an ethnographic perspective I conceptualise urban governance as "everyday governance" (Blundo et al. 2006: 1), constituted in urban politics as interactions, conflicts, negotiations, alliances, and compromises. In this sense I conceive governance as an opposition to the normative-loaded concept of good governance with its binary constructions of good or bad. The task then lies rather in grasping, understanding, and explaining the particular patterns and outcomes that I observed ethnographically in Cape Town, and locating them within global processes and debates. During my fieldwork, I followed women and men on their "everyday path to democracy", observing their activities, interactions, and networking. Furthermore, an ethnographic study delves into their accounts, interpretations, and debates of issues, concepts, policies, and practices, which are related to political micro-processes in their respective neighbourhoods. Consequently, this allows an analysis of urban politics based upon differing configurations of actors and their agencies. Here, agency articulates itself in the aptitude of social actors to develop strategies to design, organise, and manage their own lives. Social actors are always able to exercise some control over situations and are never simply victims of structural constraints or at the mercy of other actors' subjective will, even in extremely unequal positions or with constraints (Giddens 1984: 15; Long/Long 1992: 23). However, position does matter, given that different positions entail varying agencies. Processes of decentralisation and democratisation thus lead to variations of agency in the sense that political and social actors are positioned and position themselves differently within competing knowledge systems and relevant power structures in the urban governance arena. My use of the concept of arena follows the work of Bierschenk (1999) and Olivier de Sardan (2005) and analyses urban governance as a spatial process.[10] In the same vein, the book follows Turner's definition of an arena as a contested and highly politicised spatial unit where "action is definite, people outspoken; the chips are down. Intrigue may be backstage, but the stage it is back of is the open arena" (1974: 134). An arena represents a complex milieu whereby various social actors with different resources and logics of action negotiate state interventions. Particularly in Chapters 4 and 5 I expand on how the state's engagement with communities developed into progressively more procedural and technical forms of institutionalising brokers. However, rather than the consequence of this process being a depolitisation of the arena, as many authors with a focus on institutionalisation processes claim (e.g. Schuurman 2009; Mouffe 2005; Wickramasinghe 2005; Feldmann 2003), it indeed turns governance into a highly politicised arena.

Furthermore, the methodological approach takes urban politics as situated interfaces (Long 1993; Lachenmann 2010) constituted by both institutionalised and non-institutionalised encounters between various actors. Focusing on interfaces turns the attention to the significance of brokers. The concept of the broker has been discussed by a wide range of scholars who point towards the "function of brokerage" (Olivier de Sardan 2006: 176).[11] In the domain of urban governance, brokerage comprises the function of interrelating and articulating the needs, aspirations, and resources "to the corresponding demands, supplies, resources, and jural order" (Swartz 1969: 199) of the (local) state and supranational institutions. Each epoch and environment with its specific circumstances engenders specific types of brokers. Consequently, the function of brokerage in the townships of Cape Town has to be considered in the light of the post-apartheid era and understood in the particular context of the urban governance arena, which is shaped by incongruent systems of values, norms, and principles, as well as unequal power relations (Merry 2005: 40).

During fieldwork, differentiation between non-institutionalised and institutionalised brokers became evident in and outside the urban governance arena. Institutionalised brokers in this arena are embodied by ward councillors (Chapter 2) and ward committees' sector representatives and Community Development Workers (Chapter 5). Public policies concerning these institutions describe their general functions as mediating between the state and disadvantaged communities and fostering public participation. Accordingly, and applying my understanding of urban governance as an interactive process, policies are not government instruments simply for imposing conditions in order to manage the population as if from "outside" or from the top-down, but are rather negotiated at the very urban level. These negotiation processes involve (local) government representatives' and policy makers' strategic initiatives on one hand, and the public's strategies on the other. Both actors perpetually shape and mediate policy, while at the same time interpret it and put it into action (Wedel et al. 2005: 34; Shore/Wright 1997: 5). The anthropology of policy as outlined by Wedel et al. (2005) is not simply concerned with representing urban or marginalised people to policy makers and government agencies:

> Its focus instead is simultaneously wider and narrower: wider insofar as its aim is to explore how the state (or to be more exact, those policy makers and professionals who are authorised to act in the state's name) relates to local populations; and narrower to the extent that its ethnographic focus tends to privilege the goal of understanding how state policies and government processes are experienced and interpreted by people at the local level, keeping in mind that anthropologists are recasting the "local" or the "community" to capture changing realities.
>
> (ibid.: 34)

Based upon the implications of the anthropology of policy, an analysis of situated interfaces then enables us to tease out specific forms of agency related to interpreting and framing policies concerned with decentralisation and democratisation at Cape Town's periphery.

Authors such as Lachenmann (2004) and Swyngedouw (2005) point out that "while [...] innovative figures of governance often offer the promise of greater democracy and grassroots empowerment [in particular women's empowerment], they also exhibit a series of contradictory tendencies" (ibid.: 1992). According to Swyngedouw, these contradictory tendencies are characterised by actually exclusionary practices of participation, entitlement, and representation. Empirically specifying these contradictory tendencies in post-apartheid urban politics, means leaving a number of people in precarious life situations out of participatory processes in urban planning, decision-making, and formal politics. In the research, I was able to identify and understand how activists who are left out of or simply stay outside the governance arena create alternative, parallel spaces alongside the governance arena that open up perspectives on distinct social ordering. According to my understanding, non-formal brokers are crucial to this distinct social ordering process and are represented by bodies such as social movements or advocacy NGOs that challenge and contest (local) state policies and the politics of service delivery. Social movements in South Africa, as elsewhere, usually act on the basis of a shared collective identity, and are constituted by voluntary, self-organised bodies that are largely autonomous from the state, yet are primarily involved in engaging with it. Social movements are far from homogeneous, and are often characterised by internal struggles between elites with advantageous access to state power, and "challengers" with restricted access to formal channels for political and social change (see Davis et al. 2005: xv). The most important feature of the social movements discussed here is that they provide for alternative interpretations of societal problems such as water and elec- tricity cut-offs, forced removals, and other violent forms of deprivation. What unites the different fractions of these social movements is their opposition to the state, which they are able to exercise without fear of repercussions because they are not bound to it by contractual requirements, unlike say NGOs (de Wet 2012: 8). Both the social movements and some advocacy NGOs highlighted in my research share the common trait that, as non-institutio- nalised brokers, they "translate up and down" (Merry 2005: 42) between those they pretend to represent and the state. Competition in the access to the resources provided by international donors allows them to act as independent, non-institutionalised brokers. Gendered exclusionary practices and other forms of asymmetries between the various forms of brokerage and activism take centre stage in this book.

1.3 Reflections on the fieldwork methodology

Societal transformations offer new positions for actors, as shown in the push for decentralisation in the post-apartheid period in South Africa. Indeed, post-1994, the inauguration of the institution of ward councillor prompted a structural change in the political system that led local politicians to seek candidacy in such posts in the local government elections of 1995 and 1996. In doing so, not only did these candidates actively shape the devolution of power between the three spheres of government (local, provincial, and national), but also the integration of the previously excluded townships into the system of local government and broader South African society. Therefore, the "people are intrinsically involved with society and actively enter into its constitution" (Layder 2006: 159), rather than being positioned outside socie- tal and political structures, i.e. "structure is not 'external' to individuals" (Giddens 1984: 25). In this sense, people are considered capable – to some degree – of resisting societal constraints and changing their social situations (ibid.: 14–16). In other words, there is an ongoing relationship between human agency and the structuration of the different social fields, which affirms the age-old debate surrounding agency-structure dualism as the epistemological problem of grounding social action as a primary effect of either agency or structure. "Society only has form, and that form only has effects on people, in so far as structure is produced and reproduced in what people do" (Giddens/ Pierson 1998: 77), i.e. "sociability in action" is equated with reproducing structure (Meyer 2009: 419). The post-apartheid local government system's aim of integrating townships into political life is inextricably linked to ward councillors' and activists' agency, given that people are not "outside" of societal structures, and vice-versa, that structure does not exist outside of people.

The instruments chosen for analysing of political change are therefore events and trajectories. In the field, I participated in around 60 political events between 2005 and 2007.[12] My work in the field was constantly improved through the collection of data in social situations where actors participated in programmes related to decentralisation (e.g. sub-council meetings, or city council meetings) or engaged in political activism (e.g. at NGO-workshops "Democracy and Active Citizenship" in Cape Town's centre, NGO-workshops on AIDS and HIV in Mitchells Plain, or a campaign and protest march against water cut-offs in Mitchells Plain). In such social situations, which can be conceptualised as "events", actors make their actions intersubjectively accountable to the public (Meyer 2009: 16), permitting us to observe how various actors negotiate meaning, sense, and context in dialogical interactions. In all chapters, series of social situations are discussed in terms of the communicative spaces where elected local politicians and activists consider how aspects and issues are to be treated as relevant. In this sense, events are conceptualised as manifestations of social spaces, where discursive battles materialise in spatially and timely confined interactive settings and where multiple relevant actors are engaged (see Spiegel 2010). Events are treated for investigative purposes as interfaces (Long/Long 1992), i.e. face-to-face encounters between various actors, whether they be ward councillors, city council officials,[13] party politicians, NGO employees, social movement activists, and so forth. In these encounters, remembering the echoes of colonial history appeared to be essential, particularly in the former townships. In both conversations and events, people made reference to historical situations, such as the forced removals, as being crucial to their personal commitments, or for their engagement or disinterest in past and present struggles. Based on these observations, there emerged another way of constructing a comprehensive view of the topics through the construction and analysis of trajectories of ward councillors and activists. When talking with people about their current political engagements, they often explained their current commitments by referring to the past, namely to specific events and experiences during the apartheid regime. It is in this sense that

> [t]he stocks of knowledge which actors draw upon in the production and reproduction of interaction are the same as those whereby they are able to make accounts, offer reasons, etc.
>
> (Giddens 1984: 29)

My research was focused on how ward councillors and activists recounted previous and current political engagements, from a present-day perspective that "conditions the selection of memories, the temporal and thematic linkage of memories, and the type of representation of the remembered experiences" (Rosenthal 2004: 50). Narrating life histories remains a process of (re-)

constructing a self that is always emergent and incomplete. Accordingly, the material used to construct the trajectories consists of recorded conversations, observation materials, fieldnotes, and other media data collected during the 18 months of fieldwork. Naturally, the actors' life circumstances changed during the course of the research, which allowed me to directly observe the making of biographies, and ask informants about their anticipations of individual and political changes. Consequently, the trajectories are composed of positions within "social spaces permanently subjected to transformations" (Bourdieu 1990: 80).

The method of constructing political trajectories allows the researcher to identify the specific circumstances under which a subject's political engagement evolved, guided by the actors' conceptions, dispositions, and agendas. In this respect, the thematic field of urban politics is grounded in actors' socialisation in certain social milieus, day-to-day political perspectives, positioning in political events, membership of political parties, etc. These biographical aspects and life strategies correspond to a set of "resource continuit[ies]" (Goffman 1986 [1974]: 287–294), encompassing specific stocks of knowledge, records of events, symbolic meanings of public functions, memberships in institutions, and so on. Consequently, resource continuity can be regarded as a constitutional element of a political trajectory shaped by the actors' positioning and their navigation between various positions. Positioning articulates a more dynamic and active anticipation of locating oneself, or the other, in a particular position or developing a new one, and is specified by Giddens thusly: "all social interaction is situated interaction [...] interaction depends upon the positioning of individual in the time-space contexts of activity" (Giddens 1984: 86, 89).[14] Furthermore, social relations involve the positioning of actors "within a social space of symbolic categories and ties" (ibid.: 89), and thus

> [p]ositionality refers to placement within a set of relations and practices that implicate identification and 'performativity' or action. It combines reference to a social position ([...] as outcome) and social positioning (as a set of practices, actions and meanings; as process).
>
> (Anthias 2002: 501, 502)

For the construction of political trajectories, the actors' self-ascribed positioning, i.e. their self-representation and positioning of others, is naturally important in allowing us to consider the ways in which an informant "at a specific point in time and space, is able to make sense of and articulate their placement in the social [political] order of things" (Anthias 2002: 501). By focusing on people, and what they say and do, or do not say and do, this research explicitly examines the urban dynamics of democratic transformation in South Africa. In order to locate the book's analysis of political events and the construction of trajectories more precisely within the socio-economic, political, and cultural landscape, the next section briefly introduces the Western Cape and its capital, Cape Town.

1.4 Contextualising the research sites: Mitchells Plain and Khayelitsha

The Western Cape Province is one of South Africa's nine provinces and is relatively distinct from the other provinces, particularly in terms of political and social cultures, and religious confession (Giliomee et al. 1998: 108–109). It is the only province where the ANC is not currently in power (and in fact where it has only governed once post-1994, from 2001 until 2006); rather, the provincial government is led by South Africa's main opposition party, the DA. Along with the Northern Cape Province, it is the only province where the officially-registered "Coloured population" is in the majority, i.e. in greater numbers than Black Africans or Whites. The three main languages spoken are Afrikaans, English, and isiXhosa,[15] and the population follow two main religions, Christianity and Islam, plus a multitude of denominations.

As in the rest of the country, the socio-economic landscape in the Western Cape is characterised by high levels of poverty and inequality (Punt et al. 2005: 7; Adelzadeh 2003; Mattes 2002). It is worth noting that South Africa is categorised by the World Bank as an upper middle-income country (World Bank 1990, 2016), despite a vast proportion of its population living in absolute or relative poverty. Indeed, the South African NGO Coalition puts it thusly; "South Africa is poor not because it is a poor country but because the economic distance between the haves and the have-nots is enormous" (South African NGO Coalition: 2002, quoted in Poswa 2008: 5). In Cape Town, these vast disparities between the wealthiest and poorest suburbs are striking, with the latter located on Cape Town's outskirts, also known as the Cape Flats. Authors such as Davis (2006: 31) go so far as to characterise the Cape Flats as one of the world's 30 mega-slums. The Cape Flats comprise pockets of dense, informal settlements, with the number of total informal dwellings estimated to have grown from 28,000 in 1993 to roughly 100,000 in 2005 (Franklin 2011).[16] The term informal settlements is used by activists, politicians and policy makers, and the residents themselves to refer primarily to the physical housing infrastructure, not the social life of its inhabitants (also known as squatters). It is important to differentiate between types of informal settlements; some, like Site C in Khayelitsha, are allocated postal addresses, and officially represented by ward councillors, and are thus integrated into the existing political system. Conversely, there are other informal settlements that the state literally possesses no knowledge of. In addition, large parts of this urban periphery are populated with fully-serviced formal settlements where residents rent council houses or own their properties. Finally, informal settlements may convert into formalised housing areas over time, as the examples of Site C in Khayelitsha or Freedom Park in Mitchells Plain show.

In summary, Cape Town's periphery is a complex and heterogeneous area that, due to its history, encompasses differently structured former townships, and this is no less the case in Mitchells Plain and Khayelitsha. Accordingly, this book does not make use of the concept of slum, given that it does not fully capture the heterogeneity of housing and income structure in the Cape Flats. Furthermore, empirically speaking, the Cape Flats are generally not categorised as slums by local actors, whether they be politicians, policy makers, or activists, rather, they speak of township, community, town, etc.

Mitchells Plain and Khayelitsha were affected differently by apartheid segregation. In the mid-1950s, the City of Cape Town was part of a wider area demarcated as a "Coloured Labour Preference Area" (Western 1996). In terms of apartheid's grand design, the area designated as Mitchells Plain, having been built in 1973 to reduce housing shortages in the "Coloured areas" during the times of forced removals, was conceived for occupation by people classified as Coloured. Furthermore, the area called Khayelitsha was officially designated for those classified as Black Africans in 1984. The creation of this township was in line with a government decision to bring the mushrooming informal settlements under control (Tshela 2002: 47). The informal settlements in both areas are characterised by the absence of municipal services, such as sanitation and sewage systems, which means that people use buckets as toilets, and collect water from standpipes provided by local government – practices deemed unsanitary even in South African governmental reports dating back to 1942 (Report of the Department of Social Welfare 1942 [1943]). When the area of Khayelitsha was officially allocated in 1984, 23,100 of the officially estimated 206,500 classified Black residents in Cape Town were migrant workers, with hostel accommodation existing for only half this number. Additionally, it was estimated that around 76,000 people lived in the Cape Flats "illegally", namely those who did not qualify to live in the Western Cape according to the principles of the "Coloured Labour Preference Area" (Cook 1986: 58). The government officially abolished this policy in 1984, and established a leasehold-system, like the one that already existed in Mitchells Plain, where people could buy houses on credit. Squatters were allowed to build shacks on "site-and-service plots", such as those which existed in Site C in Khayelitsha (Cook 1992: 127), where this fieldwork was mainly conducted. These policies had long-term effects on the make-up of Cape Town, and the Cape Flats: "what at first sight appeared to be a policy shift, allowing [B]lack residents to live permanently in the Western Cape, had important separatist consequences" (Cook 1986: 60). The construction of Khayelitsha corresponded with the idea of creating an urban spatial enclave that would be large enough to contain numbers of classified Black Africans, alongside other enclaves for all the classified Coloured people, who were also being forcibly removed.

The two areas of Mitchells Plain and Khayelitsha were incorporated into one district, Mitchells Plain, in the mid-1980s (Ndegwa et al. 2007), and since 1994, both areas are under the jurisdiction of the Cape Town Metropolitan Municipal Council. Mitchells Plain currently has around 310,500 inhabitants (Statistics South Africa, Census 2011) and consists predominantly of formal housing, with some small informal settlements, and "backyard" dwellers scattered throughout it.[17] Despite the existence of high levels of informal (local) trading, the official unemployment rate of 16 per cent is very high, with 65 per cent of households earning less than R 3,500 a month (around 300 Euros). At the time of writing most of the wards in Mitchells Plain are represented by councillors with allegiances to the DA. Khayelitsha is the country's fastest-growing area, with approximately 390,000 residents (Statistics South Africa, Census 2011) living in both formal housing structures and informal settlements. The majority of Khayelitsha's inhabitants speak isiXhosa, have migrated from either the Eastern Cape or the former Transkei, and have come to Cape Town in order to find employment and escape rural poverty (Khayelitsha Profile, Department of Provincial and Local Government 2004). The percentage of people employed in the informal economy is considered very high at 36.0 per cent, and the average annual household income of R 21,000 (around 1,780 Euro) is significantly lower in comparison to Mitchells Plain. In contrast with Mitchells Plain, at the time of writing most of the wards in Khayelitsha are represented by ANC candidates. My interest in focusing on Khayelitsha as a contrasting case can be traced back to my acquaintance with the "Special Integrated Presidential Urban Renewal Project" (URP) in 2004. The URP discusses the future prospect of merging Mitchells Plain with Khayelitsha, locally discussed as a process to turn the areas into "Khayaplain". The City of Cape Town is also working with the provincial and national government to kick-start development in disadvantaged communities, creating economic opportunities and supporting "sustainable and habitable living environments" (South Africa Yearbook 2004/2005). As a consequence of this background, constant comparison, which emerged as crucial in understanding the dynamics of negotiation, guided the fieldwork in Mitchells Plain and Khayelitsha. Small-scale comparative analysis of categories and concepts shaped the collection of data material (Glaser/Strauss 1998 [1967]: 110).[18] The method of contrasting allowed insights into perceptions and meanings of othering, knowledge production of ward councillors and activists, meanings of belonging, as well as modes of political positioning.

Many actors, whether they be urban politicians, activists, city officials, or residents in the former segregated township areas are presented in this book. By presented I do not pretend to represent these people, but use a reconstructive approach to guide an understanding of their specific perceptions and their struggles against gendered crime, drug consumption, HIV and AIDS, water and electricity cut-offs, forced removals, and malnutrition. What became evident is that these actors all share the opinion that the tremendous hardships that people in the Cape Flats have to suffer on a daily basis stem from their precarious, historically rooted, socio-economic conditions and position within society. However, where these actors differ decisively is in the ways in which they frame and how they find reason in the actual marginalised and precarious life situations in their areas – which for some, as we will see, have given rise to the utilisation of old guises of racism as a platform for doing politics.

1.5 Structure of the book

This book is organised into six chapters. It is structured in such a way that each chapter builds upon a central argument, and comments on scholarly debates concerning the political trajectories of ward councillors and activists (Chapter 2), racism and urban politics (Chapter 3), and gendering participatory urban governance and constructing parallel spaces (Chapter 4 and Chapter 5).

Chapter 2 engages in the debate on urban governance by proposing an empirically grounded typology of ward councillors and activists, teasing out their specific modes of political positioning during the period of transition from apartheid to democracy. This typology helps to systematise specific characteristics of local politicians and activists, with the types taken as an entry point into the urban governance arena. The chapter highlights the significance of being classified as a Coloured or Black African by the apartheid state, including the associated forced removals and the development of a sense of "belonging" (Pfaff-Czarnecka 2013) to a new place, segregated along racial lines. In this chapter, I conceptualise the politics of positioning as spatially and racially circumscribed. The main argument here claims that people's attachment to places and knowledge of these places have proven to be a resource for acting politically post-1994.

Chapter 3 takes up the final point of the previous chapter, namely that everyday practices of decentralisation and development processes have enabled local actors to politicise belonging in relation to their place of living. Situating political and academic debates in South Africa within the categories of race, ethnicity, and culture, the chapter disentangles some of the dynamics and convolutions of racism within the urban governance arena. The chapter situates the making and unmaking of social boundaries in specific places and examines the everyday interactions of individuals based on an approach that stresses agency and not structural determinism (Wimmer 2008: 1027). It illustrates how ward councillors locate their work in their wards according to their political mandate, and thus almost inevitably perpetuate past racial segregations in their speeches and actions in order to maintain boundaries around their place or electorate. By contrast, many activists exercise cross-boundary networks with other translocal places; for instance, when campaigning with other (international) movements across social and spatial boundaries. In this chapter I argue that urban politics are predominantly constituted by two counter-tendencies; namely, that local government reinforces racialised divides through identity politics, while civil society blurs racialised boundaries.

Chapter 4 commences by discussing the political and academic debate on developmental urban governance raised in the introduction in more detail in order to situate the chapter's approach to the anthropology of policy. Using an example of a particular sub-council meeting, an initiative that was designed to enhance urban governance, the analysis shows how activists actively oppose such formalised institutions of local government. The chapter focuses on two contentious issues – water cut-offs and women's vulnerability – that activists consider key to creating critical spaces and opening up debates to in which they might better voice and frame their demands. The analysis here aims to temper other scholars' arguments that have pointed out the weak participatory governance system in the Cape Town's townships located at the outskirts of Cape Town. I argue that while institutionalised participation is weak, popular modes of political action illustrate how activists function as non-institutionalised brokers between residents and state actors, and challenge the state's policies and decision-making processes.

Chapter 5 builds on the preceding debates concerning developmental local government and civil society spaces. In this chapter, the main interest lies in elaborating upon three ways of fostering community-state relations and state-induced public participation, namely: the Ward Committee System, established by local government; the Community Development Worker Programme, monitored by provincial government; and the African Peer Review Mechanism, facilitated by provincial government. The intention of creating these institutions was to better include civil society activists, who should act as "mouth pieces", i.e. brokers between the state and communities. This chapter also analyses intersections and linkages between these three institutions, before offering a conclusion in how they shape the functioning of urban governance. The main argument is that the integration and coordination of civil society in developmental urban governance is by its nature conflictive, owing to contested urban agendas and divergent interests, which are geographically specific and entrenched in former apartheid divisions.

Chapter 6, in conclusion, wraps up the key findings in relation to two interrelated areas of tension that surfaced in each chapter, albeit in different ways: first, intersections of historicity and social change; and second, local, national, and global dynamics. It makes a case for linking structure with ideology, agency, and subjectivity, and for connecting local, national, and global semantics, discourses, and practices. This approach reveals how local, national, and global ideas of decentralisation and participatory governance are situated in interactions, which in turn are decisively shaped by the social positioning of local actors. Finally, I develop an agenda for future research on urban governance through the lens of the anthropology of policy and social movement theories. This allows for an engagement with global comparisons while at the same time insisting that the ways in which global ideas and discursive points of reference are localised, i.e. differently in different places, are absolutely crucial.

Notes

1 During stationary fieldwork, I lived in Rocklands, a "middle-to-low-income" area in Mitchells Plain, staying with a widower and his children from January 2006 until March 2006. Through contact with relatives of this family, I subsequently had the opportunity to live in Beacon Valley, a "low-to-no-income" area for a further two months (April 2006 until June 2006). Fieldwork was concentrated in the major areas of Mitchells Plain including Beacon Valley, Lenteguer, Rocklands, Tafelsig, and Westridge. During this period, fieldwork was also taking place in Site C, one of the oldest areas within Khayelitsha. Thereafter, from July 2006 until end of March 2007 I lived in a residence in the heart of Cape Town's city centre while continuing my fieldwork in Mitchells Plain and Khayelitsha. A more

comprehensive reflection on my positionality in this field can be found in Gukelberger (2010; 2013; 2016).

2 The first area of focus of the NGM is at the parliamentary level where the so-called "Joint Monitoring Committee on the Improvement of the Quality of Life and Status of Women" was established to foster cross-party collaboration on "women's issues". The second area of focus looks at the executive branch of government, where an "Office on the Status of Women" has been introduced in order to monitor national, provincial, and local government activities, especially in those areas relevant to women. The third area of focus of the NGM is that of civil society. For the purpose of creating closer links between civil society and government, the "Women's Budget Initiative" and the "Commission for Gender Equality" were established (Britton 2006: 71–74). Since 2009, the "Office of the Status of Women" at the provincial level has been replaced by the "Department for Women, Children and People with Disabilities" (Nord 2012: 6).

3 During the time of fieldwork urban policies, politics, and polity were being shaped by strong hetero-normative conceptions of masculinity and femininity, which strengthened concepts such as gender mainstreaming and women's empowerment. This way of seeing and doing politics is based upon static male/female binary (sex) measures as proxies for 'gender'. Same-sex and intersex people have been brutally affected and "outlawed" by apartheid policies (Swarr 2009) but due to limited data, a link between the construction of specific gender aspects (same-sex, transgender and intersexuality) and anti-apartheid activism is not dealt with in this book.

4 Local self-government emerged as a concept in countries' constitutions after the Second World War, often in connection with the return to democratic rule. The prefix of the "developmental" nature of local government is not specific to South Africa, given that it is also entrenched in the Indian Constitution in 1992, included because of developmental concerns. In this regard, integration relates to the overcoming of hierarchies not only present within the social classes, but also within government. These different meanings of integration are conflated in the notion of developmental local government.

5 Municipal Structure Act 1998.

6 In the debate on decentralisation, a differentiation is frequently made between deconcentration and devolution. Deconcentration denotes the delegation of responsibility and authority to units in the same department or at the same level of government, while devolution refers to the ceding of power to lower levels (Hagberg 2009: 11).

7 Rahnema (2001: 117) traces the first appearance of "participation" and "participatory" in development vocabulary back to the late 1950s, when it was first introduced by activists and field workers. Their requests of letting the populations concerned participate in development processes were linked to the immense failures of development aid up until that point. Years later, the semantic of participation entered the jargon of the development establishment, in part to acknowledge that there was a structural crisis, as well as to send a signal that something needed to be done about it (see also Nederveen Pieterse 1998).

8 In January 2011, the German Technical Co-operation (GTZ) merged with the German Development Service (DED) and the German Capacity Building International (INWENT), to form the German International Co-operation (GIZ).

9 The notion of a role for civil society at all levels of the political system was recognised by the ruling party, the African National Congress, in its policy document, The Reconstruction and Development Programme (RDP), in 1994 (Houston et al. 2001: 1). The RDP supported urban development as a way to integrate marginalised urban areas into local administrations and jurisdictions. The RDP Ministry was later abandoned, for reasons of efficiency, according to the national

government, making way for the introduction of the neo-liberal strategy of Growth, Employment, and Redistribution (Meyns 2000; Osmanovic 2002).

10 Scholars who work on local-level politics debate the notions of "arena" and "field"; some use them interchangeably and others differentiate between both concepts (Bailey 1957: 105–106). Similarly, Swartz's (1969) and Olivier de Sardan's (2006: 190) understanding of field is that of a configuration of objective relations between positions, such as the "development field"; containing particular institutions, specific language, etc. In contrast, arena implies a more interactive setting where "real conflicts between interacting social actors occur around common stakes" (ibid.: 190).

11 For earlier literature on brokers, see Gluckman's (1949) analysis of the positioning of the headman between villagers and colonial state representatives in British Central Africa; Press's (1969) article on the genesis of "culture broker" in social science; Boissevain's (1974) study on brokers as entrepreneurs, and his differentiation between patrons and brokers; and Tinker's (1969) contribution focusing on local government (Panchayati Raj) and middlemen in India.

12 It is worth noting that presently many social anthropologists and sociologists focus on the increasingly global scale of networks and interrelations in the name of multi-sited ethnography (Marcus 1998) or global ethnography (Burawoy 2000). In this tradition, my field research paid particular attention to place-based politics, including translocal dimensions (Lachenmann 2010: 21), whilst remaining based in the surrounds of Cape Town. Despite living in a former township, my rented VW Beetle developed into a transport resource for informants and maintained an aspect of auto-"mobile research" (Schlee 1985). Because the activists involved in the research had no private vehicle, they asked me for transport rather than taking a bus or taxi, which allowed me to "follow the people'[s] path" (Marcus 1998: 106) and participate in more informal and formal events. Such occasions provided possibilities to identify who knew whom, social networks, and last but not least to meet new relevant people.

13 In what follows, the emic term "official" used by ward councillors and activists, refers to what can be best translated into clerks, i.e. non-elected employees who work in the city administration.

14 Positioning is used in these terms particularly in the fields of social anthropology and sociology, ranging from a researcher's methodological reflexions on their own positioning (Gould 2004), to an actor's positioning within the research arena (see Pfaff-Czarnecka 2009: 2). Interestingly, there exists a method explicitly called positioning analysis, derived from Anglo-Saxon discursive psychology (Hollway 1984; Harré/van Langenhove 1999). This has been elaborated upon in the context of narrating by the psychologist Bamberg (1997) (Lucius-Hoene/Deppermann 2004: 168).

15 IsiXhosa is a Southern African language spoken in South Africa and is part of the Nguni language group. It is closely related to the other major languages in this group, isiZulu, isiSwati, and isiNdebele. In 1994, isiXhosa was recognised as one of nine indigenous languages in the South African Constitution (Alexander 2003).

16 Informal settlements consist of shacks, defined by the current government as housing units constructed out of wood and metal sheets (often of a temporary nature).

17 A backyard dwelling is different from other forms of informal housing as it is built on a demarcated plot within a formal, fully-serviced housing area. One such type of backyard rental is constructed by the landlord with the intention of renting it out to tenants such as migrants or family relatives. Another type of backyard rental relates to those dwellings built by tenants on plots which they themselves have rented (see Lategan 2012: 74).

18 Primary data was gathered in face-to-face interactions using three main methods: (1) informal, unstructured, and semi-structured interviews (see Whitehead 2005, Spradley 1979); (2) participant observation and observing participation (see Spradley 1980; Wolcott 1999); and (3) organising focus group discussions (Morgan/Spanish 1984). Fieldwork was further supported by memo writing and the collection and archiving of secondary data, which included newspaper articles, political pamphlets of political parties, NGOs, and social movements, minutes of sub-council and council meetings, etc. Data material was coded following the guidelines of Grounded Theory, inspired in particular by Strauss (1987: 55–81). The interviews, focus group discussions, and social and political events are all documented in detail in my dissertation (Gukelberger 2013). This includes a comprehensive overview of all the empirical material used for the construction of the trajectories of ward councillors and activists.

References

Adelzadeh, A. (2003). *South Africa Human Development Report 2003. The Challenge of Sustainable Development in South Africa: Unlocking People's Creativity*. Oxford: University Press.

Albertyn, C. (1995). Mainstreaming Gender: National Machinery for Women in South Africa. *Center for Applied Legal Studies, Occasional Paper* 24.

Alexander, N. (2003). *Language Education Policy, National and Sub-National Identities in South Africa*. Reference Study for Language Policy Division. Strasbourg: DG IV – Directorate of School, Out-of-School and Higher Education Council of Europe.

Alvarez, S. E. (2005). The Politics of the Place, the Place of Politics: Some Forward-Looking Reflections. In: W. Harcourt and A. Escobar, eds. *Women and the Politics of Place*. Bloomfield: Kumarian Press, pp. 248–256.

Anthias, F. (2002). Where Do I Belong? Narrating Collective Identity and Translocational Positionality. *Ethnicities* 2(4), pp. 491–514.

Appadurai, A. (2007). Hope and Democracy. *Public Culture* 19(1), pp. 29–34.

Bailey, F. G. (1957). Political Change in the Kondaals. *Eastern Anthropologist 11*, pp. 88–126.

Benz, A. and Dose, N. (2010). Governance-Modebegriff oder nützliches sozialwissenschaftliches Konzept? In: A. Benz and N. Dose, eds. *Governance-Regieren in komplexen Regelsystemen: Eine Einführung*. Wiesbaden: VS Verlag, pp. 13–36.

Benz, A., Luetz, S., Schimank, U. and Simonis, G. eds. (2007). Einleitung. In: A. Benz, S. Luetz, U. Schimank and G. Simonis, eds. *Handbuch Governance. Theoretische Grundlagen und empirische Anwendungsfelder*, pp. 9–25.

Blundo, G., Olivier de Sardan, J. and Arifari, N. B. (2006). *Everyday Corruption and the State. Citizens and Public Officials in Africa*. London: Zed Books.

Boissevain, J. (1974). *Friends of Friends – Networks, Manipulators, and Coalitions*. Oxford: Basil Blackwell.

Bourdieu, P. (1990). Die Biographische Illusion. *BIOS, Zeitschrift für Biographieforschung and Oral History* 1, pp. 75–81.

Britton, H. E. (2006). South Africa Mainstreaming Gender in a New Democracy. In: G. Bauer and H. E. Britton, eds. *Women in African Parliament*. London: Lynne Rienner Publishers, pp. 59–84.

Burawoy, M. (2000). *Global Ethnography: Forces, Connections, and Imaginations in a Postmodern World*. Berkeley: University of California Press.

Cameron, R. (1998). *Democratisation of South African Local Government: A Tale of Three Cities.* Pretoria: J. L. van Schaik.

Cloete, J. J. N. (1982). *Towns and Cities. Their Government and Administration.* Pretoria: J. L. van Schaik.

Cook, G. P. (1986). Khayelitsha: Policy Change or Crisis Response. *Transactions of the Institute of British Geographers* 11(1), pp. 57–66.

Cook, G. P. (1992): Khayelitsha: New Settlement Forms in the Cape Peninsula. In: D. M. Smith, ed. *The Apartheid City and Beyond. Urbanization and Social Change in South Africa.* London: Routledge, pp. 125–135.

Crook, R. C. and Manor, J. (1998). *Democracy and Decentralisation in South Asia and West Africa: Participation, Accountability and Performance.* Cambridge: Cambridge University Press.

Davis, G. F., McAdam, D., Scott, W. R. and Zald, M. N. (2005). *Social Movements and Organisation Theory.* Cambridge: Cambridge University Press.

Davis, M. (2006). *Planet of Slums.* London: Verso.

de Wet, J. (2012). *Friends, Enemies or 'Frienemies': Development and Civil Society Organizations' Relations with the State in a Democratic South Africa. Working Paper* 367. Bielefeld University, Faculty of Sociology.

du Toit, P. and Kotzé, H. (2011). *Liberal Democracy and Peace in South Africa: The Pursuit or Freedom as Dignity.* New York: Palgrave Macmillan.

Evans, S. (1969). *New Management Committees in Local Government.* Wynberg: Juta.

Feldman, S. (2003). Paradoxes of Institutionalisation: The Depoliticisation of Bangladeshi NGOs. *Development in Practice* 13(1), pp. 5–26.

Fuster, T. (1998). *Die "Good Governance" Diskussion der Jahre 1989 bis 1994. Ein Beitrag zur jüngeren Geschichte der Entwicklungspolitik unter spezieller Berücksichtigung der Weltbank und des DAC.* Bern: Haupt.

Giddens, A. (1984). *The Constitution of Society. Outline of the Theory of Structuration.* Berkeley: University of California Press.

Giddens, A. and Pierson, C. (1998). *Conversations with Anthony Giddens. Making Sense of Modernity.* Stanford, CA: Stanford University Press.

Giliomee, H. and Schlemmer, L. (1998). *From Apartheid to Nation Building.* Cape Town: Oxford University Press

Glaser, B. G. and Strauss, A. L. (1998). *Grounded Theory. Strategien qualitativer Forschung.* Bern: Huber.

Gluckman, M. (1949). The Village Headman in British Central Africa: Introduction. *Africa* 19(2), pp. 89–94.

Gukelberger, S. (2010). Violence in the Field. *Working Paper* 367. Bielefeld University, Faculty of Sociology.

Gukelberger, S. (2013). Whose Rainbow Nation? Local Politics and Belonging in Cape Town, South Africa. Dissertation. Faculty of Sociology. Bielefeld University.

Gukelberger, S. (2016). La chercheuse en prise avec les différentes formes de violence sur le terrain au Cap. In: E. Perera and Y. Beldame, eds. *In Situ: situations, interactions et récits d'enquête.* Paris: L'Harmattan, pp. 91–100.

Goffman, E. (1986 [1974]). *Frame Analysis. An Essay on the Organization of Experience.* Boston, MA: Northeastern University Press.

Gould, J. (2004). Positionality and Scale. Methodological Issues in the Ethnography of Aid. In: J. Gould and H. Secher Marcussen, eds. *Ethnographies of Aid. Exploring Development Texts and Encounters.* Roskilde: The Graduate School International

Development Studies Roskilde University, Occasional paper, *International Development Studies* 24, pp. 266–293.

Haferburg, C. and Huchzermeyer, M. (2015). *Urban Governance in Post-Apartheid Cities: Modes of Engagement in South Africa's Metropoles*. Stuttgart: Borntraeger Science Publishers.

Hagberg, S. (2009). *Inventer et mobiliser le local. Inventing and Mobilizing the Local.* Berlin: LIT Verlag.

Harré, R. and van Langenhove, L. (1999). *Positioning Theory*. Oxford: Blackwell.

Hearn, J. (2000). Aiding Democracy? Donors and Civil Society in South Africa. *Third World Quarterly* 21(5), pp. 815–830.

Hollway, W. (1984). Gender Difference and the Production of Subjectivity. In: J. Henriques, W. Hollway, C. Urwin, C. Venn and V. Walkerdine, eds. *Changing the Subject. Psychology, Social Regulation and subjectivity*. London: Methuen, pp. 223–261.

Houston, G., Humphries, R. and Liebenberg, I. (2001). *Public Participation in Democratic Governance in South Africa*. Cape Town: Jacaranda Printers.

Lachenmann, G. (1999). Entwicklungssoziologie: Geschlechterforschung in der Entwicklungspolitik. In: B. Dausien, M. Herrmann, M. Oechsle, C. Schmerl, M. Stein-Hilbers, eds. *Erkenntnisprojekt Geschlecht. Feministische Perspektiven verwandeln Wissenschaft*. Opladen: Leske + Budrich, pp. 72–95.

Lachenmann, G. (2004). Researching Local Knowledge for Development: Current Issues. In: N. Schareika and T. Bierschenk, eds. *Lokales Wissen. Sozialwissenschaftliche Perspektiven*. Berlin: LIT Verlag, pp. 123–148.

Lachenmann, G. (2010). Methodische/methodologische Herausforderungen im Globalisierungskontext: komplexe Methoden zur Untersuchung von Interfaces von Wissenssystemen. *Working Paper* 364. Bielefeld University, Faculty of Sociology.

Lategan, L. G. (2012). *A Study of the Current South African Housing Environment with Specific Reference to Alternative Approaches to Improve Living Conditions*. Master's thesis North West University.

Layder, D. (2006). *Understanding Social Theory*. London: Sage.

Long, N. (1993). Handlung, Struktur und Schnittstelle: Theoretische Reflektionen. In: T. Bierschenk and G. Elwert, eds. *Entwicklungshilfe und ihre Folgen: Ergebnisse von Untersuchungen in Afrika*. Frankfurt am Main: Campus Verlag, pp. 217–248.

Long, N. and Long, A. (1992). *Battlefields of Knowledge. The Interlocking of Theory and Practice in Social Research and Development*. London: Routledge.

Lucius-Hoene, G. and Deppermann, A. (2004). Narrative Identität und Positionierung. *Gesprächsforschung – Online-Zeitschrift zur verbalen Interaktion*, pp. 166–183.

Marcus, G. E. (1998). *Ethnography Through Thick and Thin*. Princeton, NJ: Princeton University Press.

Mathekga, R. and Buccus, I. (2006). The Challenge of Local Government Structures in South Africa: Securing Community Participation. *Critical Dialogue – Public Participation in Review: IDASA*, pp. 11–17.

Mattes, R. (2002). South Africa: Democracy Without the People? *Journal of Democracy* 13(1), pp. 22–36.

Merry, S. E. (2005). Transnational Human Rights and Local Activism. Mapping the Middle. *American Anthropologist: Journal of the American Anthropological Association* 108(1), pp. 38–51.

Meyer, C. (2009). Ereignisethnographie und Methodologischer Situationalismus: Auswege aus der Krise der Ethnographischen Repräsentation. In: P. Berger, J.

Berrenberg, B. Fuhrmann, J. Seebode and C. Strümpel, eds. *Feldforschung. Ethnologische Zugänge zu sozialen Wirklichkeiten*. Berlin: Weissensee Verlag, pp. 401–436.

Meyer, J. (1978). *Local Government Law*. Durban: Butterworth.

Meyns, P. (2000). *Konflikt und Entwicklung im südlichen Afrika*. Opladen: Leske and Budrich.

Misra-Dexter, N. and February, J. (2010). Introduction. In: N. Misra-Dexter and J. February, eds. *Testing Democracy: Which Way Is South Africa Going?* Cape Town: ABC Press for Idasa, pp. vii–xxiv.

Morgan, D. L. and Spanish, M. T. (1984). Focus Group: A New Tool for Qualitative Research. *Qualitative Sociology* 7(3), pp. 253–270.

Mouffe, C. (2005). *On the Political*. London: Routledge.

Muiu, M. W. (2008). *The Pitfalls of Liberal Democracy and Late Nationalism in South Africa*. New York: Palgrave Macmillan.

Ndegwa, D., Horner, D., and Esau, F. (2007). The Links between Migration, Poverty and Health: Evidence from Khayelitsha and Mitchell's Plain. *Social Indicators Research* 81(2), pp. 223–234.

Nederveen Pieterse, J. (1998). My Paradigm or Yours? Alternative Development, Post-Development, Reflexive Development. *Development and Change* 29, pp. 343–373.

Nord, A. K. (2012). Mehr Geschlechtergerechtigkeit? Zur Frauenquote in Afrika. *GIGA Focus Afrika 5*. Hamburg: GIGA, pp. 2–7.

Olivier de Sardan, J.-P. (2006). *Anthropology and Development: Understanding Contemporary Social Change*. London: Zed Books.

Osmanovic, A. (2002). *Transforming South Africa*. Hamburg: Hamburg African Studies.

Parnell, S. (2016). Defining a Global Urban Development Agenda. In: *World Development 78/2*, pp. 529–540.

Parnell, S., Pieterse, E., Swilling, M. and Wooldridge, D. (2002). *Democratizing Local Government. The South African Experiment*. Cape Town: University of Cape Town.

Pfaff-Czarnecka, J. (2009). Die Sprache der Ethnizität: Südasiatische Perspektiven. In: *Bi.research. Forschungsmagazin der Universität Bielefeld*, pp. 64–68.

Pfaff-Czarnecka, J. (2013). Multiple Belonging and the Challenges to Biographic Navigation. *MMG Working Paper* 13–05. Göttingen: Max-Planck-Institut zur Erforschung multireligiöser und multiethnischer Gesellschaften.

Press, I. (1969). Ambiguity and Innovation: Implications for the Genesis of the Culture Broker. *American Anthropologist* 71, pp. 205–217.

Punt, C., Pauw, K. and van Schoor, M. (2005). A Profile of the Western Cape Province: Demographics, Poverty, Inequality and Unemployment. *PROVIDE Project Background Paper* 1(2). Elsenburg: The Provincial Decision-Making Enabling Project.

Rahnema, M. (2001). Participation. In: W. Sachs, ed. *The Development Dictionary*. London/ New York: Zed Books, pp. 116–131.

Rosenthal, G. (2004). Biographical Research. In: C. Seale, G. Gobo, J. F. Gubrium and D. Silverman, eds. *Qualitative Research Practice*. London: Sage, pp. 48–64.

Schlee, G. (1985). Mobile Forschung bei mehreren Ethnien. Kamelnomaden Nordkenias. In: H. Fischer, ed. *Feldforschungen: Berichte zur Einführung in Probleme und Methoden*. Berlin: Dietrich Reimer Verlag, pp. 203–218.

Schuurman, F. (2009). Critical Development Theory: Moving Out of the Twilight Zone. *Third World Quarterly* 30(5), pp. 831–848.

Shore, C. and Wright, S. (1997). *Anthropology of Policy: Critical Perspectives on Governance and Power*. London: Routledge.

Spiegel, A. F. (2010). *Contested Public Spheres. Female Activism and Identity Politics in Malaysia.* Wiesbaden: VS Verlag für Sozialwissenschaften.

Spradley, J. P. (1979). *The Ethnographic Interview.* New York: Holt, Rinehart and Winston.

Spradley, J. P. (1980). *Participant Observation.* New York, Chicago, IL and San Francisco, CA: Holt Rinehart & Winston.

Strauss, A. L. (1978). *Negotiations. Varieties, Contexts, Processes, and Social Order.* San Francisco, CA: Jossey-Bass.

Strauss, A. L. ([1987] 2008). *Qualitative Analysis for Social Scientists.* Cambridge: Cambridge University Press, pp. 55–81.

Stytler, N. (2005). Local Government in South Africa. Entrenching Decentralised Government. In: N. Stytler, ed. *The Place and Role of Local Government in Federal Systems.* Johannesburg: Konrad-Adenauer-Stiftung, pp. 183–220.

Swarr, A. L. (2009). "Stabane," Intersexuality, and Same-Sex Relationships in South Africa. *Feminist Studies* 35(3), pp. 524–548.

Swartz, M. J. (1969). The Middleman. In: M. J. Swartz, ed. *Local-Level Politics: Social and Cultural Perspectives.* London: University of London Press, pp. 199–204.

Swyngedouw, E. (2005). Governance Innovation and the Citizen: The Janus Face of Governance-Beyond-the-State. *Urban Studies* 42(11), pp. 1991–2006.

Tinker, H. (1969). Local Government and Politics, and Social Theory in India. In: M. J. Swartz, ed. *Local-Level Politics: Social and Cultural Perspectives.* London: University of London Press, pp. 217–226.

Tshela, B. (2002). Non-State Justice in the Post-Apartheid South Africa: A Scan of Khayelitsha. *African Sociological Review / Revue Africaine de Sociologie* 6(2), pp. 47–70.

Wedel, J., Shore, C., Feldman, G. and Lathrop, S. (2005). Toward an Anthropology of Public Policy. *Annals of the American Academy of Political and Social Science* 600, pp. 30–51.

Western, J. (1996). *Outcast Cape Town.* London: George Allen and Unwin.

Whitehead, T. L. (2005). Basic Classical Ethnographic Research Methods. Secondary Data Analysis, Fieldwork, Observation/Participant Observation, and Informal and Semi-structured Interviewing. Ethnocraphically Informed Community and Cultural Assessment Research Systems Working Paper Series. University of Maryland: Department of Anthropology.

Wickramasinghe, N. (2005). The Idea of Civil Society in the South: Imaginings, Transplants, Designs. The Deep Structure of the Present Moment. *Science & Society* 69(3), pp. 458–486.

Williams, J. J. (2006). Community Participation. Lessons from Post-Apartheid South Africa. *Policy Studies* 27(3), pp. 197–217.

Wimmer, A. (2008). Elementary Strategies of Ethnic Boundary Making. *Ethnic and Racial Studies* 31(6), pp. 1025–1055.

Wolcott, H. F. (1999). *Ethnography as a Way of Seeing.* Lanham: ALTAMIRA Press.

Wooldridge, D. (2002). Introducing Metropolitan Local Government in South Africa. In: S. Parnell, E. Pieterse, M. Swilling and D. Wooldridge, eds. *Democratizing Local Government. The South African Experiment.* Cape Town: University of Cape Town, pp. 127–140.

State and non-state sources

Government Communications. (2004). *South Africa Yearbook 2004/2005*. Pretoria: Government Communications (GCIS).

Ministry of Local Government (2009). *White Paper on Local Government*. Draft. Pretoria: Government Printer.

Poswa, N. (2008). *Characteristics of Households Living in Poverty*. Cape Town: Strategic Development Information and GIS Department.

World Bank (1990). *World Development Report 1990: Poverty*. New York: Oxford University Press.

World Bank (2016). *Poverty and Shared Prosperity 2016: Taking on Inequality*. Washington, DC: World Bank.

UNHabitat (2003). *The Challenge of Slums – Global Report on Human Settlements 2003*. London: Earthscan Publications Ltd.

Union of South Africa (1943). *Report of a Committee of Enquiry Appointed to Enquire into Conditions Existing on the Cape Flats and Similarly-Affected Areas in the Cape Division in 1942*. Pretoria: Government Printer.

Websites

Franklin, S. (2011). Enabled to Work? The Impact of Housing Subsidies on Slum Dwellers in South Africa. Unpublished manuscript. Available at: https://editorialexp ress.com/cgibin/conference/download.cgi?db_name=res_phd_2012&paperid=165 [30.09.2017].

Municipal System Act 32/2000 (Section 16, 17). Available at: http://extwprlegs1.fao. org/docs/pdf/saf93030.pdf [30.09.2017].

Sarr, F. (2007). Toutes les tâches non productives relèvent de la responsabilité des femmes. Décentralisation et Développement local au Sénégal. Available at: Le Quotidien, www.sendeveloppementlocal.com/PLUS-LOIN-AVEC-Pr-Fatou-Sarr-So w-directrice-du-laboratoire-Genre-de-l-Ucad-Toutes-les-taches-non-productives-rele vent_a634.html [30.09.2017].

South African Constitution (1996) (Section 152(1) (e)). Available at: www.justice.gov. za/legislation/constitution/SAConstitution-web-eng-07.pdf [accessed 30.09.2017].

South Africa Statistics. Census (2011). Mitchells Plain. Available at https://census2011. adrianfrith.com/place/199039 [30.09.2017].

South Africa Statistics. Census (2011). Khayelitsha. Available at https://census2011. adrianfrith.com/place/199038 [30.09.2017].

2 From a violent past to democratic futures

And then in the '90s when Nelson Mandela was released, my husband and I were sitting in front of the TV watching the gathering. We didn't think much of it, aside from saying 'now there's gonna be big trouble in this country'. We didn't bother when the NP [National Party] opened up for all races; we were two of the first people who joined the NP.[1]

(Ward councillor Ms Thompson[2], 20.12.2005)

While others were on the streets celebrating the historical moment of South Africa's liberation, Ms Thompson witnessed Mandela's release from prison on the 11th February 1990 on TV. She evidently felt threatened by Mandela's release, which initiated the end of apartheid and heralded the start of the new democratic era. She explained that this event prompted the beginning of her political career as a member of the NP, a party that had severely subjugated those classified as non-Whites for more than 50 years. Among others, Ms Thompson's trajectory in politically positioning herself in the new democratic South Africa is discussed in relation to her rationale in becoming an elected ward councillor on behalf of her former oppressor, the NP.

This chapter adopts the perspective of conferring meaning to the past from the present, i.e., relating the past to the present, by dealing with individual histories of political engagement during apartheid. Indeed, such biographic narratives of how persons situate themselves with respect to salient events, and use retrospection as a rationale to explain present agency, form part of what I would call the politics of positioning. By proposing to give attention to the political trajectories of ward councillors and activists, who are discussed through limited, selective characterisations in studies on the governance system (Parnell et al. 2002; Mhone/Edigheji 2003; Thompson/Tapscott 2010; Haferburg/Huchzermeyer 2015), I show the need to include the experiences of these people and thereby develop a historicising perspective from below in order to understand the fostered interconnections, loyalties, as well as frictions and fissions between the individual actor and larger society.

The actors' ways of positioning themselves within past and present political arenas, as well as local engagements in or rejections of specific political events, reveal relevant practices and perspectives on concepts, ideas, and values, i.e. on doing politics and even doing urban governance. Accordingly, the way in which actors recapitulate their political trajectories during the time when they were oppressed shapes how they relocate themselves in post-apartheid public spheres.

The institution of ward councillor was established post-1994, as part of the process of decentralising power and integrating townships into the political system (Cameron 1998). Ward councillors in South Africa have been the subject of many studies on democratising local government, focusing on their technical function (Stytler 2005; Wooldridge 2002), and also in relation to participatory governance (Pieterse 2002; Mogale 2003), including activism (Bond/Guliwe 2003; Habib/Kotzé 2003). At this point, it suffices to say that "developmental local government" (Chipkin 2002: 57–79) after 1994 foresaw systematically building up lines of communication and forms of cooperation with civil society in certain policy sectors, such as health and security, in order to enhance urban development in the previously disadvantaged townships. The studies discussed in Chapters 4 and 5 analyse forms of cooperation between local government representatives and activists (e.g. Millstein 2010), albeit not from the perspective of their political trajectories. Hence, this chapter contributes to the ongoing debate on urban governance by adding a new historicising perspective, based upon the political trajectories of ward councillors and activists. The trajectories relate to the construction of the political self (Pfaff-Czarnecka 2011), i.e. the modalities of individual positioning, shaped by violence, and gendered and racialised discrimination. This approach enhances this debate in illuminating the knowledge stocks of these actors, which explain somewhat the logic of the actions they follow on their path to independence. The narratives reveal the process of becoming racially classified by the apartheid state as a youth as a brutal experience of discrimination of the self. At the same time, the biographic accounts provide further insights into how these individuals tell us about the social structuration of "the wider society or social segment of which they are also part" (Arnold/Blackburn 2005: 43, quoted in Jeffrey/Dyson 2008). Based on these narratives, the chapter argues that after the segregation policies of the forced removals, people began to develop urban ties and a sense of attachment to the new places, which turned out to be resources in acting politically after 1994.

The chapter is structured into five main parts. In the first part, the focus lies on the political trajectories of four elected ward councillors as local government representatives. The second part introduces the most important aspects of being ward councillors, emphasising their perspectives on their current political mandates. Third, four trajectories of activists highlight how they contributed to shape a civil society in the ideals of strengthening principles of public debate and making the state accountable. Fourth, a discussion wraps up the differences and commonalities between ward councillors' and activists' understandings of state, society, and gendered politics, while the fifth section elaborates upon the shift from the politics of positioning to the politics of attachments or "urban ties".

2.1 Paths to becoming a ward councillor

In what follows, the trajectories of three ward councillors from Mitchells Plain and one from Khayelitsha are presented. As clarified above, these ward councillors are elaborated upon as different types, linked to modes of self-positioning in the apartheid and democratic eras. The first type of trajectory, of Mr Kal-El Check, presents itself as one marked by pragmatic considerations, as shown by the way he adjusted his position alternately between diverse right-wing and left-wing political parties. Ms Thompson represents the second type, as someone who was politically active in the 1970s, silent through the 1980s, and re-entered politics on behalf of the NP after 1994. Eventually, she formed and built her own political party. The youngest and third type, Mr Beauty, embodies a former passionate "stone-throwing" youth from the 1980s, who voted for the ANC in the first democratic elections. Shortly afterwards, disillusioned by the "romance of democracy", he became a conservative politician. While these three ward councillors only supported the liberation movement for a short period, Ms Parrow, the fourth type, can be considered as a longstanding ANC compatriot, whose political actions are deeply rooted in her activism and the liberation movement.

Given that ward councillors are elected based on their party-political programme, it is necessary to briefly sketch and contextualise the political arena. In the Western Cape, the merging of the New National Party (NNP) and the Democratic Party (DP) in July 2000, formed the Democratic Alliance (DA), thus making the NNP and DP the ruling coalition. The NNP was formerly known as the NP, which ruled throughout the apartheid era from 1948 to 1994. The DP was launched by Afrikaner intellectuals in 1989, its founding supported by reform-oriented groups and business people with British backgrounds. At its first executive meeting, it decided to campaign for a majoritarian democracy committed to non-racial democracy, civil liberties, and private enterprise (Terreblanche 2001: 79; Wood 2000: 179).

In October 2001, the NNP withdrew their support from the DA, owing to the incompatibility of political programmes, and throwing Western Cape politics into turmoil. This political feud led to re-elections, which ultimately brought the ANC to power from 2001 until 2006, for the first time since the introduction of local government elections in 1995–1996.

At the time of fieldwork, the ANC was the governing party on both a national and provincial level in the Western Cape, whereas the 2006 newly-elected local government in Cape Town was headed by a mayor allied with the DA. Interestingly, the majority of South Africans classified as Coloured by the apartheid regime voted for the NNP in the first two democratic parliamentarian elections (Mattes et al. 1996; Pickel 1997; Jensen 2001; Reddy 2001, 2015), while those previously classified as Black Africans voted overwhelmingly for the ANC. The NNP suffered a devastating defeat in the parliamentary elections of 2004, which resulted in the dismantling of their party structure directly afterwards (Schwikowski 2004). However, the majority of people in Mitchells Plain voted for the NNP in the same elections. Today, most communal politicians in Mitchells Plain are affiliated with the DA, which they joined following the NNP's dissolution. In the parliamentary elections in 2009, the DA returned as the governing party in the Western Cape Province, while the ANC won a clear majority nationwide.

The defector: from the political right to the political left

Mr Kal-El Check (KEC) was a ward councillor in low-to-no-income areas of several township communities including Mitchells Plain (Lentegeur) until 2006. He is 55 years old and portrays himself as being married according to Muslim law and the father of two children.

Mr KEC began his involvement in politics in the 1976 Soweto Uprising, as a stone-throwing youth opposing the apartheid state's repressions in the Cape Flats, targeted towards classified Black African students protesting against the use of Afrikaans as a medium of instruction. Introduced in 1974, this regulation had forced all Black schools to use Afrikaans and English as languages of instruction in a 50–50 mix, while languages such as isiXhosa were only to be used for instruction in religion, music, and physical education. Resistance to the regulation spread nationwide and persisted for several months resulting in arrests, deaths in detention, and criminal trials.[3] According to Mr KEC, in order to become part of the liberation movement, he felt obliged to reject the Coloured identity given to him by the apartheid state, and its related privileges. His perspective corresponds to those classified Coloured people who became part of the struggle against apartheid by identifying themselves as being "black of a special type" (Erasmus 2001: 19). However, his subsequent arrest and detainment by the police under severe conditions changed Mr KEC's political attitude:

> My very first time when I got locked up in jail I was a minor kid of thirteen years old, but I just got off with a few lashes, you know, six cuts, I have still the scars today. Then when I was seventeen years old I got caught up again by the security police. I was interrogated and held under what we called 'the Security System Act'. It stood for 'detention without trial' where again they kept you for an amount of days, years, months as long as they wanted – without having a fair trial on that matter. When I ended up in jail that's where my political career started because I met other activists with political experience and we exchanged ideas. I decided instead of being killed or being shot by the police, I decided to put my ideas and my living expertise for what I believed in – and this is the freedom and the justice for everybody.
>
> (Kal-El-Check, 20.12.2005)

Rather than getting more involved in anti-apartheid politics, he started to work for the apartheid government after his release. He realised that counteracting the apartheid state meant living on the edge, and "instead of being killed" he thus changed sides, leaving the liberation movement and becoming a member of the Labour Party. The Labour Party was officially accepted as a legal political party in the 1980s and was organised by classified Coloureds to ensure the representation of "Coloured affairs" in the Tricameral Parliament. Classified Black Africans were, however, not represented by this body (Terreblanche 2001).[4] In contrast to his fellow ward councillors who did not vote to support the Tricameral Parliament, Mr KEC became a member of this disputed form of government.

Mr KEC explained his engagement in local government during apartheid thus:

> I did not want to enrich myself but it was to empower myself with the knowledge, to learn how the system can be manipulated to suit not myself but the people out there without education.
>
> (Kal-El-Check, 20.12.2005)

Therefore, on the one hand he wanted to bridge the political cleavages that were tearing society apart, while he was simultaneously eager to gain the expertise and knowledge that might help stabilise the political system.

Mr KEC's trajectory shows that he rejected and then re-adopted the racialised categories of apartheid, reacting to different related opportunities and life chances. In this respect he represents a special type of politician, in contrast to many of his fellow ward councillors who were largely apolitical during apartheid, and who rejected the Labour Party as a "puppet" of Whites, and the apartheid government.

In 2002, when the NNP still existed, he switched allegiances to the DA, and in 2005 to the newly-established Independent Democrats (ID). While the NNP and the DA generally promote rather conservative values, such as support for the death penalty, the ID, in contrast, promotes itself as a newly-progressive centrist party with left-wing sensibilities.[5]

The founder of a new political party

Ms Thompson is 53 years old, married and a mother of three children, and grew up in a number of townships in the Cape Flats before moving to Mitchells Plain (Eastridge). Ms Thompson was a Muslim until she was 20 years old; she converted to Christianity after her marriage, but does not belong to any specific church.

Similar to Mr KEC's trajectory, Ms Thomson also participated as a teenager in the 1976 uprising:[6]

> I was part of the riots in '76, the uprising. So we stood with the Black Africans because they wanted freedom but after that in the '80s I deci-ded, no way, I am not interested in politics anymore. Because you fight and you fight – but what were we fighting for? And we brought the fights here to our Coloured neighbourhood that damaged our roads and everything, burnt down the shops. We suffered in the end. Generally I still

say that when the apartheid government was in power we Coloureds were much better off [...] The NP government, gave us these houses so I am proud that my children can be raised in a proper house whereas we were raised in shacks. So they have done something for me – they gave me a better house, not a shack [...] I am favouring anytime the old South Africa without apartheid but as a free person.

(Thompson, 20.12.2005)

Despite Ms Thompson talking about her initial phase of political activism against racialised inequality, she explained in the same breath why she later distanced herself from the resistance movement. As part of her reasoning, she referred to the social mobility experienced by her family and the classified Coloureds in general. She pointed to the privileged access to social services, such as housing and education, which presented classified Coloureds with the possibility of developing their areas socially and economically, in stark contrast to former Black African townships.[7] For Ms Thompson, the struggle negatively affected the classified Coloured areas, where she claimed that the battles taking place between activists and police "on her roads" destroyed the infrastructure, such as street pavements and shops. Furthermore, she mentioned elsewhere that raising her children during apartheid caused her to abandon her political involvement in the struggle against it.

During apartheid, she was neither involved in the UDF nor voted for the Labour Party, whose elected members represented the Assembly for "Coloured Affairs" in the Tricameral Parliament. She silently accepted her privileged status being classified as a Coloured, yet did not actively support the Tricameral system by voting for it – "I am favouring anytime the old South Africa, but as a free person".

Like many of her fellow ward councillors, Ms Thompson joined the NP in 1993. Later, in 1995/1996, she stood for election as a ward councillor under the banner of the NP in the first local government democratic elections in South Africa, successfully organising the NP's election campaign in Mitchells Plain. In her role as ward councillor, people in serious need did not hesitate to visit her in her private home, for instance when they were confronted with evictions, water being cut off, family-related problems, etc. In this respect, I witnessed on several occasions how her home turned into a pseudo "council office", where she offered immediate help to these people, even using her own private resources to solve their problems. When the NP suffered a devastating defeat in the parliamentary elections in 2004, which resulted in the dismantling of their party structure directly afterwards, she was unable to find another political party with a similar conservative programme. This suggests the reason why Ms Thompson then founded her own political party in 2011, "The Community Coalition" (Comco), which closely follows the (former) NP's moral issues, principles, and values: "against abortion, prohibition of prostitution and homosexuality, establishment of the death penalty" (Thompson, 12.11.2006).

The disillusioned comrade: a former UDF youth turned conservative

Mr Beauty is quite different from the urban politicians discussed here, in several aspects. At 34 years old, he is the youngest, and given that the Mitchells Plain township only came into being in the 1970s, he belongs to its first generation. Furthermore, he is the only one of the councillors who graduated from College, in 1989. He is divorced and a father of three children, who live with his ex-wife. At the time of fieldwork, he was in his second term as a ward councillor, for a ward that encompasses middle and low-income areas in Mitchells Plain (i.e. Westridge and Beacon Valley), where he grew up. From 2006 until 2011, he was the chairperson of the sub-council, a sub-municipal body.

As a classified Coloured, Mr Beauty was an active member of the youth movements of the 1980s, fighting against apartheid, and started his political activism as a stone-throwing youth supporting the UDF movement. In significant contrast to his colleagues, as a member of the ANC he also voted for the ANC in the first democratic parliamentarian elections in 1994. He also worked for the ANC government in 1999, "appointed as a National Youth Commissioner by President Thabo Mbeki", but then turned conservative for various reasons, and has since aligned himself with the DA. Since the last local government elections in 2011, Mr Beauty has become a mayoral committee member in the City Council of Cape Town and the chairperson of the DA's Cape Town Metro Region. He explains that:

> In 1994, I voted for the ANC. You know it was like the big thing, just we fought for so long and it was the whole romance of democracy and our dreams which came true [...] But then soon after that things changed. A lot of changes did occur in our country and we all had our expectations into this new found democracy. The promises that we have been made, they will create jobs for all and there will be this, there will be houses – nothing would be realised. Obviously it was unrealistic of the naïve public, sort of, to believe that things would happen overnight. But I didn't become involved in the Youth Movement and then realising that certain individuals were benefiting – everybody made sacrifices – and I couldn't ally myself with that.
>
> (Beauty, 31.01.2006)

Mr Beauty details the disparities in the promises of democracy that aimed to triumph over the autocratic apartheid system yet according to him left the majority disempowered. He highlights the hopes and expectations connected with the political shift towards democracy, although this romantisation of democracy brought him only disappointment and disillusionment, which resulted in him ending his ANC membership in 1999. When speaking of hope and expectations, Appadurai reminds us that "hope [...] is a collectively mobilised resource that defines a new terrain between the temptations of utopia and the arrogance of technocratic solutions to change" (ibid. 2007:

33). Mr Beauty's narrative emphasises the discrepancy in democratic speech between proposed technocratic solutions for change and the resulting enrichment of a few elite groups that sees inequality and marginalisation endure. Similar attitudes of the citizenry can be found in many studies on democratisation processes in post-colonial countries, where there are high expectations about democratisation on one hand, but ultimately remaining inequalities and the profiting of a few elites on the other (Beall 2013; Harvey 2008; Paley 2002; Aké 1994). This is particularly the case in South Africa, where activists similar to Mr Beauty first aligned themselves with the ANC in 1994, but later distanced themselves because "we didn't fight against apartheid only to enrich a few. We fought apartheid to ensure that all of the South Africans have freedom in this country". During fieldwork this tendency to break with the former liberation movement is more prevalent among activists than ward councillors in Mitchells Plain, many of whom never voted for the ANC. As indicated previously, with his past of ANC membership and related activism, Mr Beauty represents a unique case among ward councillors in Mitchells Plain.

The loyal ANC comrade

Ms Parrow has been elected twice as a ward councillor in one of the oldest informal settlements in Khayelitsha, located in Site C, where she has lived for 20 years. She was born in Cape Town, but left with her mother for their former "homeland" of Transkei, now known as the Eastern Cape, when her parents separated. After growing up in the Transkei, she moved as a single mother to the outskirts of Cape Town in order to live with her father. Ms Parrow explained that she was confronted with harsh circumstances in organising her everyday life during apartheid:

> My son Mapelo was born 1986 in the church in Wynberg [Cape Town] – that time was very bad in Cape Town for me and the other comrades. That time they killed the people in Nyanga [Black African township]. That time was very, very bad in Cape Town. You know, those people [in power], they burned the houses in Crossroads [Black African township], and all of us we had to flee to the church. The people of the church they took us, the people, to the churches, Anglican churches. Mapelo, you know, the last one was born in 1986 in this church – because at that time it was very, very bad. My son grew up here in Khayelitsha, he grew up here. But my other two children grew up in the Eastern Cape and then came back to Cape Town, like I did.
>
> (Parrow, 25.04.2006)

Ms Parrow shares her migratory background in which she left the Eastern Cape in order to find a job in Cape Town and to escape rural poverty, as is the case with most of those living in Khayelitsha. In contrast to the ward councillors in Mitchells Plain, she was categorised as a Black African, and therefore had no civil rights, no work permit, and limited permission to stay in urban areas such as Cape Town. She was effectively "on the run" and received refugee help from the Anglican Church; it was these experiences that lead her into politics:

> Long ago, I joined the UDF, later I came to the ANC, I joined the ANC Women's League [ANCWL][8] and its civic structures, you know [...] we [UDF] worked hand in hand with the street committees and the civics, [which operated under] Sanco. It was very, very hard.
>
> (Parrow, 04.05.2006)

Ms Parrow became a political activist involved in different civic organisations, and a member of the ANCWL. After 1994, she kept working in organisations such as the street committees as well as Sanco, on a voluntary basis. During the 1980s, "street committees"[9] were active at the lowest levels of "informal rule" in the townships, ordered beneath executive committees, known as "civics", and subsequently an umbrella body (Burman 1989: 154) termed the "South African National Civic Organisation" (Sanco). Sanco is a broad, mass-based organisation that was at its peak organising popular mobilisations against the apartheid state (Zuern 2004), and presently maintains a weak yet still significant presence as a national body with local branches. In areas such as Site C the organisation remains strong and highly active, and as is later noted, functions as a sort of gatekeeper for development projects. In Khayelitsha itself, residents of several "streets", i.e. neighbouring shacks, make up the current street committees and meet weekly to organise safety concerns and security within the neighbourhood, as well as deal with social and economic issues.

In 2000, Ms Parrow was approached by the ANC, and asked if she would become their candidate for ward councillor in her area, and subsequently won election to the post. In her capacity as a local government representative, she works closely with institutions, many of which trace their histories back to apartheid, to organise everyday life. This points to the intricate and lasting networks linking former activists of the liberation movement with ward councillors today. In contrast to the ward councillors discussed thus far, Ms Parrow's trajectory explains how she remains an activist, through her historically-shaped positioning through which she belongs to both civil society and the state, which decisively shapes her political manner of cooperation and networking between state actors, civic organisations, and NGOs.

2.2 Robin Hoods and fire fighters: the ward councillor's mandate

All the urban politicians presented thus far have established themselves, for different reasons, as opponents of the current ruling party, with the exception of Ms Parrow, who described herself as a longstanding ANC comrade. Mr KEC overtly positioned himself against the liberation movement in the 1980s by joining the Labour Party, which stood exclusively for "Coloured interests";

Ms Thompson became largely apolitical in the same period, but still accepted her status as a classified Coloured in order to gain privileged access to resources; and Mr Beauty, the youngest ward councillor, becoming fed up with his party's comrades after they ascended to power in 1994, turned his back on them. In their function as ward councillors they make the state "work" at the urban level, and therefore represent the governing state differently through the lens of their ward. In fact, the different types of ward councillor illustrated here indicate that the local state (Cockburn 1977) "is more than simply an agent of the central state" (Duncan/Goodwin 1988: 34), and that these ward councillors enhance the party-political tensions between central and local states in the specific context of the Western Cape.

There is the widespread assumption within academic circles that ward councillors in the Cape Flats post-1994 have generally had pasts as apartheid sympathisers, because

> [...] most of the Coloureds, when they voted, voted for the old apartheid party. The New National Party councillors' relationship to the rest of the organisations, which were mostly ANC-affiliated, was strained to say the least. Most of them came from the old Labour Party that participated in the apartheid endorsed Coloured politics of the House of Representatives and the Management Committees.
>
> (Jensen 2004: 189; see also Cameron 1998: 77–78)

This quote asserts that most urban politicians in the Cape Flats who became ward councillors in the post-apartheid era, almost inevitably have a background connected to the Labour Party, and thus as so-called collaborators with the old regime. However, with one exception, most ward councillors encountered in Mitchells Plain were not members of the Labour Party. In this respect, the reconstruction of trajectories offers a more differentiated perspective on political positionings towards the apartheid regime, adding the types of classified Coloureds who remained impartial to or fought against the system.

Furthermore, as will become evident in Chapters 4 and 5, another opinion about ward councillors widespread in academic studies contends that as elected agents they do not really represent their ward communities (e.g. Jensen 2004). Even in the general debate about the urban poor, elected (local) government representatives and officials are constructed as being alienated from the problems and hardships of their electorate (Das/Randeria 2015). In the case of the Cape Flats, they are constructed as the scapegoats for ward residents' dissatisfaction with their ailing infrastructure, with distrust consequently shaping the relationships between the two sides. The following quotation highlights the contrasting images of ward councillors by painting themselves as "Robin Hoods" and "fire fighters", suggesting that they are the ones that people trust and have confidence in, due to the fact that they, and they alone, address many of their issues and problems:

When you become a councillor you are not only involved on the municipal side but you are also getting involved in the personal side, in the
social side of the people. And then sometime you are confronted with
community members who tell you 'I got HIV/Aids', so you got to get
help for HIV/Aids patients and I have to refer the person to another
structure again, so it goes from the raids aspect to the social aspect to the
health aspect, and it goes on and on. And that's why I say, a councillor is
in the first line of fire and he is the last one in defence [...] If the street
lights don't work, people never phone the government, they go to the
councillor. For example the police are working under provincial government. But if something happens in the communities, they don't want the
police, they don't phone the provincial government or the minister of
police, they phone the councillor. That's why I use the expression first line
of fire within the system. And even if the government takes issues to the
people, the people refer it back to the councillors. It is very, very, complex
and also very exciting, very interesting and very challenging.

(Ward councillor Mr Kal-El Check, 15.12.2005)

In fact, all ward councillors emphasised the social side of place-based politics
in relation to their political mandate. What is striking in their descriptions is
the social component of the ward councillors' work, where they face difficult
and violent situations on a daily basis. In this sense, the restructuring of the
previous local government regime represents an attempt to establish democratic structures, particularly in townships where the social conditions are
generally regarded as the causes of violence, i.e. where "the situation is
already violent" (Coronil/Skurski 2006: 4). Mr KEC uses the metaphor of
being in the "first line of fire within the system", thus describing the ward
councillor simultaneously as the fire fighter and the target, intervening locally
and functioning as an intermediary to outside state agencies such as the
police. According to ward councillors, their main task is that of a

[...] translator, arbiter, "fixer" and so forth, [their] status might reasonably
be labelled intermediary, interpreter, mediator, or broker [...] although
"middleman" seems the most appropriate cover term for [this] species.

(Swartz, 1969: 203)

Furthermore, their self-descriptions of what it means to be a ward councillor
could be read as reflecting a sense of "deep democracy" (Appadurai 2001),
"rooted in urban context and able to mediate [...] forces in ways that benefit
the poor" (ibid.: 23). In this instance, their way of positioning themselves
within certain political spheres is to impute importance to the category of
ward councillor. Moreover, it also reflects a perception of the dynamics of
encounters at different interfaces (Long 1996: 58); on one hand with citizens,
and on the other with representatives of the different spheres of local, provincial, and national government. All ward councillors mentioned here refer

to the complexity and difficulty of balancing obligations to council, provincial, and national governments with the expectations of their ward residents. According to them, local government is closest to the people and therefore more easily reachable, which is why their constituents continuously raise all sorts of issues, including personal ones, with ward councillors. For instance, ward residents would rather report HIV and AIDS infections to councillors than to the health care system, and generally expect to be helped out of their fragile situation by them. Residents and activists expect councillors to develop the area, deliver services, and enhance participatory governance by including them in decision-making processes and so forth. This means that ward councillors are also expected to act as Robin Hoods, and accordingly their positioning is open to contest. In this sense, ward councillors acting as translators (Behrends et al. 2014) and "knowledge brokers" (Merry 2006: 40) are both vulnerable and powerful. Due to their intermediary positioning, they channel the stream of information between (local) state and ward levels, which results in their loyalties appearing ambiguous and equivocal. This is why ward councillors can easily generate suspicion among ward residents, activists, and officials, because they can be seen as being not fully in one world or the other.

Ward councillors generally depicted the complexity of their job by stating that their work overload resulted from ward residents' ignorance of how the political system functions. Given that ward residents are not knowledgeable about which government body or level is responsible for which aspect, they simply identify the ward councillor as the person responsible for everything and thus ignore what ward councillors are, in fact, supposed to do. Similarly, some scholars also state that poor residents lack specific knowledge concerning the functioning of the political system. Meanwhile, Williams (2006: 210) questions whether ward councillors are sufficiently engaged in community issues, including educating and informing their citizenry, thereby implicitly making ward councillors complicit in residents' assumed naivety and ignorance.

These views stand in stark contrast to the perceptions of ward councillors themselves, who felt that members of provincial and national government are simply not visible in the Cape Flats, which is why residents know little about them and instead approach their ward councillors:

> [...] because at the end of the day it's my picture that goes up on the posters, my little leaflets with my face goes for 'vote for me', I am representing you at local government.
>
> (Ward councillor Mr Beauty, 31.01.2006)

This is why school directors addressed conditions of overcrowded classes, broken windows, violence and drug-related problems of pupils, etc. to ward councillors rather than to the provincial government representatives responsible. In addition, as opposed to "these guys" who work in higher levels of government, are employed on a full-time basis, and receive a much higher income, ward councillors are formally considered as part-time state employees. Some ward councillors associated the Cape Flats with "hell", pointing towards the precarious socio-economic conditions and its associated problems, which obliged them to give up their second job and work as a ward councillor on a full-time basis. In contrast to the male ward councillors discussed here, it is important to note that the female ward councillors have no "fallback" in terms of a profession or paid activity apart from their post as a ward councillor. Both female ward councillors are in their fifties and raised their children during apartheid; a time that restricted their citizens' rights in terms of educational possibilities, both as classified Coloureds and as Black Africans.

As indicated previously, some studies on urban politics (Millstein 2010; Esau 2007, 2008) have acknowledged the manifold expectations of diverse actors concerning ward councillors' performance. Additionally, following the narratives of the ward councillors presented here it is necessary to pay attention to the socially-precarious and violence-prone setting where ward councillors have to work, perform, and fulfil these expectations.

> We have got three druglords in our neighbourhood. I have got one, two, three druglords just here, at the corner of the road on that side. One who is in his thirties stays at the corner over there and the other two in the next street. They work together with the gangsters, the Dixie Boys, who are all bosses now, they are the druglords, the business people. The Americans and the Fancy Boys are on the other side, and on this side and the old Tafelsig we have the Americans. But the Americans are all over now, don't worry.[10]
>
> (Ward councillor of a low-to-no-income ward in Mitchells Plain, 31.01.2006)

Crime and violence are intrinsic phenomena of the social order and reality that ward councillors in townships engage with. In contrast to their counterparts in better-off areas, the violent circumstances make it more challenging for ward councillors in townships to administrate their wards and deliver basic services effectively. The "mind-mapping" of hotspot areas as described in the aforementioned quotation is of significance for all ward councillors, enabling them to identify the common issues their ward members face as harsh reality on a daily basis, when for instance their children get involved in gangsterism or "doing drugs". This detailed knowledge could be described as a spatial orientation that locates druglords and gangs within the wider area of townships. Ward councillors need to share this perspective with their electorate in order to communicate on the same level, and this specific knowledge and habitus of the place legitimises them to work as politicians in the townships.

Moreover, the female ward councillors argued that they had to fight twice as hard to maintain their positions within the male-dominated spheres of local government, due to entrenched beliefs that men are more capable politicians than women. The gendered composition of the sub-council in Mitchells Plain underwent changes after the 2006 elections, with fewer female politicians represented, a change mirrored by local governments in South Africa in general. Despite this reduction in female ward councillors, the sub-council was headed by a woman, with Ms Thomson as the chairperson. In the local government elections of 2001 and 2006, despite women also heading many party lists for high-profile mayoral positions, only approximately one-third of all candidates were women, far from the goal of equal gender representation, as defined in the White Paper on Local Government. The same picture is seen in provincial government politics, with the ratio of 1:2 remaining virtually unchanged since the end of apartheid. Despite some gains, the overall under-representation of women in local government persists (Local Government Bulletin Vol.8/1, March 2006, 6). The ANC has addressed the under-representation of women in local government by introducing a quota policy.[11] For the 2006 local government elections, 50 per cent of the candidates fielded by the ANC were women.

Many political analysts, such as Fesseh and Jordan (2005), criticise party policies on equal gender representation in local government, the reasoning being that generally lower levels of education among women could result in representation at local government levels becoming somewhat less qualified.

> If the ANC makes the mistake of putting women on the lists on the basis that they are women, and not because they have the skills that are required, local government will sink into a deeper crisis, says political analyst Aubrey Matshiqi.
> (Local Government Bulletin 2005, cited in Fessah/Jordan, 2005)

This is a very common view of women candidates who are perceived as entering local government only due to quotas, rather than as capable politicians. This assessment of female politicians' "incompetence" corresponds with the worldwide construction of "feminised systems of ignorance" (Lachenmann 2009: 8; Strulik 2004, 2013). As shown in this chapter, this perception is not only prevalent in local government but also in civil societal spaces.

2.3 Constructing civil society

Constructing civil society in South Africa reflects a complex conjuncture of almost 50 years of anti-apartheid movements and Western ideas of a moral community, public sphere, bourgeois society, citizenship, civility, and so forth. As becomes evident, the liberation movement laid the foundation for the constitution of a (to a great extent) non-racialised, post-apartheid civil society, including such considerations as gender justice. Activists who fought against apartheid and continued their activism in various ways after independence were thereby actively engaged in the building of South African civil society:

> In short, in Africa as in other places 'civil society' evokes a polythetic clutch of signs. An all-purpose placeholder, it captures otherwise inchoate – as yet unnamed and unnameable – popular aspirations, moral concerns, sites and spaces of practice [...] Also in life on the street.
> (Comaroff/Comaroff, 1999: 4)

After 1994, civil society became not only a category referenced in the international and transnational development aid agenda but also a local byword symbolising a space for novel structures, and a "new cultural fabric" (ibid.: 3) proclaimed to be able to change existing wealth and power relations, particularly in the Cape Flats. In what follows, the political imagination of civil society is looked at from the point of view of "life on the street" by introducing four trajectories of activists, indicating how actors successively contributed to build up and strengthen social spaces after 1994 "through which a normative civil society is being moulded in [South Africa and in general in] countries in the South" (Wickramasinghe 2005: 481). As argued by Seekings (1996), the period immediately following 1994 was first characterised by a weakening of civic organisations. Until the so-called new social movements – for example, those organised around campaigns for electricity, water, AIDS, and the privatisation of government services in general – emerged after 2000, many civic groups, i.e. grassroots associations, NGOs, and community-based organisations, concentrated on fighting gender-specific crime. Therefore, the first two types of activists are those engaged in violence prevention: the first trajectory presents an activist who built up an NGO, whereas the second shows how activists are capable of embedding a German-financed urban development project in their local neighbourhood. The third trajectory shows how new social movements might be built up and integrated into local government, and the fourth gives prominence to an activist, student, and researcher focusing on advocacy.

The founder of an NGO through links to government

Ms Roosevelt lives in the ward of councillor Ms Thompson, the so-called low-to-no-income section of Mitchells Plain (Eastridge). She shares a council-owned social housing project apartment with three of her daughters, and is dependent upon government grants for her grandchildren as well as her children's irregular income. Based on her longstanding experiences of working with ex-prisoners, Ms Roosevelt developed a rehabilitation and resocialisation programme involving the Department of Correctional Services. In 2005, she founded her own NGO, the Community Correction Care Organisation in Mitchells Plain, based upon the aforementioned programme, and financed by the Department of Social Services.

Ms Roosevelt identifies the Group Areas Act as a benchmark in her life, reflecting on its consequences as resulting in her first experience of being classified as a Coloured, and socially discriminated against by the apartheid system. Being forcibly relocated to the Cape Flats, according to her, she had to adapt to the new conditions of a rude and violent neighbourhood. In this context, she spoke about her son, who was arrested by the police in the late 1980s for selling Mandrax,[12] and who ended up in prison. She maintains that the youths who were socialised under these conditions during apartheid are now those who currently violate and criminalise her neighbourhood:

[…] it is sometimes a hard way to educate your child and teach them not to get involved with crime. It is our children who do the armed robberies and murders; it's got to do a lot with poverty and living conditions.

(Roosevelt, 28.02.2006)

Ms Roosevelt identifies herself as a social and human rights activist, who looked after prisoners and their families and organised communication links between them during apartheid, and since the end of apartheid has worked for many organisations, mainly on a voluntary basis, dealing with issues related to violence in different neighbourhoods.

According to Ms Roosevelt, the South African Police Service (SAPS) has not been able to effectively handle crime in the Cape Flats in the years following 1994, when "the situation even got worse". This is why she has continued to work in this sector by assisting in the rehabilitation and reintegration of prisoners back into society. Through her work in reintegrating gang members into society, she broke with the prevalent stereotypical thinking surrounding *"skollies"*, which treats "gangsterism" as a social disease that needs to be eliminated.[13] The SAPS has decentralised its competences step-by-step beginning in 1994, a process based on the White Paper on Safety and Security (1998). This occurred particularly during the democratic transformation period, when security institutions began to build up partnerships with citizens and different civil society organisations. The decentralising of the SAPS followed a dominant mantra of participatory governance that claims the overall intention was to reposition the SAPS as a democratic state institution, thereby overcoming its apartheid past where it committed severe human rights violations. Accordingly, this aim will supposedly be achieved by the provision of participatory forums at the urban level, creating what has been called "the local ownership for securing neighbourhoods" (excerpt from an NGO brochure, cited in Mncadi 1995), i.e. security enforcement together with civilians, rather than against them, as was the case during apartheid. State and non-state actors have framed the decentralisation of the SAPS as an effort to install "peace of mind" in South Africa.

Similarly, Ms Roosevelt mentioned her activities in the Community Police Forums (CPFs), which aim to facilitate cooperation between police and communities.[14] Ms Roosevelt represents a type of activist who has never questioned her ANC membership, participating in every ANC meeting, as well as workshops and conferences organised by both the ANC and other bodies. She is well-informed about political programmes and institutions, and maintains contact with NGO activists and ANC members in Khayelitsha, following a rights-based approach to development. She is also engaged in what she referred to as a "global network" of civil societies, which structure translocal political spaces.[15] Ms Roosevelt emphasises her practical knowledge gained from longstanding community work, which she wants to be recognised by the state, explaining why she applied (unsuccessfully) for the government's Community Development Worker Programme (see Chapter 4). After her application was rejected, however, she subsequently established her own NGO, whose board members are all ANC members who fought against the apartheid system in Mitchells Plain during the 1980s.

We will meet Ms Roosevelt again in Chapter 4, showing how she has shaped non-institutionalised spaces for public participation through her activism.

The transnational activist: embedding an urban development project in the community

Mr Khumalo lived with his mother in the informal settlement in Site C, the ward where Ms Parrow has her mandate as a councillor. He grew up in the Eastern Cape (former Transkei), being classified as a Black African, and became politicised as a schoolboy, encountering the apartheid state's repression at school in the form of behavioural restrictions, violent treatment, and arrest. These experiences led him to join the underground movement, where he became an active member of the African National Congress Youth League, overseen by the Lilian Ngoyi African National Congress Branch.[16] Mr Khumalo received military training in the so-called Self Defence Unit, which was formed by "*Umkhonto We Sizwe*" combatants linked to the ANC branch in Khayelitsha, following their military training in Cuba.

After the abolition of apartheid, he initially found employment as a body-guard. Despite receiving a regular salary and enjoying full citizenship, which allowed him to move freely and leave the informal settlement of Site C, he decided to stay there, a point to which I will return later.

He was actively engaged in community-based organisations and was a leading figure in the aforementioned Sanco in Khayelitsha. Mr Khumalo heard about the Peace and Development Project (PDP) in the neighbouring township of Nyanga, and approached the GTZ directly with a request to conduct such a project in what he referred to as his community. Because of Mr Khumalo's direct contact with the GTZ, a transnational development agency, and his continued involvement as director of the subsequent project, he was perceived by the local community as a transnational activist. The PDP was initiated by the GTZ as an innovative crime prevention strategy in the two neighbouring townships Nyanga and Crossroads in February 1997 (Sub-klew 2002: 88). However, in 2003, due to the specific histories of both town-ships as well as party-political frictions and cases of corruption, the GTZ ceased the PDPs in these areas.

Before approaching the GTZ, Mr Khumalo pursued a strategy of imple-menting the project in his neighbourhood by first presenting it to the respec-tive ward councillor Ms Parrow, as well as to Sanco, and to other community based organisations.

Ms Parrow remembered Mr Khumalo as a youth involved in the ANC Youth League branch within their area during apartheid, which gained her respect. As the local government representative, she immediately supported the project together with Sanco, and both were the driving forces that helped

Mr Khumalo to establish a PDP in Site C. All the local parties involved in the project were aligned with the ANC, which may have helped to convince the GTZ to launch a PDP in Khayelitsha and thereby avoid party-political frictions or fracturing. Once working in the PDP and promoting peace within his neighbourhood, he made the decision to get rid of his gun, which had become instrumental in the exertion of power in his life:

> I thought that when talking about peace I have to forget about my fire-arm and promote this peace thing. But to be honest with you I was so scared in the first year – you know when you are used to carrying a gun with you and because before I really believed in firearms, really I did, because I told myself I am untouchable, nobody can touch me, maybe harm me. But then I thought, no man, I can't be untouchable within my community and at the same time contributing to this community, not scaring people anymore.
>
> (Khumalo, 24.04.2006)

Towards the end of this fieldwork, Mr Khumalo was fired from his position as project manager of the PDP project, due to his alleged misuse of project funds. Shortly afterwards, he started work for the Department of Social Services.

The career-changer: from new social movements to local government

Mr Jeferson is 42 years old and lives where he grew up, in the poorest area of Mitchells Plain (Tafelsig), with his partner and second son.

Similar to Mr Khumalo, he became radicalised in the apartheid struggle, but unlike Mr Khumalo he was a classified Coloured. According to Mr Jeferson, political activists like him were trained to be robbers, with the pro-ceeds from their crimes maintaining the ANC's underground activities, describing this process as the criminalisation of activism. He spent 16 years in prison for several attempted murders. Activists like him were not ready to end the revolution when the ANC-leadership went into the negotiation process at the end of apartheid.[17] Mr Jeferson's mistrust, particularly of the ANC elite, manifested itself during this period, which was also defined by trouble in the townships, and still endures in the post-apartheid era.

His resistance against the post-apartheid ANC government was renewed in the late 1990s when they introduced the "Growth, Employment and Redis-tribution" (GEAR) plan. He considers GEAR to be a neoliberal strategy, with the associated liberalisation of the economy having caused increased poverty and unemployment in the Cape Flats. His political line of argu-mentation is based on an anti-neoliberal approach that is widespread among leftist activists. Mr Jeferson argued that globalisation, retrenchments, and the casualisation[18] of employment kick-started the restructuring of various industries, especially in the textile, clothing, footwear, and agricultural sectors, as well as in public services. According to him, economic policies based on

GEAR have been accompanied by cutbacks in the government's social services expenditure in areas such as health care, education, childcare, and the provision of basic services.

Both just prior to and during the World Summit for Sustainable Development in Johannesburg in 2002, a number of new social movements came into being, for example the Anti-Privatisation Forum, the Soweto Electricity Crisis Committee, and the Landless People's Movement (Workers World News 2002: 1; Nyman 2001), all of which oppose GEAR. As indicated previously, new social movements in South Africa have historical roots in the youth and civic movements in the 1980s, as well as the labour movement in the 1970s and 1980s. According to Mr Jeferson, militancy combined with socialist perspectives became the principles of left-wing opposition to the ANC's transformation into a bourgeois party.

> It started in 2000, when government started credit control. I went to buy a box of eggs for my mum and when I got there I saw a whole contingency of army and police forces busy with evicting a family, ok, so I started questioning what is really happening there, and that is when we started mobilising the people and that's when I got involved and I became the co-coordinator of this organisation, the Anti-Eviction Campaign.
>
> (Jeferson, 24.11.2005)

Mr Jeferson's frustration with the ANC government culminated in his activities as one of the founders of a new social movement, the Anti-Eviction Campaign (AEC), in 2001. At this time he saw ward councillors per-se, because they do not serve their communities and deliver benefits to them, as enemies of social movements, which is why they needed to be attacked, even with physical violence. During fieldwork, the AEC's protest actions included those using violent means,[19] such as the burning of car tyres, to express aggression towards the post-apartheid state and the ANC.[20] Interviewees who were openly critical of the current ANC government described such actions as ironic, due to their resemblance to the former tactics used by ANC-political activists themselves in mobilising township residents to fight for access to social services during apartheid.

Mr Jeferson faced tremendous financial difficulties as an everyday activist with no regular income, and consequently left the AEC in 2005 after receiving an offer of a paid position in local government as a personal assistant to the mayoral committee member, Mr Star. Mr Star was able to convince members of the wider AEC-network, like Mr Jeferson and Ms Cube, to join his newly-formed Universal Party (UP) and run for ward councillors in the 2006 local government elections. Mr Jeferson campaigned unsuccessfully as an UP candidate in a byelection in his ward.

Mr Jeferson always differentiated between political movements and NGOs. He argues that internationally funded NGOs use the activities of social movements to acquire funds from international donors such as the Rosa

Luxemburg Foundation (RLS), which is "committed to the mainstream ideology of democratic socialism".[21] In his opinion, social movements do the groundwork, organise grassroots activities, mobilise people for protest actions and so forth, without getting paid. In contrast, NGO staff which pretend to support social movements' struggles, for instance through programmes of political education, receive a regular income.[22] Furthermore he criticises these NGOs for using social movements as sources of information for research reports for donor communities, and then failing to share their research results with the same social movements. Mr Jeferson sums up his feelings towards NGOs, thus: "So, people from NGOs you can't trust. We can't trust them and we don't trust them."

The advocacy-worker: activist, student, and researcher

Ms Smith is 34 years old and grew up in Bontheuwel, a former Coloured township bordering Mitchells Plain and Khayelitsha. She has relatives in Mitchells Plain and networks with activists from Mitchells Plain and Khayelitsha. She is a single parent of one child, who was born in 1994, "when our country was reborn". Ms Smith's own history of political activism is based on memories of personal experiences with crime and violence, including sexual abuse at home, and rapes in her neighbourhood. She left school during grade nine at the age of 19, and since that time (i.e. 1991), has been politically active in her local area, reflected by her engagement in various organisations as an ANC member. Ms Smith became involved in many different youth organisations, predominantly on a voluntary basis, with one of them being the Youth Peace Academy. In 2003, she went to Northern Ireland for one year on their behalf, in order to conduct a comparative study on youth work. When she returned, she continued with activities in her neighbourhood and became involved with Sanco.

> Through Sanco I got involved with the Congress of South African's Trade Union's (COSATU) Jobs and Poverty campaign. COSATU formed a social movement to look at issues of service delivery from the municipality. At first Sanco was very eager to become part of this campaign, but later as it came time to take action Sanco became very reluctant. I started to investigate, why the sudden shift? And discovered that Sanco was not prepared to take on the issues of people because it is in alliance with the ANC– of which we all were members – which was in control of the city at the time. I had major issues with this and in the process tried to convince this organisation and my comrades that it is about the issues of the people irrespective of who is in power.
> (Autobiography written for a job application, Ms Smith 2006)

Ms Smith left Sanco and cancelled her ANC membership shortly afterwards. Her political positioning shifted considerably, and she distanced herself from the party that she had previously identified with for more than two decades. In 2009, disappointed party members split from the ANC, essentially given their perception of the ruling party being unable to make participatory democracy possible, something that will be expanded upon in Chapters 4 and 5 of this book. Since 2006, Ms Smith has been employed by the NGO International Labour Resource and Information Group (ILRIG)[23] as a researcher, working on the subjects of local government and youth. She described the main activities of this NGO as serving labour and new social movements in their activities and protests against national and global attacks against people's livelihoods, and supporting community structures, for example through political education. She saw ILRIG's deeply entrenched idea of promoting socialism in its educational work with marginalised areas as a response to current government policy and related globalisation processes.

Parallel to her researcher position, in 2007 she began a Bachelor degree in social sciences at the University of the Western Cape, in order "to further develop [the] skill of working with people".

2.4 Historical webs, conflicts, and opportunities

In a similar way to ward councillors, the trajectories of activists illustrate how their repositioning in democratic political spheres is shaped by historical entanglements, conflicts, and opportunities.

First of all, the activists' and ward councillors' accounts show how their past definitely affects the way in which they imagine post-apartheid statehood in relation to their place in it. However, in contrast to ward councillors, all activists opposed the former apartheid system and were all involved in the struggle against it. Moreover, they all referred to the apartheid legal system, and particularly to the Group Areas Act, as the crucial state intervention that racially segregated and categorised the South African landscape into rich and poor territories. Ward councillors and activists pointed to the racialised divisions in this context: experiences of forced removals, discrimination at school, going underground, imprisonments, rapes, being on the run, differing housing provisions for classified Coloureds and Black Africans, and forging "territories of difference" (Escobar 2008: 25).[24] Indeed, the segregated provision of housing functions as a lasting spatial and racialised marker through which the apartheid state remains symbolically visible, and through it, is remembered, embodied, and materialised. This symbolic dimension is also reflected in the way that residents and ward councillors highlight the spatial divisions through references to the different cultures and languages that characterise different regions. Moreover, some urban politicians remember their childhood in mixed neighbourhoods as a positive experience, which was the case in South Africa before the NP came to power in 1948. In this sense, ward councillors and activists hold a diachronic perspective, where apartheid politics are pertinent to understanding that former Black African and Coloured townships continue to be hierarchically interconnected. On the one hand, apartheid segregation politics treated the concept of place as a territorial configuration dividing townships along racialised lines; while on the other, these political processes of place-making (Gupta/Ferguson 1997: 6) led to inhabitants developing senses of attachment to these places and their respective segregated groupings. Following the forced removals, inhabitants themselves became involved in place-making through their political engagement, their building up of urban ties and networks, their cultural practices, and their social and economic lives. Through these activities, the individuals gained richly textured knowledge of their places. These knowledge reservoirs function as resources to enter the political arena, as they related them to the work of improving the socio-economic status of their neighbourhoods. In this vein, place-making has enabled actors to re-position themselves as ward councillors, NGO employees, project managers, etc. in the years after 1994. Accordingly, all trajectories demonstrate how politics are place-based (Harcourt/Escobar 2005; Alvarez 2005), and in this respect politics is identified as being, per se, attached to place and as one activist said, not focussed on the bigger picture. Despite "the urban" appearing to be constructed in terms of place, the four types of activists, particularly, illustrate through their work how place becomes translocal. The NGO activist Ms Roosevelt spoke of the global network of civil society, while the project manager Mr Khumalo explained how the GTZ intervened to make his place safer. The social movement activist Mr Jeferson talked about networking his campaign with an international forum. Conversely, the ward councillors did not refer to any international connections. Reflecting more closely upon their places of work, however, they cannot be considered simply as isolated urban enclaves. For example, the ward councillor Ms Parrow in Site C in Khayelitsha interacted on a regular basis with the project manager and the coordinators of the Peace and Development Project based in her ward, which was financed by the GTZ. The manuals used in the ward councillors' introductory training, which all ward councillors are obliged to attend, were conceptualised and financed in part by the GTZ. Ward councillors interpret global ideas about good governance, transparency, and accountability during these workshops, and with reference to these manuals. In this sense, "places are hardly self-contained, and after all are constituted at the crossroad of global forces" (Alvarez 2005: 249). These examples show how the same place may become differently translocally connected in various contexts.

Violence and ruptures

All trajectories illustrate how violence is spatially embedded in the Cape Flats as a structural element that shapes feelings of insecurity in the everyday lives of residents. These trajectories reveal that violence took place both in the public arena, such as in the streets, as well as in the private domains, such as the home (see Moser 2001: 34; Jimeno/Roldan 1996). Violence materialised in the accounts in different ways, and referencing Moser (2001: 36), can be placed into economic, social, or political categories. Economic violence encompasses that associated with robberies, carjackings, drug trafficking, etc., and is motivated by economic gain; social violence concerns itself with conflicts mainly at the interpersonal level, such as domestic violence, with the aim of keeping or gaining social power and control; and political violence becomes manifest in armed conflicts between political parties, or sexual abuse and rape as political acts, with the will to achieve, increase, or uphold political power. These different forms of violence are deeply concerned with agency and power, exhibiting "the type of forces that consciously and unconsciously uses violence to gain or maintain power" (ibid.). Additionally, the trajectories presented here highlight that these categories are often interconnected, as illustrated by the social movement activist Mr Jeferson when they recounted the attempted murders and armed robberies which they performed in order for the underground movement to survive. Hence, depending on the social context and life circumstances, the boundaries between social, economic, and political violence become blurred and diffuse.

Furthermore, ward councillors and activists in the townships consider the handling of violence in its different forms as an intrinsic part of their job. It is also evident that peace-making programmes are linked to many civil society organisations and the (local) state, and attempts to enhance cooperation between these two levels of representation. In these contexts, forms of political violence in apartheid and post-apartheid South Africa emerged as issues in all the trajectories, either in the form of physical violence or as aspects related to (political) work. Some ward councillors like Mr KEC and activists like Mr Jeferson had experienced physical violence exerted by the apartheid state as a crude response to their adolescent activism. After their respective prison terms, one joined a military wing of the underground movement, the other an organ of the apartheid regime, i.e. the Tricameral Parliament. In both cases, the exercise of state violence did not hinder their political engagement with the apartheid state, although this engagement ended up taking opposing forms. Furthermore, the NGO activist explained how her support for the families of apartheid prisoners was the foundation of her political awakening. Such examples demonstrate that experiences with political violence leads people to become involved in politics or prompts them to continue their political work even after the dispensation.

The accounts also demonstrate that violent conflict is a gendered activity, and gender is a pertinent factor in social, economic, and political violence. Many activists experienced gender-specific social and political violence during apartheid, and according to them, the police did not take action against the offenders. They explained this as being due to a significant absence of justice, and thus of the state, in the Cape Flats. This represents one of the main grounds cited for their activism in challenging the state. Domestic and sexual violence remains "epidemic" in post-apartheid society (Kadalie 1995: 67; Abrahams 2004: 4–6), further illustrated by the number of civic associations and organisations engaged with gender-specific violence-related issues in the Cape Flats, such as the NGOs Network Opposing Women Abuse, and Crisis Line. Despite considerable advancements in legislation against sexual violence,[25]

NGO activists criticise the fact that offenders are only convicted in less than 10 per cent of reported rapes (Nord 2012: 6). The common reproach is that parliament, and its departments responsible for gender issues, is a "toothless tiger" that fails to exercise its control function vis à vis the executive, instead focusing on party-political interests.

Up until this point, I have discussed conflicts with references to violence, ignoring the fact that conflicts can also be non-violent. Authors like Cockburn (1999) argue the need to distinguish conflict from violence. Despite violent and non-violent conflicts both being fundamentally concerned with power, non-violent conflict does not necessarily impose physical or mental harm on others, "while violence does by its very nature" (Moser/Clark, 2001: 6). As the trajectories demonstrate, conflict implies the pursuit of discordant objectives by different individuals, collectives, or political parties. In this sense, political positioning infers situating oneself vis à vis others who do not (necessarily) share the same ideas, values, norms, etc. Indeed, party-political differences caused non-violent conflicts in many of the cases, even drawing social boundaries between neighbours and families and influencing their social interaction. For instance, even though a ward councillor and an activist mentioned here lived in the same ward, their children were not allowed to play with each other, as both parties looked upon such interaction with a critical eye. The ward councillor explained that the reason why she wanted to maintain a social distance from her activist neighbour was due to the neighbour's family's longstanding ANC membership. Similarly, the activist was critical of her neighbour's allegiance with the NP. In addition, the activist didn't want her daughter to be in contact with the ward councillor's sons, due to their alleged abuse of the drug Tik-Tik (crystal meth or methamphetamine[26]). This example shows how the ward is indicative of a dynamic and contested field representing a number of interests and actors, rather than an all-inclusive community. In the blueprint of the local government transition phase, the White Paper of Local Government (1998), the electoral ward was to have developed into the main space for community representation and participation, through elected ward councillors, in order to improve social and economic development, especially in townships. However, the policy-makers and planners did not take into account that communities are contested fields, with non-cooperative interactions between different actors involved in such developmental issues. Despite this point having been raised in the aforementioned studies on urban politics in the Cape Flats, one has to be aware that it is not only about the lack of lines of interaction between ward councillors and activists, but rather the deepness of the ruptures polarising peoples' positionings and hence their willingness to interact. These ruptures are the result of hard-fought community politics during apartheid, where one neighbour fought against the regime while the other remained silent or collaborated. These ruptures now shape their social relations; the urban ties between neighbours, between members of different political parties, or between different civil organisations, reflect the fractured picture of spaces of place-based politics in modern South African society.

Claims for equality and multiplicities of justice

Modes of activism are far from uniform, given that they differ in their political positionings with regards to the various political parties and the ANC government (de Wet, 2012). In the Cape Flats, members of the new social movements claim to belong to the "real" grassroots movement and to being political movements, whereas they view the broader NGO movement as being aligned with the ANC government and thus acting as accomplices of the state. According to them, there also exists another branch of NGOs that should contest statecraft by promulgating alternatives to state governance. However, these NGOs actually use the struggles of social movements for their own gains, i.e. to obtain funds from international donors. All the activists mentioned in this chapter confirm the urban discourse about ward councillors who, being despite elected by the people, do not truly represent their wards in the Cape Flats (Jensen 2004; Millstein 2010). This is also evident in the way new social movements address their criticism to state representatives at the local level. While this makes the state appear a tangible target and therefore able to be attacked, I contend that it is therefore also more open to negotiation. In this case, the production of difference (Gupta/Ferguson, 1992: 11, 14) between ourselves (activists) and the others (ward councillors), i.e. society and the state, takes place within common, shared and connected, yet also contested, places and spaces.

The two aforementioned categories of NGOs – those aligned with the ANC government and those aligned with the international donor community – make up part of the so-called intermediary or third sector, which acts as a broker between the state and society (see also Neubert, 1997; Olivier de Sardan, 2006). This third sector is largely financed through the ANC government, and thus has to follow its rules and directives. However, as shown by Ms Roosevelt's case, there is still sufficient room for manoeuvre in establishing projects according to specific needs at the local level. Despite both types of organisation being positioned as brokers between the state and society, it could be argued that service providers, allied as they are with the ANC in some way, provide state patronage to the grassroots level. By contrast, government-critical NGOs, financed mainly by international donors, take on issues from the urban level that challenge the very notions of how the state works. Accordingly, at first glance these organisations and their followers constitute two groups, based upon their socio-political positioning; namely, whether they are for or against the current idea of statehood. As discussed in Chapters 4 and 5, this polarisation hinders vertical cohesion between the ward level, and the local and national state, rendering the lines of communication at the different interfaces as laden with conflicts.

Some ward councillors hierarchically categorise the political landscape on the basis of gender distinctions, for example into civil society organisations dominated by women or spheres of government dominated by men. Accordingly, they tacitly portray civil society organisations as being less powerful than state structures, which according to their "masculine" natures are strong, controlling, and effective.

The fact that the majority of civil society organisations, also in the broader sense of the term, are dominated by female leaders and members, has been noted by a number of authors (Benjamin 2004; Friedman 2004; Wittmann 2005). However, it is also a commonly-held view that men generally dominate leadership structures in the new social movements in South Africa (Benjamin 2004: 87; ILRIG 2006: 8). According to these authors, while the movements are aware of this deficiency, they have not been able to change it. Conversely, my field observations maintain that many female activists show awareness of this problem and challenged the order of things to certain extents:

> And we did face the problem. They [the male leadership] are quiet now. They don't contact us such a lot like before. They were the leaders but we are more educated now.
>
> (Female leader of the "United Civic Organisation", a new social movement, 15.12.2005)

As a result of becoming involved in urban politics, many female activists have gained experience and knowledge, and thus are able to observe gendered positioning within the civil society arena more critically.

Hence, the trajectories illustrate how the actors' life-strategies have equipped them with resources over time, including rhetorical skills, knowledge about their place, and the establishment of networks. As previously argued, actors use such resources in order to access and participate in the political arena to become more integrative. According to the trajectories, both ward councillors and activists are linked to and active in several organisations participating in urban politics. This indicates their social competencies in maintaining relationships and networks.

However, critical and intellectual activists regard the new political system as an exclusive sphere where "it is not about the issues of the people anymore, it is about power and money at the expense of the people" (Fieldnote, Ms Smith, 26.09.2006). Despite the political system being perceived as exclusive by the ward councillors and activists, all actors are actively engaged in transforming old mechanisms of gendered and racialised discrimination and segregation into inclusive ones. While most of the actors discussed here demand inclusiveness, the differences between the notions of inclusiveness of activists and those of conservative ward councillors are striking. For instance, the latter demands more inclusive state actions, particularly in reference to "the Coloureds", based upon a conservative conceptualisation of gender order, i.e. a "housewife concept", where men are providers and women mothers. By contrast, the activists use non-racialised human rights language, taking up the claims of the Women National Council,[27] which promoted a woman's right to emancipation and equality in political, economic, social, and cultural spheres during the 1990s. Therefore, the historical continuity of excluding certain groupings from the sharing of power remains, yet it is also challenged through actors' divergent claims for equality in the democratic terms of diversity, social justice, and citizenship. Despite some of these claims for equality fundamentally contradicting each other at the urban level, they forge part of a continuous process of social change in becoming contested and negotiated in day-to-day practices.

2.5 The contentious politics of belonging

This chapter introduced empirically-grounded types of ward councillors and activists based upon typical trajectories and particular modes of positioning from apartheid to present-day politics. Therefore, while the typology is not exhaustive, it can be used to illustrate different modes of political action[28] related to specific characteristics, distinct perceptions, interpretations, contentions, standpoints, and coping strategies of being a ward councillor and an activist (see Rosenthal/Fischer-Rosenthal 1997: 147–156). In the case of the research sites from this fieldwork, and based upon the construction of people's trajectories, the categorical differentiation between ward councillor and activist can become blurred, specifically with activists who became ward councillors or those who remained activists after 1994. Although the latter now work in NGOs or are active in new social movements, some of them have tried to switch their "doing politics" sphere by entering local government. Field observations relate the dynamics of the overlapping positional logics of both types of actors, in which their ways of doing politics are continually being revised and modified. Such emergent narratives, i.e. those that change depending on particular situations, entail dynamic aspects of contradiction and struggle (Yuval-Davis 2006: 205). This is particularly the case because actors change and add positions, consequently moving within the social hierarchy during the courses of their lives.

It is worth noting that while activists' work in new social movements is unpaid, NGO employees and ward councillors receive a regular income. Therefore, the incentive of regular income and social security can be seen as significant for the socio-political mobility of those activists who want to enter local government (a point raised by many interviewees). This holds true for activists in social movements and community-based organisations who work on a voluntary basis, where becoming a ward councillor would secure income for at least their term of office.

While the concept of the politics of positioning grasps the dynamics of actors' re-positionings from apartheid and into the democratic era, belonging, and the related concept of the "politics of belonging", advanced by Crowley (1999), Yuval-Davis et al. (2006), and Pfaff-Czarnecka (2011), evolved as a mechanism in urban politics after 1994. The politics of belonging presupposes the sense of people belonging together "when they share values, relations and practices" (Anthias 2006: 21) and attachment to a particular place (Rodman 1992). As shown thus far by the trajectories, segregation politics, forced displacements, and violent uprisings constantly contributed to a detraction from and the destabilisation of a sense of belonging to particular places in peripheral urban environments. It was only after the forced relocation processes to the Cape Flats in the 1960s and 1970s that the actors started to develop a sense of "specialised channels of knowledge" (Lachenmann 2004: 127) in their newly-inhabited spaces. The trajectories revealed that since most of the actors had always been actively engaged in community-based organisations and urban politics within their area since apartheid, they developed a sense of responsibility towards their neighbourhoods. Sharing the common apartheid past bonded them to their particular places and enabled them to become engaged in urban politics against the backdrop of the perils of living in the townships. Despite activists receiving regular salaries as NGO researchers or GTZ project managers, and enjoying full citizenship, which allows them to move freely and theoretically leave the dangerous sites of township life, they still stay there. Some of these persons have been victims in their townships, being raped, robbed, or carjacked, yet even these experiences have not made them leave their homes. This phenomenon has been confirmed many times during fieldwork in Mitchells Plain and Khayelitsha, where inhabitants with regular incomes such as policemen choose to stay in areas with poor housing and sanitation, despite their financial situation improving, which might allow a social "upgrade". Accordingly, the next chapter also focuses on positioning, albeit emphasising attachment to a place and its role in urban politics.

Notes

1 From the beginning of fieldwork I chose to transcribe my data material in such a way that idiosyncratic elements of speech (e.g. nonverbal mannerisms, involuntary vocalisations, stutters, or pauses) were removed. My research interest centered upon meanings and perceptions within speech that construct social realities, rather than linguistic aspects (see Kowal/O'Connell 2000; Davidson 2009).

2 The names of persons have been changed to allow interviewees to remain anonymous. In accordance with the interviewees the name of geographical areas, political parties, NGOs and social movements are not treated anonymously.

3 Ndlovu (1998) points out that a variety of explanations for the Soweto uprising have been proposed. "Some highlight structural changes in the economy and society, including political changes brought about by apartheid [since 1948]; some stress the emergence of youth subcultures in Soweto's secondary schools in the 1970s; some emphasise the transformative role of Black Consciousness and its associated organisations" (Ndlovu 1998: 317). It is important to take all of these explanations into consideration when trying to understand why the Soweto uprising occurred.

4 At the time, the government made separate countries for Black Africans, who thus did not belong to the Republic of South Africa, and the so-called "Bantustans" were turned into "independent homelands". Furthermore, people classified as

"African" were only allowed to vote for the national government of their own "homeland". The Tricameral parliament was constituted of segregated chambers for "Coloured, Indian, and White voters" (Seekings/Nattrass 2006: 21). By partly integrating classified Coloureds and Indians into the political system, the intention was to prevent any further alliances between these groups and classified Black Africans.

5 In 2014 the ID merged with the DA in order to challenge the governing ANC just before the national elections.

6 This confirms that the 1976 revolt can be seen as an event that politicised not only classified Black African township residents but also solidarised, to a certain extent, classified Coloured and Black African areas to act together against the state's (education) policies (see TRC 1998: 392; Chapter 3).

7 In what follows, I mention townships as formerly Coloured or Black African only in reference to the way that they were conceived of in the past, i.e. in the context of segregation politics during apartheid; I do not mention the townships in this way as a reference to racial categories in the current South African context. Nevertheless, the racialisation of townships as either Coloured or Black African remains prevalent in everyday life and urban politics.

8 Before the formation of the ANCWL, the Bantu Women's League was the women's branch of the ANC from 1931 and mainly engaged in resistance against women's lack of free movement (Wells 1993: 54).

9 Street committees have operated since the 1980s, particularly in former Black African townships, as informal courts that settle disputes and attend to the daily affairs of the townships. In Cape Town, a single form of street committees did not and does not exist; townships have been created at different times and under different circumstances, and consequently each has developed their own type of committees (Burman 1989: 153, 154).

10 For a detailed account of gangsterism in the Cape Flats see Jensen (2008).

11 As indicated in Chapter 1, the ANC was the first party to introduce a 30 per cent quota just before the national elections in 1994, which considerably changed the political landscape. Today, more than 45 per cent of the members of parliament and 40 per cent of ministers of government are women (Nord 2012: 6).

12 According to some internet sources, South Africa is the world's largest abuser of Mandrax, a synthetic drug mainly sold in the form of a tablet which is highly addictive. The active ingredient in Mandrax is Methaqualone, www.drugaware.co.za/mandrax.html, accessed 08.11.2011.

13 Jensen (2008) highlights in his study on gangs and politics that crime is a racialised and gendered phenomenon in the Cape Flats, analysing how the construction of Coloured men as *skollies* has functioned as a type produced and maintained by both the (apartheid) state and township dwellers.

14 In 1997, the Department of Safety and Security published a formal policy through which a detailed framework for community policing was established (Pelser 1999: 4). The Metro Police in Cape Town was established in 2005, introducing the global concept of community-based structures of the Sector Policing Forum (SPF) and the Community Police Forum (CPF) at the urban level. The policy draws attention to the aims of the SPF and CPF to involve multiple stakeholders within the community, including both state and non-state actors. This collaboration is depicted as a way of creating participatory spaces, where organisations on the ground, together with the police, build up cooperation strategies for the establishment of more secure environments (Pelser 1999: 4).

15 Ms Roosevelt is the Vice Chairperson of the NGO Crisis Line, Vice Chairperson of the Community Police Forum, Virtual Coordinator of the Peace and Development Platform of South Africa, and Project Coordinator of the NGO Community Correction Care Organisation.

16 This branch was named after Lilian Masediba Ngoyi (1911–1980), a politician and anti-apartheid activist, and President of the African National Congress (ANC) Women's League.

17 The ANC, representing almost 80 years of liberation movement, and the NP, representing the massive economic capacity of South African business and state resources, entered into a negotiation arena based around the National Peace Accord of 1991. These negotiation processes involved a complex network of actors and organisational structures, most noteably the internal factionalism of the main political parties, their different philosophies, and compromises (Baker 1990; Muiu 2008; Wood 2000; Seekings 2000). Significantly, the NP could only position itself as an influential actor in the new democratic setup owing to a lasting compromise originally suggested by the ANC, known as the "sunset clause". The sunset clause guaranteed continued employment and pensions for white civil servants, police, and military, as well as the potential to be involved in policy-making, if the NP won more than 20 per cent of seats in the first democratic election (Wood 2000; Muiu 2008), which it subsequently did. The ANC argued publicly that this concession had been strategically necessary to facilitate the smooth transition of government.

18 According to a research report for the Danish Federation of Workers in 2006, "casual labour refers to work conducted for a defined period and during a peak business period. Casual workers will be called to supplement full time workers in times of high business activity, particularly in retail. Most labour laws in the region [southern Africa] still rely on this definition of casual work" (Bodibe 2006: 4). This report was written by the National Labour & Economic Institute, formed in 1993 as an initiative of the Congress of South African Trade Unions (COSATU).

19 The AEC organised a protest in Ms Thompson's ward, where tyres and furniture were burnt to demonstrate against the lack of commitment from the Cape Town Community Housing Company in ensuring safe, decent, and stable housing conditions. The protests started due to families being left homeless after an alleged electrical wiring fault caused a fire and damaged their homes. See Barnes, Clayton, "Smarty Town Rage", in: Mitchells Plain MetroBurger, 30.11.2005, p. 1.

20 During apartheid, the burning of tyres was known as the "necklace", and involved placing a tyre soaked in petrol around the victim's neck and setting it alight. The victims of "necklacings" were supposed to be collaborators, witches, murderers, or rapists – who were punished for betraying the social solidarity of their neighbourhood (Ball 1994: 1).

21 www.rosalux.de/english/foundation.html, access 02.03.2011.

22 Mr Jeferson mentioned in this context the NGO International Labour and Information Group, which, together with the Rosa Luxemburg Foundation, organised a seminar entitled with "State, Party and Popular Power" (01.03.2006) and a conference called "The Globalisation School" (25.09.2006–29.09.2006) for activists of different NGOs and social movements, including also activists from other African countries. While he clearly sees the positive sides of such encounters and networks, he argues that he alone does not have the resources to maintain such networks, which creates one-sided dependencies and therefore asymmetries between individuals and these kinds of NGOs.

23 ILRIG was founded in the 1980s as a project by David Cooper from the Industrial Sociology Faculty of the University of Cape Town. After 1994 it was officially registered as an NGO – during the apartheid era no state-critical NGOs existed. ILRIG considers itself primarily a research and information centre. It has been responsible for a series of publications on trade union movements in Latin America, Africa, and Europe, of which several volumes have been published in African languages. Due to disagreements surrounding ILRIG's focus between its founder and other members, ILRIG ended its cooperation with the university in the early

2000s in order to "follow the demands of the trade union and wider resistance movement more closely, carrying out more narrowly defined commissioned research" (Keim 2017: 131).

24 Similar to Escobar's analysis (2008), different concepts of place as "territories of difference" or "social environments" are applied in this study. Escobar analyses a political organisation that represents the interests of Afro-Colombians who were geographically, economically, and politically excluded from the dominant Colombian political system until the 1990s. His research focuses, among other things, on the different concepts of the places of Afro-Colombians. Afro-Colombian activists portray their places as social environments, while development actors and big enterprises construct the same places as developmental "territorial configurations".

25 The Domestic Violence Act of 1998 can be considered an important milestone against the prevalence of domestic violence, as can the official recognition of traditional marriages, which became manifest in the Recognition of Customary Marriages Act of 1998.

26 Like Mandrax, Tik-Tik is used mainly by youth, and has been constructed as a serious problem in recent years in the townships, reflected by the headlines of local newspaper articles which point to the widespread drug problem in Mitchells Plain: Staff Reporter, "Tafelsig [Area in Mitchells Plain] Now Western Cape drug capital", in: Plainsman, Independent Community Newspaper, 28.06.2006, p. 17; Barnes, Clayton, "Families of 'Tik Users' Bear Brunt of Drug Habit", in: Metro-Burger, 01.02.2006, p. 4; Williams, Alicia, "Big Tik Haul. Police Seize R400,000 Drugs in Portland [Area in Mitchells Plain]", in: Plainsman, Independent Community Newspaper, 15.03.2006, p. 1; and so forth.

27 The formation of the Women National Council (WNC) in 1991 brought together individuals from various economic and social backgrounds, political parties, and various women's organisations including those representing the church, welfare, and health sectors. It could be said that the inclusion of women as a category in the preamble to and in the South African Constitution itself was the result of challenges made by the WNC and others during the transition period (Meintjes 1996: 47).

28 Conceptually speaking, "modes of political action" stems from Bayart, who does not use it in gender-specific terms – "*politique par le bas*" (Bayart et al. 1992).

References

Abrahams, N. (2004). Sexual Violence Against Women in South Africa. *Sexuality Africa Magazine* 1(3), pp. 4–6.

Aké, C. (1994). *The Democratisation of Disempowerment in Africa*. Lagos: Malthouse Press.

Alvarez, S. E. (2005). The Politics of the Place, the Place of Politics: Some Forward-Looking Reflections. In: W. Harcourt and A. Escobar, eds. *Women and the Politics of Place*. Bloomfield: Kumarian Press, pp. 248–256.

Anthias, F. (2006). Belonging in a Globalising and Unequal World: Rethinking Translocations. In: N. Yuval-Davis, K. Kannabiran and U. Vieten, eds. *The Situated Politics of Belonging*. London: Sage, pp. 17–31.

Appadurai, A. (2001). Deep Democracy: Urban Governmentality and the Horizon Politics. *Environment & Urbanisation* 13(2), pp. 22–43.

Appadurai, A. (2007). Hope and Democracy. *Public Culture* 19(1), pp. 29–34.

Arnold, D. and Blackburn, S. (2005). *Telling Lives in India: Biography, Autobiography, and Life History*. Bloomington: Indiana University Press.

Baker, P. (1990). A Turbulent Transition. *Journal of Democracy* 1(4), pp. 8–24.

Ball, J. (1994). *The Ritual of the Necklace*. Research Report. Johannesburg: Centre for the Study of Violence and Reconciliation.

Bayart, J.-F., Mbembe, A. and Toulabar, C. (1992). *Le politique par le bas en Afrique noire: contributions à une problématique de la démocratie.* Paris: Karthala.

Beall, J. (2013). Invention and Intervention in African Cities. In: B. Obrist, V. Arlt and E. Macamo, eds. *Living the City in Africa. Process of Invention and Intervention.* Zürich: Lit-Verlag, pp. 23–44.

Behrends, A., Park, S.-J. and Rottenburg, R. (2014). *Travelling Models in African Conflict Management. Translating Technologies of Social Ordering.* Leiden: Brill.

Benjamin, N. (2004). Organisation Building and Mass Mobilisation. *Development Update* 5(2), pp. 73–94.

Bodibe, O. (2006). *The Extent and Effects of Casualisation in Southern Africa: Analysis of Lesotho, Mozambique, South Africa, Swaziland, Zambia, Zimbabwe.* Research Report for the Danish Federation of Workers, National Labour and Economic Development Institute.

Bond, P. and Thulani, G. (2003). Governance in the New South Africa. In: Mhone, G. and O. Edigheji, eds. *Governance in the New South Africa.* Lansdowne: University of Cape Town Press, pp. 313–345.

Burman, S. (1989). The Role of Street Committees: Continuing South Africa's Practice of Alternative Justice. In: H. Corder, ed. *Democracy and the Judiciary. Proceedings of the National Conference on Democracy and the Judiciary.* Mowbray: IDASA, pp. 151–166.

Cameron, R. (1998). *Democratisation of South African Local Government: A Tale of Three Cities.* Pretoria: J. L. van Schaik.

Chipkin, I. (2002). A Developmental Role for Local Government. In: S. Parnell, E. Pieterse, M. Swilling and D. Wooldridge, eds. *Democratising Local Government. The South African Experiment.* Landsdowne: University of Cape Town, pp. 57–78.

Cockburn, C. (1977). *The Local State: Management of Cities and People.* London: Pluto Press.

Cockburn, C. (1999). Gender, Armed Conflict and Political Violence. Background Paper for Conference on Gender, Armed Conflict and Political Development. Washington, DC: World Bank, 9–10 June.

Comaroff, J. and Comaroff, J. L. (1999). *Civil Society and the Political Imagination in Africa. Critical Perspectives.* Chicago, IL: University of Chicago Press.

Coronil, F. and Skurski, J. (2006). Introduction: States of Violence and Violence of States. In: F. Coronil and J. Skurski, eds. *States of Violence.* Ann Arbor: University of Michigan Press, pp. 1–32.

Crowley, J. (1999). The Politics of Belonging: Some Theoretical Considerations. In: A. Geddes and A. Favell, eds. *The Politics of Belonging: Migrants and Minorities in Contemporary Europe.* Aldershot: Ashgate, pp. 15–41.

Das, V. and Randeria, S. (2015). Politics of the Urban Poor: Aesthetics, Ethics, Volatility, Precarity. An Introduction to Supplement 11. *Current Anthropology* 56(11), pp. 3–14.

Davidson, C. (2009). Transcription: Imperatives for Qualitative Research. *International Journal of Qualitative Methods* 8(2), pp. 1–52.

De Wet, J. (2012). Friends, Enemies or 'Frienemies': Development and Civil Society Organisations' Relations with the State in a Democratic South Africa. *Working Paper* 367. Bielefeld University, Faculty of Sociology.

Duncan, S. and Goodwin, M. (1988). *The Local State and Uneven Development.* Cambridge: Polity Press.

Erasmus, Z. (2001). Re-imaging Coloured Identities in Post-Apartheid South Africa. In: Z. Erasmus, ed. *Coloured by History, Shaped by Place. New Perspectives on Coloured Identities in the Cape.* Cape Town: Kwela Books, pp. 3–28.

Esau, M. (2007). *Deepening Democracy through Local Participation. Examining the Ward Committee System as a Form of Local Participation in Bonteheuwel in the Western Cape.* Project: Policy Management, Governance and Poverty Alleviation in the Western Cape. Cape Town: University of the Western Cape.

Esau, M. (2008). Contextualizing Social Capital, Citizen Participation and Poverty through an Examination of the Ward Committee System in Bonteheuwel in the Western Cape, South Africa. *Journal of Developing Societies* 24(3), pp. 355–380.

Escobar, A. (2008). *Territories of Difference: Place, Movements, Life, Redes: New Ecologies for the Twenty First Century.* Durham, NC: Duke University Press.

Fessah, Y. and Jordan, J. (2005). South African Local Government Bulletin. Electing Women Councillors 50/50 Representation. *Local Government Bulletin* 8(1), p. 3.

Friedman, S. (2004). A Voice for All: Democracy and Public Participation. *Critical Dialogue: Public Participation in Review* 1(1), pp. 22–26.

Gupta, A. and Ferguson, J. (1992). Beyond "Culture": Space, Identity, and the Politics of Difference. *Cultural Anthropology* 7(1), pp. 6–23.

Gupta, A. and Ferguson, J. (1997). *Culture, Power, Place. Explorations in Critical Anthropology.* Durham, NC: Duke University Press.

Habib, A. and Kotzé, H. (2003). Civil Society, Governance and Development in an Era of Globalisation: The South African Case. In: G. Mhone and O. Edigheji, eds. *Governance in the New South Africa. The Challenges of Globalisation.* Cape Town: UCT Press, pp. 246–270.

Haferburg, C. and Huchzermeyer, M. (2015). *Urban Governance in Post-Apartheid Cities: Modes of Engagement in South Africa's Metropoles.* Stuttgart: Borntraeger Science Publishers.

Harcourt, W. and Escobar, A. (2005). *Women and the Politics of Place.* Bloomfield: Kumarian Press.

Harvey, D. (2008). The Right to the City. In: *New Left Review* 53, pp. 23–40.

Jeffrey, C. and Dyson, J. (2008). Introduction. In: *Telling Young Lives: Portraits of Global Youth.* Philadelphia, PA: Temple University Press, pp. 1–14.

Jensen, S. (2001). *Claiming Community, Negotiating Crime: State Formation, Neighborhood and Gangs in a Capetonian Township.* PhD dissertation. Roskilde University, International Development Studies.

Jensen, S. (2004). Claiming Community: Local Politics in the Cape Flats, South Africa. *Critique of Anthropology* 24(2), pp. 179–207.

Jensen, S. (2008). *Gangs, Politics & Dignity in Cape Town.* Chicago, IL: University of Chicago Press.

Jimeno, M. and Roldan, I. (1996). *Las sombras arbitrarias: Violencia y autoridad en Colombia.* Santa Fe de Bogotá: Editorial Universidad Nacional.

Kadalie, R. (1995). Women in the New South Africa. From Transition to Governance. In: S. Liebenberg, ed. *The International Covenant on Economic, Social and Cultural Rights and Its implications for South Africa.* Cape Town: The Community Law Centre, UWC in association with David Phillip, pp. 64–78.

Keim, W. (2017). *Universally Comprehensible, Arrogantly Local: South African Labour Studies from the Apartheid Era into the New Millenium.* Bielefeld: transcript Verlag.

Kowal, S. and O'Connell, D. C. (2000). Zur Transkription von Gesprächen. In: U. Flick, E. von Kardorff and I. Steinke, eds. *Qualitative Forschung. Ein Handbuch.* Hamburg: Rowohlts Enzyklopädie, pp. 437–447.

Lachenmann, G. (2004). Researching Local Knowledge for Development: Current Issues. In: N. Schareika and T. Bierschenk, eds. *Lokales Wissen. Sozialwissenschaftliche Perspektiven.* Berlin: LIT Verlag, pp. 123–148.

Lachenmann, G. (2009). Engendering Knowledge in Organisations. Negotiating Development in Local and Translocal Social Spaces. *Working Paper* 362. Bielefeld University, Faculty of Sociology.

Long, N. (1996). Globalisation and Localisation: New Challenges to Rural Research. In: H. L. Moore, ed. *The Future of Anthropological Knowledge.* London: Routledge, pp. 37–59.

Mattes, R., Hermann, G. and Wilmot, J. (1996). The Election in the Western Cape. In: R. W. Johnson and L. Schlemmer, eds. *Launching Democracy in South Africa: The First Open Election, 1994.* New Haven, CT: Yale University Press, pp. 108–167.

Meintjes, S. (1996). The Women's Struggle for Equality during South Africa's Transition to Democracy. *Transformation* 30, pp. 47–64.

Merry, S. E. (2006). Transnational Human Rights and Local Activism. Mapping the Middle. *American Anthropologist* 108(1), pp. 38–51.

Mhone, G. and Omano, E. (2003). *Governance in the New South Africa. The Challenges of Globalisation.* Cape Town: University of Cape Town Press.

Millstein, M. (2010). Limits to Local Democracy: The Politics of Urban Governance Transformations in Cape Town. *Working Paper* 2. Stockholm: Swedish International Centre for Local Democracy.

Mogale, T. M. (2003). Developmental Local Government and Decentralised Service Delivery in the Democratic South Africa. In: G. Mhone and O. Edigheji, eds. *Governance in the New South Africa.* Lansdowne: UCT Press.

Moser, C. O. N. (2001). The Gendered Continuum of Violence and Conflict: An Operational Framework. In: C. O. N. Moser and F. Clark, eds. *Victims, Perpetrators or Actors? Gender, Armed Conflict and Political Violence.* London: Zed Books, pp. 30–51.

Moser, C. O. N. and Clark, F. (2001). Introduction. In: C. O. N. Moser and F. Clark, eds. *Victims, Perpetrators or Actors? Gender, Armed Conflict and Political Violence.* London: Zed Books, pp. 3–12.

Muiu, M. W. (2008). *The Pitfalls of Liberal Democracy and Late Nationalism in South Africa.* New York: Palgrave Macmillan.

Ndlovu, S. M. (1998). The Soweto Uprisings: Counter-Memories of June 1976. In: M. Seeber and L. Callinicos, eds. *Ravan Local History Series.* Randberg: Ravan Press, pp. 317–368.

Neubert, D. (1997). Demokratisierung ohne Zivilgesellschaft? Zur Rolle von Patron-Klient-Beziehungen in den neuen Mehrparteiensystemen. In: H.-J. Lauth and U. Liebert, eds. *Im Schatten demokratischer Legitimität: Informelle Institutionen und politische Partizipation im interkulturellen Demokratievergleich.* Opladen: Westdeutscher Verlag, pp. 258–276.

Nord, A. K. (2012). Mehr Geschlechtergerechtigkeit? Zur Frauenquote in Afrika. *GIGA Focus Afrika* 5. Hamburg: GIGA, pp. 2–7.

Nyman, R. (2001). Globalisation and the South African Economy – Does It Benefit the Working Class? In: N. Pape, J. Newman and H. Jansen, eds. *Is There an*

Alternative? South African Workers Confronting Globalisation. Cape Town: International Labour Resource and Information Group, pp. 108–130.

Olivier de Sardan, J.-P. (2006). *Anthropology and Development: Understanding Contemporary Social Change.* London: Zed Books.

Paley, J. (2002). Toward an Anthropology of Democracy. *Annual Revue Anthropology* 31, pp. 469–496.

Parnell, S., Pieterse, E., Swilling, M. and Wooldridge, D. (2002). *Democratising Local Government. The South African Experiment.* Cape Town: University of Cape Town.

Pelser, E. (1999). *The Challenge of Community Policing in South Africa.* ISS Paper 42. Pretoria: Institute for Security Studies.

Pfaff-Czarnecka, J. (2011). From 'Identity' to 'Belonging' in Social Research: Plurality, Social Boundaries, and the Politics of the Self. In: S. Albiez, N. Castro, L. Jüssen and E. Youkhana, eds. *Ethnicity, Citizenship and Belonging. Practices, Theory and Spatial Dimensions.* Frankfurt am Main: Iberoamericana-Vervuert, pp. 199–219.

Pickel, B. (1997). *Coloured Ethnicity and Identity. A Case Study in the former Coloured Areas in the Western Cape/South Africa.* Berlin: LIT Verlag.

Pieterse, E. (2002). Participatory Local Governance in the Making: Opportunities, Constraints and Prospects. In: S. Parnell, E. Pieterse, M. Swilling and D. Wooldridge, eds. *Democratising Local Government. The South African Experiment.* Cape Town: University of Cape Town, pp. 1–17.

Reddy, T. (2001). The Politics of Naming: The Constitution of Coloured Subjects in South Africa. In: Z. Erasmus, ed. *Coloured by History, Shaped by Place. New Perspectives on Coloured Identities in the Cape.* Cape Town: Kwela Books, pp. 64–79.

Reddy, T. (2015). *South Africa, Settler Colonialism and the Failures of Liberal Democracy.* London: Zed Books.

Rodman, M. C. (1992). Empowering Place: Multilocality and Multivocality. *American Anthropologist* 94(3), pp. 640–656.

Rosenthal, G. and Fischer-Rosenthal, W. (1997). Narrationsanalyse Biographischer Selbstpräsentation. In: R. Hitzler and A. Honer, eds. *Sozialwissenschaftliche Hermeneutik*, pp. 133–164.

Seekings, J. (1996). The Decline of South Africa's Civic Organisations, 1990–1996. *Critical Sociology* 22(3), pp. 135–157.

Seekings, J. (2000). *The UDF. A History of the United Democratic Front in South Africa, 1983–1991.* Athens: Ohio University Press.

Seekings, J. and Nattras, N. (2006). *Class, Race, and Inequality in South Africa.* Scottsville: University Press of KwaZulu-Natal Press.

Strulik, S. (2004). Engendering Local Democracy Research. Panchayati Raj and Changing Gender Relations in India. Unpublished Paper presented at the International Workshop on Local Democracy, organised by the EU-Asia Link Programme "The Micro Politics of Democratisation: European-South Asian Exchanges on Governance, Conflict and Civic Action". Tribhuvan University, Kathmandu.

Strulik, S. (2013). *Politics Embedded: Women's Quota and Democracy – Negotiating Gender Relations in North India.* Berlin: LIT Verlag.

Stytler, N. (2005). Local Government in South Africa. Entrenching Decentralised Government. In: N. Stytler, ed. *The Place and Role of Local Government in Federal Systems.* Johannesburg: Konrad-Adenauer-Stiftung, pp. 183–220.

Subklew, F. (2002). *Local Peace Work in a Transforming Society as a Challenge for Social Work – Two Project Examples from Cape Town, South Africa.* Diploma Thesis. Department of Social Service. Potsdam: University of Applied Sciences.

Swartz, M. J. (1969). The Middleman. In: M. J. Swartz, ed. *Local-Level Politics: Social and Cultural Perspectives.* London: University of London Press, pp. 199–204.

Terreblanche, S. (2001). *A History of Inequality in South Africa 1652–2002.* Scottsville: University of Natal Press.

Thompson, L. and Tapscott, C. (2010). Mobilisation and Social Movements in the South: The Challenges of Inclusive Governance. In: L. Thompson and C. Tapscott, eds. *Citizenship and Social Movements. Perspectives from the Global South.* London: Zed Books, pp.1–34.

Wells, J. C. (1993). *We Now Demand! The History of Women's Resistance to Pass Laws in South Africa.* Johannesburg: Witwatersrand University Press.

Wickramasinghe, N. (2005). The Idea of Civil Society in the South: Imaginings, Transplants, Designs. The Deep Structure of the Present Moment. *Science & Society* 69(3), pp. 458–486.

Wittmann, V. (2005). *Frauen im Neuen Südafrika. Eine Analyse zur gender-Ger-echtigkeit.* Frankfurt am Main: Brandes & Apsel.

Wood, E. J. (2000). *Forging Democracy from Below: Insurgent Transitions in South Africa and El Salvador. Insurgent Transitions in South Africa and El Salvador.* Cambridge: Cambridge University Press.

Wooldridge, D. (2002). Introducing Metropolitan Local Government in South Africa. In: S. Parnell, E. Pieterse, M. Swilling and D. Wooldridge, eds. *Democratising Local Government. The South African Experiment.* Cape Town: University of Cape Town, pp. 127–140.

Zuern, E. (2004). *Continuity in Contradiction? The Prospects for a National Civic Movement in a Democratic State: SANCO and the ANC in Post-Apartheid South Africa.* Paper of a joint project between the Centre for Civil Society and the School of Development Studies. Durban: University of KwaZulu-Natal.

State and non-state sources

Government Communications (2004). *South Africa Yearbook 2004/2005.* Pretoria: Government Communications (GCIS).

ILRIG (ed.) (2002). Faizel Brown of the Western Cape Anti-Evictions Campaign. *Workers World News.* Cape Town: Workers World, pp. 4–5.

ILRIG (ed.) (2002). *Workers World News.* Cape Town: Workers World, p. 1.

ILRIG Report (2006). *ILRIG Public Forum: Building Women's Activism.* Cape Town.

Minister of Local Government (1998). *White Paper on Local Government.* Ed. v. Pretoria: Government Printer. Republic of South Africa.

Mncadi, M. (1995). Towards Effective Community Safety. Perspectives on Community Safety. *NICRO Research Series* 1, pp. 30–42.

MsSmith (2006). Autobiographical Learning History. Truth and Reconciliation Commission. (1998). *TRC Report, Volume Three.* Cape Town: Truth and Reconciliation Commission.

Newspaper articles

Barnes, C. (2006). Families of 'Tik Users' Bear Brunt of Drug Habit. In: *Mitchells Plain MetroBurger,* 01.02.2006, p. 4.

Barnes, C. (2005). Smarty Town Rage. In: *Mitchells Plain MetroBurger,* 30.11.2005, p. 1.

ILRIG-Newsletter, 02. 01. 2013.
Schwikowski, M. (2004). Der letzte Seufzer. In: *Die Tageszeitung*, 02.09.2004, p. 10.
Staff Reporter (2006). Tafelsig, Now Western Cape Drug Capital. In: *Plainsman, Independent Community Newspaper*, 28.06.2006, p. 17.
Staff Reporter (2006). Somali Offer Lessons, but We Prefer Violence. In: *Cape Argus*, 01.09.2006, p. 16.
Williams, A. (2006). Big Tik Haul. Police Seize R400,000 Drugs in Portland. In: *Plainsman, Independent Community Newspaper*, 15.03.2006, p. 1.

Websites

Mandrax. Available at: www.drugaware.co.za/mandrax.html [08.03.2017].
Rosa Luxemburg Foundation. Available at: www.rosalux.de/english/foundation.html [02.03.2017].

3 Old racism in new guises

Given the history of racism in South Africa, where it existed as an ideological mindset at the centre of state apartheid policies, the ideas of belonging in and to former racialised townships are maintained in present-day urban politics. The preceding chapter concluded that the politics of belonging presuppose a sense of people belonging together "when they share values, relations and practices" (Anthias 2006: 21) and an attachment to a particular place (Rodman 1992). However, it is important to differentiate between "belonging" and "the politics of belonging", when analysing racism as a contemporary form of the politics of belonging (Yuval-Davis 2006: 197). Belonging relates to feeling "at home", "safe", and "secure" (Pfaff-Czarnecka 2011a, 2013),[1] whereby people can start to develop feelings of being at home and a sense of belonging to their place, despite living on the urban periphery, and even in insecure socio-economic conditions or unsafe environments. In addition, townships in post-1994 South Africa emerged as spaces of democratisation and urban development intervention, and the aim to integrate them into larger society. The attachment to place that emerged as a part of the democratisation and development process converted townships into arenas of conflict concerning access to resources. Particularly, the positions of ward councillors, employment in government-funded housing or violence prevention programmes, or working in the third sector offer in-demand paid positions to actors seeking economic security within their own township society. With democratisation, the foundations were laid for various actors, especially ward councillors, to politicise belonging in order to maintain communication with their constituency through convincing rhetoric and practises, as well as to position themselves within the governance arena. This chapter examines how racism influences political action; as an important element for mobilising voters and state support; as a means to further one's own interests and causes; and a way to blame the other for the existence and perpetuation of poverty and other social problems.

Since colonialism, racism in South Africa has manifested itself as a societal phenomenon, in manifold and changing forms, on all levels of social relations. In this sense, racism is not (only) an individual phenomenon but also a societal structural problem (see Mecheril/Melter 2009: 15). In accordance with Hall (1994), I conceive racism as functioning on the basis of markers of differences, i.e. material and non-material demarcations that are used against the other in the fight for access to (basic) resources (see Solomos 2015). At the same time, these markers draw social boundaries between groupings and can be seen as "objectified forms of social differences manifested in unequal access to and unequal distribution of resources (material and nonmaterial) and social opportunities." (Lamont/Molnár 2002: 168). These demarcations are used by some urban politicians as legitimation or justification for their social, political, and economic actions. This chapter will highlight how these narratives of material and nonmaterial demarcations have developed as key areas for micro politics in post-apartheid Cape Town in structuring the urban governance arena.

The subsequent analysis of empirical material adopts the use of Pfaff-Czarnecka's (2011a) heuristic triad of commonality, attachment, and mutuality, as being the constituting elements of belonging among members of a collective. This concept therefore links perceptions, narratives, and cultural practices of commonality that create and reproduce attachment and mutuality as the basis for individuals to locate themselves within a collective (ibid.: 201). As will become evident, the actors' social location is embedded in the Cape Flats, where "multiple axes of differences" (Yuval-Davis 2006: 200) intersect, including gender, generational, economic, and political categories. Urban politicians build their rhetoric around their knowledge of actors' locations, including their specific electorate and the socio-economic situation in the Cape Flats, to further their own causes and agendas.

I argue that urban politics are predominantly shaped by two opposing tendencies; namely, that politicians form their arguments based upon racial and territorial divides, while activists attempt to go beyond racial criteria and territorial borders. Despite racism looming everywhere – with places of contention still being ostensibly constructed as either "Coloured" or "Black African" – it must be seen in the context of historically situated interactions and everyday practices. In this sense, focusing on different forms of political engagement and activism will allow us to explore the multi-layered processes of belonging to a place through aspects of gendered, political, cultural, and religious positioning, rather than simply by primarily racialised identifications.

The chapter is organised into five sections. The first section introduces academic and political debates and approaches concerning the construction of race. The categorical shifts from race to culture and ethnicity are dismantled as strategic political attempts to split South African academia during apartheid into two schools. The second section pays attention to similar categorical shifts at the urban level, and teases out urban views on processes of othering, by considering current narratives and practices within the townships. These views are then specified in regard to notions of switching from racialised to culturalist ascriptions. The third section concentrates exclusively on the sphere of local government, where racial and economic differences have become more pronounced since the end of apartheid. In contrast, the fourth section focuses on analysing varying forms of activism as ways of creating spaces, where racial boundaries dissolve and become blurred. The final section summarises the results and highlights some of the dynamics and intricacies of racism in urban politics.

3.1 Situating racism, culture, and ethnicity

This section situates the concepts of race, culture, and ethnicity in the context of public and academic debates in South Africa. The racialised classification system emerged in 1903 and continued to permeate through the South African political and social systems. Following the inception of apartheid in 1948, social sciences in South Africa, and particularly the Afrikaans-speaking discipline of social anthropology ("*volkekunde*"), played an important role in conceptualising and substantiating cultural models of race classification for the Ministry of Bantu Affairs.[2] Apartheid theorists were devoted cultural relativists,[3] understanding humanity as separate cultural groups that "required" separate development. Referring to Leo Kuper's thesis (1965),[4] Gluckman (1975: 23–22) states that:

> This does not appear blankly as a theory that indigenous cultures are inferior, even if some of them argue that the people are less intelligent in terms of biogenetic endowment: their contention is that indigenous culture is excellent in its own right, not only appropriate for its bearers, but indeed something they should cling to and fight for, as Afrikaners fought for their language and culture against the might of English culture.

Therefore, the Afrikaner academic perspective on the uniqueness of culture as a hermetic closed entity, i.e. one that is resistant to intercultural exchange and social change, complemented apartheid's ideology of separate development. The NP entrenched race and culture as socio-legal concepts, in the sense that they are bounded communities with shared beliefs and practices.

The apartheid government subsequently replaced race with ethnicity in the 1970s, representing an attempt to redefine a segregated signifier beyond mere racial criteria, i.e. to substitute it with a more "legitimate and saleable surrogate" (Adam 1995: 426), and to correct the judgements of previous national governments and their policies. In this sense, and especially during the late-apartheid era, politicians in power rather used the concept of ethnicity when appealing to international audiences. The use of the term ethnicity "as a discourse strategy aimed at legitimating late-apartheid ideology – has tended to devalue and malign the term, the concept, and the questions which underpin it" (Bekker 1993: 26). As a result, liberal scholars involved in studying South Africa, activists involved in the anti-apartheid movement, socialists, communists, and social democrats vehemently rejected the use of the terms race and ethnicity, with the terms developing into virtual taboos. Some South African scholars who actively fought against apartheid, including the educationist Neville Alexander, historian Mohamed Adhikari, social anthropologist David

Webster,[5] and the well-known anti-apartheid figure Archbishop Desmond Tutu not only denied the existence of ethnicity and related concepts of race and culture, but also devoted their activism to "execrat[ing] ethnicity with all our being" (Tutu, quoted in Lijphart 1989: 14). In this vein, scholars critical of White supremacy theory described Coloured as a category imposed by the apartheid regime during the final decade of apartheid (Lewis 1987; Goldin 1987, 1989). They replaced "Coloured" with the term "so-called Coloured", thus effectively rejecting the categorisation system. However, it should be said that those active in this debate were mainly political activists, intellectuals, and academics who had been in some way involved in the struggle against apartheid and who identified with the Black African experience. From their perspective, those who adopted the category Coloured, even as a self-identification, were cooperating with the system and its segregated naming politics.

Immediately following the 1994 elections, "Race talk" was considered obsolete in government circles and as an issue that belonged to the past (Wilson 2002: 225). From the government perspective it was seen as necessary to make a major break with old apartheid thinking, despite the fact that the concept of race still played a significant role in the organisation of South African politics and society. After 1994, the post-apartheid government took over the apartheid ethnic classification system, in the hope that during the process of nation-building the country would come to terms with previous ethnic classifications and divisions. Rather than imagining ethnicity in terms of exclusive and conflict-laden boundaries, the aim was to perceive it as a bearer of culture (Aké 1993: 8–9). The concept of the "rainbow nation", coined by Archbishop Desmond Tutu, was originally used as a metaphor to promote the equal integration of multicultural diversity in society, and achieve social cohesion amongst a diverse population. Moreover, Tutu championed "*ubuntu*", a term found in all Bantu languages that reflects a romanticised vision of "the rural African community", one based upon reciprocity, respect for human dignity, community cohesion, and solidarity. Indeed, ubuntu became a *leitmotif* of Tutu's rainbow nationalism (Wilson 2002: 216).[6]

Alongside this public debate, more studies started to gradually emerge, beginning in the 1990s, acknowledging that many people in South Africa did indeed live their lives in terms of the apartheid-era racialised categories (Jensen 2008: 15) and readily identified themselves as such (Erasmus 1998, 2000, 2001; Salo 2003, 2004; Adhikari 2005). The majority of scholars who worked on identification processes with respect to the category "Coloured" accept its existence as a social fact, and one that results from historical developments since the beginning of White settlement in South Africa (Lewis 1987; Norval 1996; Reddy 2001; Jensen 2001). Several academic and governmental commissions[7] were initiated by successive apartheid governments in order to construct and produce knowledge of so-called Coloured people as a separate group. The main role in the creation of the category Coloured was arguably played by the so-called Wilcocks Commission of Inquiry into the Cape Coloureds (1937), which stated that:

A [C]oloured in this view, is a person living in the Union of South Africa, who does not belong to one of its aboriginal races, but in whom the presence of [C]oloured blood (especially due to descent from non-Europeans brought to the Cape in the 17th and 18th century or from aboriginal Hottentot stock, and with the admixture of European or [B]antu blood) can be established with at least reasonable certainty, a) from knowledge of the genealogy of the person during the last three or four generations; and/or b) by ordinary direct recognition of characteristic physical features […] by an observer familiar with these characteristics.

(Wilcocks Commission of Inquiry into the Cape Coloureds, 1937, par. 14, quoted in Jensen 2008: 23)

The classified Coloureds were constructed as a mixed *"bredie"* (breed), with this term developing into a common colloquialism highlighting their racialised and cultural hybridity (Adhikari 2005: 13), and colonial government built on these pseudo-scientific discourses by introducing a legal framework to politicise collective identity on the base of race. Consequently, the Coloured group was officially subdivided into three classes, as identified by the Wilcocks Commission (1937): the undesirable classes, i.e. the underclass, habitual convicts, ex-convicts, and drunkards at lowest level; farm and unskilled labourers, factory workers, and household servants, positioned in the middle; and relatively well-to-do and educated people at the top (Lewis 1987; Asforth 1990; Jensen 2001).

The construction of identification with the category Coloured must be considered from a relational perspective (Erasmus 1998). Government ascriptions about being Coloured have not only been imposed, but also negotiated within population groups that are not homogenous and static entities (Adhikari 2005; Jensen 2008), as is often imagined. In this sense this chapter situates the "making" and "unmaking" of social boundaries in specific places, and examines the everyday interactions of individuals based on an approach that stresses agency and not structural determinism (Wimmer 2008a: 1027). As the South African sociologist Zimitri Erasmus (1998: 3) emphasises, the construction of Coloured should be understood as "a fluid process involving agency and shaped by time and place".

According to Jensen (2008: 8), studies often offer readings on the conceptualisation of Coloured identification processes as either positive or negative. The first reading can be understood as being similar to the idea of "Black is beautiful" in the terms of the Black consciousness movement (Erasmus 2001), thus articulating the endeavour to overcome the negative connotations of the concept race by imposing positive attributes, in the sense of ethnicity as a bearer of culture, i.e. a clear shift away from race to culture. By contrast, negative perceptions are reflected in the racial stereotyping of Coloureds as lazy, poor, drunkards, and criminals or *"skollies"* (Jensen 2004, 2008; Adhikari 2005). Perceptions and ideas with positive and negative connotations certainly play into the hands of politicians, as shown in the next section.

3.2 Remaking differences and spatial ordering

It is necessary to extend our perspective beyond a broader differentiation of racial classification into situated positive and negative readings, to show how both at times simultaneously shape actors' political agency in the particular urban contexts of the Cape Flats. This is achieved by analysing how politicians, activists, and residents have internalised the classifications of being Coloured and Black African, i.e. paying attention to how they interpret, use, and re-interpret these categories situatively. It should be noted that while concepts of race and culture are part of their social life-worlds, i.e. of their active vocabulary, the terminology of ethnic or ethnicities is not used by either politicians, activists, or residents.

The in-between logic

The interesting point of departure lies in the particular history of South African politics. As betwixt and between the White and Black categories, the concept of Coloured initially functioned as a metaphor for the unclassifiable, for the "mixture of races" (Horrell 1958; Dubow 1995) during the apartheid era. The term Coloured today, still relies on notions of the mixed and the other (Reddy 2001: 65), with the dominant social construction referencing a lasting societal in-between position when contrasting Whiteness and Blackness. Ward councillors of the opposition parties, such as the DA and the former ID, particularly sustain this "sandwich" identification logic, reflecting the general feelings and tendencies within their wards.

> In fact, in the old system we were called the peanut butter – the in between position – like I said, when I was with the Blacks I was told 'you are not black enough to be Black', you are mallow, you are Coloured, and then I came to the Whites and they said 'you are not white enough to be white', so we always were in-between and still are .
>
> (Ward councillor from Mitchells Plain, 15.12.2005)

Additionally, self-defined Coloureds from Mitchells Plain frequently used the term *"Kafir"*[8] in conversations when speaking about the other, which maintains this perceived in-between position. *"Kafir"* is an offensive and abusive term, not only used in South Africa but also in other African countries to speak of or address Black Africans derogatively. Othering provides the self with an internal sameness and imposes an external difference or otherness (Werbner 2000 [1997]: 228). The usage of the term *"Kafir"* thereby imputes a positive connotation to the social category Coloured, while simultaneously serving to imagine Black Africans as inferior.

Conversely, people from Khayelitsha construct their neighbours as being Coloureds, and inferior. The importance of skin colour also plays a vital role in drawing the boundaries between themselves and the others. One prevalent narrative of Coloured that I heard from people who themselves identified as Coloured went like this:

> Xhosas had been raped by Dutchies [the Dutch] that's how Coloured came into effect. So they are part of us, we are their uncles. They came out of criminal acts. I wouldn't say that's why they are criminal but they have inherited part of us and part of those criminals.
>
> (Fieldnote, resident from Khayelitsha 24.04.06)[9]

This account perpetuates the idea of Coloureds being peoples of mixed blood, in this case through miscegenation between Xhosas and White settlers. These images of Coloureds additionally encompass notions of moral and physical degeneration, such as drunkenness and criminality (see Dubow 1995: 187).[10] They echo historical stereotypes of mixed-blood being associated with "biological disharmony", as was the case in former eugenic literature, views that became manifest in several segregation policies in South Africa, such as the Prohibition of Mixed Marriage Act of 1939, in order to preserve "racial purity and pride" (Dubow 1995: 182, 187).

It is also important to note that this construction of Coloureds in scientific discourses from the 1930s until at least the 1970s also associated them as more prone to criminality than Black Africans. The inference of "Black" criminality as such was interpreted as a proof of Coloureds inferiority. In general criminality among Coloureds and Black Africans was thought to be much higher than among Whites, and was attributed to their lack of social order and organic community bonds (Dubow 1995: 159, 160).[11] During occasions in the field, residents from Mitchells Plain and Khayelitsha described several examples of Black Africans committing crimes, where the crimes were characterised as barbaric and cruel. These examples contrasted Black Africans' criminal practices, such as cutting off tongues or ears, or stoning people to death, to those of Coloureds, whose criminal activities were characterised by organised crime or syndicates.[12] As shown by such narratives apartheid-era scientific and governmental discourses linking race to economic and social violence are still translated in various ways into modern-day discourses, along the lines of ideas of superiority and inferiority reproducing a racialised hierarchy.

In the following quote, the lack of intermarriage between groups is understood as "common-sense", i.e. a type of mutual agreement to maintain boundaries:

> When it comes to the intermarriage, very seldom you see a Coloured marry a Black person, maybe marry a person with darker skin but also Coloured, but he would never marry a person with a darker skin who is Black. That is what the system has done to us.
>
> (Fieldnote, resident from Mitchells Plain, 12.06.2006)

First of all, this quotation further illustrates how Coloured persists in everyday use as a category for classifying people with both fairer or darker skin.[13] The statement "that is what the system has done to us" attributes apartheid as being responsible for introducing the racist regulation of marriage as being only possible within the respective categories. After the Prohibition of Mixed Marriage Act, forbidding marriages between Whites and non-Whites, or classified Coloureds and Black Africans (Sherman/Steyn 2009: 64, 65), a series of other acts followed, which rendered intermarriages between the three categories almost impossible. These acts foresaw segregated access to the education system, to housing, in the labour market, etc. Against this background, the concept of belonging to a racialised group became manifest through the machinery of laws and rules that govern social relations between the racialised categories. By the same token, marrying within the same grouping can be considered as helping to stabilise mutual values. In this case, the sense of mutuality (Pfaff-Czarnecka 2011b: 3) marks a compliance with the rules governing social relations between people considering themselves as Coloureds or Black Africans, and thereby excludes social relations with other groups, i.e. it reinforces racism.

The education systems in Khayelitsha and Mitchells Plain still operate separately to a great extent, mainly recruiting pupils from their respective areas. Since 1994, the responsibility for the governance of schools has moved from a racially segregated departmental system to a centralised model of control through the Provincial Department of Education,[14] based on the ideal of "People's education for People's Power" (Kallaway et al. 1997: 1). However, while youths from the Cape Flats now have access to the previously White-only education system, and especially to the so-called Model C schools, education, including higher education, remains a question of affordability. Model C schools are semi-privatised state schools in the former Whites-only sector, mostly located in middle income suburbs. While such schools have followed a non-racialised approach since 1994, due to their high fees, it "is still true that the vast majority of students come from the immediate neighbourhood" (Kallaway 1998: 47), i.e. middle-income settlements. Furthermore, the schools in Mitchells Plain and Khayelitsha differ in schooling standards, with many citizens in Khayelitsha considering the school system in Mitchells Plain as much better in terms of equipment and the qualifications of so-called Coloured teachers.[15] This perception has evident links with the apartheid era, when the school system for classified Coloureds received more financial support than that for classified Black Africans (Kallaway 1997: 47). Even today only a few families from Khayelitsha have sufficient and stable financial means to be able to afford the costs of transport and school fees that might allow their children to attend schools in Mitchells Plain; "less than 5 per cent of the school-going population of Khayelitsha is on the move to schools outside of the township" (Clark 2015: 10). Therefore, the divided school systems in Mitchells Plain and Khayelitsha still reproduce historically rooted ideas of segregation, representing public spaces where little intermixing takes place.

The same holds true for many local markets in both places, which are predominantly occupied by local traders from the respective areas.[16] In fact, positionality within the townships "refers to placement within a set of relations and practices that implicate identification and 'performativity' or action" (Anthias 2002: 501, 502; Chapter 2), and which are directly linked to the enduring constructions of belonging to apartheid-era racialised categories.

From race to culture

Ward councillors and residents of Mitchells Plain and Khayelitsha substantiate and strengthen the apartheid-era discourse of identity through racialised categories by expressing differences between the townships with reference to cultural and social institutions (Anthias 1992: 421). The rhetoric used to express social difference is therefore adopted from apartheid-era protagonists, who entrenched race and culture as socio-legal conceptions: bounded communities based upon communal beliefs, principles, and practices.

> We [Coloureds] have a culture of a certain way of dancing, the Blacks also have a certain culture of dancing [...] we dance like the Europeans dance, ok, like we do the waltz, the rumba and the samba, the tango, that's how we dance. The Blacks again they do what we call 'bushmans jumping up and down' [...] – so that is a culture to them, to them it's beautiful, not to us, we don't see it that way [...] The other thing is the culture that we sing, we would sing more like the European style and American system than the Blacks, they have their own, what we call 'township language' and linguistics [...] And the major problem that we are having is, despite the 40 or 50 years that we have been together as Coloured persons that can speak the African language, that is also what you call the culture. Our Coloured people, we have also our own little slang, what you call 'township talks', our 'township language' that's how we talk, ok, and because we talk that way, the Blacks they can never identify the kind of language that we are speaking, even if they speak the Afrikaans language the slang they are using immediately shows that 'hey, that's a Black guy'.
>
> (Ward councillor from Mitchells Plain, 15.12.2005)

A special bond between those who are considered as being Coloured or White was a common understanding of belonging of inhabitants in Mitchells Plain, where they pointed to their way of dancing and singing, similar lifestyle, or speaking Afrikaans, the dominant language of apartheid, as all being practises similar to those of Europeans, in the sense of "acting White". Furthermore, the passion for karaoke, jazz dance, and the Cape Town Minstrel Carnival, known locally as the brass band festival "Coon Carnival", all reflect cultural institutions that belong exclusively to Coloureds, albeit with connections to "civilised" Europe. At the same time, the culture of Black Africans is imbued with negative connotations. On many occasions, people from

Mitchells Plain addressed the supposed primitive attitudes of Khayelitsha's residents with references to *"sangomas"* (natural healers), belief in witchcraft, and the fact that goats are slaughtered on the pavements and their heads sold as delicacies. The same stereotypes devaluing the cultural practices of the other also exist in Khayelitsha: "African people would always feel that Coloured people don't have a culture." The aforementioned Cape Town Minstrel Carnival, attended by Coloured people living in the Cape Flats, is more-or-less depicted as a cultural practice where the only aim is to get "drunk and silly".

Language represents another cultural marker and is perceived among inhabitants of both areas as the most deep-rooted historically evolved barrier to breaking down racial divisions, due to its embedded nature. Language embodies and constructs racialised differences and is regarded as a specific texture of relations. Most people from Mitchells Plain, including ward councillors and political activists are unable to speak any African languages fluently, whereas most residents of Khayelitsha that grew up under apartheid know to communicate in Afrikaans and English.

In this context, inhabitants from Mitchells Plain argued that their inability to speak African languages decisively reduced their opportunities within the labour market, given that many job positions require applicants to speak an African language. In this regard, the belonging to Coloureds can also be seen as a construction of economic exclusion and inequality, promoted through post-apartheid policies such as "Black Economic Empowerment" (BEE), which alienated voters from the ANC (van Kessel 2009: 476).[17]

In this fieldwork, references to "Africanness" were used as a marker to maintain boundaries between protagonists and "others". However, concepts of Africanness differed according to the migratory backgrounds of people in Khayelitsha. As discussed in the context of the political trajectories, the majority of people in Khayelitsha have migratory backgrounds, involving the leaving of the Eastern Cape and rural poverty in order to find jobs in Cape Town. In cases where people believe in the cultural practices of *"imbeleko"* or *"umqombothi"*,[18] ties to the rural society remain very strong, and rural ritual practices become ingrained in what they understand as Africanness. For instance, Mr Khumalo from Chapter 2 maintained an exclusionary understanding of Africanness:

> I am not religious, I am having a problem here, when somebody is saying that Jesus Christ is the King of Judah, so I am not here for Jesus Christ – this makes me so angry. I can't say that Jesus Chris is my king – I am an African [...] African people would always feel that Coloured people don't have a culture.
>
> (Khumalo, 24.04.2006)

This construction of Africanness in terms of a racialised understanding of Blackness involves notions of authenticity in terms of being African while resisting Christianity. In contrast to Africanness, Whiteness is linked to the European continent, and reflects domination and subordination (Erasmus

2001: 20). This construction further denies the existence of a Coloured culture per se, thus also excluding it from being defined as Black or "African".

Another extreme notion of Africanness is that imagined in cases where there is less maintenance of relationships with ancestral places, and fusions with other forms of cultural practices and values take place:

> I'm a born Xhosa in Gugulethu [former black African Township in Cape Town], there are families who stick to "*imbeleko*", it is a tradition, it was done by the forefathers and so on. You cannot speak about a general Xhosa culture, exactly, we are mixed now, for example truly speaking in my family we don't believe and we don't adhere to these customary things and worshipping the forefathers and all those things, we don't do that and I know there is some people who don't like to hear that. We are Christians as well, you know, we adhere to Christian values.
>
> (Coordinator of the Social Development Fund Urban Renewal Programme & Expanded Public Works Programme, 24.05.2006)

In township slang, this kind of mindset is circumscribed with the concept of a coconut, a "Black acting White", which implies the loss of Xhosa culture and language.[19] According to the fieldwork, many people in Khayelitsha, and particularly in Site C, could be located somewhere between these two extreme cases, embracing a subset of various cultural norms and values.

Although the mode of ascription has shifted from racialised to culturalist concepts, the implications of inferiority and superiority remain, with the mutual devaluing of the other's culture reaffirming racialised boundaries. Although aligning himself somewhat with European culture, a ward council-lor from Mitchells Plain also speaks of a specific Coloured culture: "when the system was imposed upon us, we adopted not just the identity but also the culture, what we call in Afrikaans '*Eie aan onself*' 'own to ourselves', it is a culture that we have." In this sense, speaking of one's own culture involves connoting Coloured-ness in positive terms, rather than the betwixt and between category of "racially mixed and other" (Reddy 2001: 65). Nonetheless, through this definition of a specific Coloured culture, racialised difference is implicitly articulated in cultural and social terms (Anthias 1992: 421). In this vein, practices of social locating by Coloureds and Black Africans vary according to how racialised categories intersect with economic and gender categories (Yuval-Davis 2006: 200). Following these ethnographic insights, I argue that "the cultural" has developed into a crucial arena for micro-politics.[20]

3.3 Urban politicians fostering social differences

Dynamics of divergence affect political action, standpoints, and representation within local government, characterised by the polarisation of council and municipal institutions (e.g. sub-councils) along racial lines.

Under the Apartheid system, the Coloureds ate, slept and drank one message from the apartheid propagandists, "they were better than the Africans, the natives of this land" [...] Coloured leaders in the Western Cape have not tried to bring about a racial understanding by talking about the social engineering of the apartheid system and how Coloureds must undergo ideological transformation if their race is to prosper and not die a drunken death.[21]

This is an excerpt of a speech by a former media advisor to the ANC mayor of Cape Town, published on his website in July 2005, which elicited a subsequent scandal among the local government representatives of Cape Town's city council. In his remarks, the media advisor, who identifies himself as a isiXhosa-speaking Black African, assumes that Coloureds have adopted a mindset engineered by decades of apartheid propaganda. During fieldwork, urban politicians in the former Coloured townships in the Cape Flats often referred to this scandal, which was referred to as a reason for their marginalisation and the area's social problems.

The media advisor's statement addresses the leaders of Coloured people in the Western Cape Province, by whom he is referring to Premiers of the Western Cape Province, mayors of cities, as well as ward councillors in former Coloured townships. The media advisor expects them to facilitate changes in the self-definition of Coloured people. The two following aspects are central to the further interpretation of this statement: 1) the unique political arena of the Western Cape Province; and 2) the opinions of ANC politicians and activists that Coloured leaders especially promote racist attitudes amongst their constituents. The Western Cape Province can be considered more heterogeneous than any of South Africa's other eight new provinces, with reference to administrative categories such as the ethnicity and religion of the population. While the state officially recognises Coloureds as the majority ethnic group since 1994, the Western Cape Province has a diverse history in terms of political culture. Up until the present day, there have been two elected premiers in the province who consider themselves as Coloured, one of whom belonged to the ANC and another who belonged to the conservative opposition party, the DA. As is the case with the provincial government, local governments in the Western Cape Province have largely consisted of members of the national opposition parties, such as the NP or the DA. Since 2011 the governing mayor of Cape Town has been the former leader of the ID party, which merged with the DA in the same year. Besides the premiers and mayors, ward councillors who consider themselves as Coloured particularly felt that they were being addressed as leaders in the media advisor's remarks. The majority of the Western Cape's ward councillors are not supporters of the ANC and are instead aligned with opposition parties, especially the DA. In short, the DA and other opposition parties form the core of local government in the former Coloured townships, whereas the ANC govern almost all former Black African areas.

Particularly in Cape Town, racism represents a resource for politicians, i.e. a specific method through which to communicate and address divides and belonging. The most obvious reason for this is that the former Coloured areas represent the majority of potential voters (Goldin 1989). In 1994, the majority of citizens in Mitchells Plain voted for the NP/NNP alliance, but the years that followed saw a shift to opposition parties, primarily the DA.[22] However, particularly during the time of this fieldwork, i.e. in the national and local elections in 2004 and 2006, and in subsequent election campaigns, all parties specifically addressed the "Coloureds" in their speeches. This is explicitly referred to as the "Coloured vote" among urban politicians. Against this backdrop, racialised belonging has developed as an indelible political issue that mobilises public spheres of activism against the (local) state. To understand this point, it is first necessary to observe how ward councillors in Mitchells Plain promote racism as Coloured leaders, which is achieved with reference to their political trajectories as discussed in Chapter 2. Critical political activists label such acts as "playing the race card".

Embracing religious diversity while "playing the race card"

It is important to note that ward councillors in Mitchells Plain see their electorate as being inherently racist, which forms a part of their knowledge of their wards as political units. Despite urban politicians being aware of the deep cleavages and power relations among their constituents, they use the "in between" metaphor to position themselves personally vis-à-vis the ANC government. Ward councillors repeated such positionings not only during election campaigns but also in their daily work. In their function as representatives of local government, they possess detailed knowledge of how to play up to the different belongings of the residents from Mitchells Plain.

An example of this behaviour is that of a ward councillor who ran for local government office on behalf of the ID party in 2006, when he appeared with his family in support of his new party leader Patricia de Lille at a rally in Tafelsig, the poorest area of Mitchells Plain. His main argument for his shift from the political right to left essentially revolved around the need to endorse the newly-formed ID in the "Coloured communities", disregarding some of the leftist ideas that this party proclaimed at that time. During this rally, he ensured that a brass band accompanied the politicians, with the musicians wearing T-shirts with the ID emblem. He depicted the brass band as a typical cultural institution that was highly valued among Coloureds. He also regularly organised huge brass band festivals in his ward, as a way of creating feelings of commonality and mutuality between ward residents and himself as ward councillor. Organised and financed by a ward councillor, these kinds of events were unique during fieldwork, because they didn't clearly relate to the developmental role of local government (Chipkin 2002) per se. However, even though his political rhetoric always included the phrase "we Coloureds" (a trait he shared with all ward councillors in the Cape Flats), when asked directly

whether he considered himself to be a Coloured, he asserted that on an individual level he is a Muslim, and that Islam is a colour-blind religion. In this
context, it should be noted that residents in the townships in the Cape Flats
recognise themselves as Muslims, born-again Christians, Jehovah's Witnesses,
Catholics, Baptists, etc.[23] Accordingly, religious practices in political settings,
such as council, sub-council, or even party political meetings and events
during election campaigns are to an extent "homogenised", for example when
politicians and their followers of diverse religious backgrounds pray together
in order to symbolise unity. As shown by the empirical data, most ward
councillors do not instrumentalise their respective religious convictions in
their way of doing politics, owing to the religious diversity represented within
their own wards and therefore the risk of alienating certain potential voters.[24]
While one ward councillor highlighted that he is a Muslim only on an individual
level, another pointed out that he believed in the bible but did not belong to
any specific Christian church, and another emphasised being raised as a
Baptist but no longer being a practising one; and all made sure to organise
their election campaigns with supporters from diverse religious backgrounds.

Planning integration and the creation of a new sense of place

While urban politicians in Mitchells Plain saw the diversity of religious
belongings within their wards as non-problematic, they constructed the issue
of social cohesion between the localities of Mitchells Plain and Khayelitsha as
one laden with problems.

The idea to integrate these two areas as "cohesive communities" and to
create "more liveable environments" (Donaldson et al. 2013: 630) arose out of
the Special Integrated Presidential Urban Renewal Programme (URP) in
2001. The URP "was identified as one of the first Presidential Lead Projects"
initiated in 1994 (South Africa Year Book 2004/2005: 380). Mitchells Plain
and Khayelitsha were two of eight townships targeted in a 10-year initiative.
An area-based approach (ABA) to urban renewal was, at the time, in line
with emerging international policies on participatory urban governance. The
ABA not only aimed to enhance intergovernmental cooperation and public-
private partnerships, but also foresaw the integration of the community in
local planning processes. It aimed at "renewing eight urban nodes of deprivation in six South African cities and [...] addressing poverty and underdevelopment [...] by involving residents and other interest groups who have a
stake in its future" (Donaldson et al. 2013: 630, 631). In general, the projects
included the provision of "hard" infrastructure such as housing, shopping
centres, electricity, street-lighting, medical clinics, roads, etc., as well as "soft"
infrastructure such as the clearing of bush in order to make the surroundings
safer, particularly for women, urban beautification programmes, and youth
and family centres.

Aligned with the ABA, Urban Renewal Offices were established in both
Mitchells Plain and Khayelitsha, and each was headed by an Urban Renewal

Manager. The manager of the Mitchells Plain office depicted the Urban Renewal Nodes, so-called "presidential nodes", as follows:

> I think if you look to Mitchells Plain clearly and this is not, this is not 'I think or perceived', one can see with the blatant eye you cannot compare Mitchells Plain to Khayelitsha. You cannot compare development that is happening in Mitchells Plain to Khayelitsha, as night and day. Khayelitsha is at least 15 years behind Mitchells Plain so in real it's a fact, clearly there is a need to prioritise development within Khayelitsha.
>
> (Urban Renewal Manager of Mitchells Plain, 12.04.2006)

In contrast to this official's perspective, many residents of Mitchells Plain complain about unequal investments in local development, arguing that Khayelitsha benefits more than Mitchells Plain from the URP. According to the official, it is these types of attitudes that hinder the social cohesion between Mitchells Plain and Khayelitsha, and hamper the creation of a new shared sense of place. According to him, these attitudes are due to the specific history of privileged housing allocation for Coloured townships in the Western Cape Province during apartheid.[25] From recent data the total expenditure for URP projects was approximately 1.2 billion Rand (approximately 76.3 million Euros) in Khayelitsha and 610 million Rand (approximately 38.8 million Euros) in Mitchells Plain in the period from 2002 to 2009 (Donaldson/du Plessis 2011: 47).

The policy makers involved in the URP also considered collaboration with local leaders, especially ward councillors, as playing a crucial role in assisting the community in capacity-building processes. During fieldwork, however, the URP became one of the most hotly-debated topics in local council and sub-council meetings. One dominant perspective among the ward councillors in Mitchells Plain was that officials and planners responsible for the URP at the local level are disconnected from the "Urban Renewal Nodes", i.e. the townships. This accusation questions the implementation approach of the URP as a hierarchal, "top-down" organisation, rather than one that equally integrates local knowledge systems:

> Currently what is happening with regard to Urban Renewal is that decisions are being made by officials, right, community has very little input in what programmes and projects are being run. Now we need that public engagement, we need public's influence in how we are developing and how the money is being spent and what projects it's gonna be implemented [...] currently they are sitting there on their own and they have created for themselves an empire of their own, they can decide what to do, when to do, how to do and how to spend money without consulting and answering to anybody, to be accountable to anybody.
>
> (Ward councillor from Mitchells Plain, 18.07.2006)

This ward councillor considers the URP as the platform for an "empire", i.e. a decision-making body where no checks and balances are in place to exert control over the selection of projects and expenditure. In fact, the URP is seen as representing "knowledge of domination" (*Herrschaftswissen*) (Lachenmann 2009: 18), i.e. wisdom that is passed down without consulting ward councillors or concerned ward residents. The ward councillor counter-argues that, as citizens, ward residents should actively participate in the whole process of renewing urban spaces, and some responsibilities should be delegated to local government and sub-council levels. This critical perception might also be connected to what Donaldson and Du Plessis (2011) reference as an overload of restructuring and participatory development programmes following the end of apartheid. According to these authors the URP was introduced in 2001, soon after South Africa had accomplished a structural government reform process at the sub-national level, which included the establishment of local governments, municipal elections, and so forth. The introduction of the URP, therefore, "had an impact on the institutional psyche at the time of having to deal with yet another nationally-imposed institutional structure" (ibid.: vii). An initiative that ward councillors in Mitchells Plain constructed as an agenda driven by their political opponents in the ANC.[26]

Ward councillors from Mitchells Plain further described the URP as a political initiative of the governing party ANC that would "hijack community initiatives".

> The other thing about the Urban Renewal is that Urban Renewal officials, they initiate development by taking over community's initiatives, they will hijack it and flag it as an Urban Renewal project. And I have a problem with this. For example in my area, if an Urban Renewal official came to me and said, 'councillor, what are your needs in your area?', then I would take initiative and I would go to them and say 'look, I need funding because I have this project' and then they would hijack it and say 'ok, thank you very much' but we will run it under Urban Renewal flag. For example, the Westgate Mall Housing, that was my initiative, my project, when I say my project with my community, we identified the land, we identified the beneficiaries and everything, we did all the ground work, we say the donkey work, and we did all the donkey work.
>
> (Ward councillor from Mitchells Plain, 20.12.2005)

In this statement, the URP is converted into a criminal arena where projects become "hijacked", i.e. appropriated for political gains, which leads to a distrust of state institutions and national programmes. Furthermore, the usage of the expression "donkey work" points to the perceived lack of acknowledgement of the ground work done by ward councillors, work that they see as key to the URP conducting useful projects.

With respect to the overarching topic of social cohesion and integration, different modes of violence and crime are highlighted as one reason as to why integration between the two communities will ultimately not work.

And I believe integration must not be forced upon people, it must be a voluntary thing. If we want to be integrated with Khayelitsha we must decide 'we want to be integrated', not have a government who forces this process upon us. Then we are just as bad as we say the old NP government was by removing people out of areas [...] we lived, I said earlier, with black neighbours in Kensington peaceful, no problem. But it should be a voluntary thing not a forced one because that will only create animosity amongst them and fights. One example, 'the Noon' in Milnerton, it's a black area but these Nigerians, the immigrants, they also live amongst them, and I mean they were killing each other because the Blacks don't want them in their communities. Just as the Coloureds, just remember we have gangsters, murderers, rapists [sic], they have there what they call "*tsotsies*", they also will rape and murder and all that – it's gonna be clashes because they gonna fight over territories. But in any case racism is rife [sic] in South Africa and integration must be voluntary.

(Ward councillor from Mitchells Plain, 20.12.2005)

From this perspective, although integration has the intent of mixing the residents of both areas, it brings with it increased potential for fights over territories between rival gangs or "*tsotsies*" to escalate, and thus is perceived as being largely impracticable.

Following this argument, ward councillors bring with them another significant perspective, as they relate inherent racism to the levels of unemployment and the marginalised economic situation of residents living in the low-to-no-income areas. According to them, these residents cannot "escape" the history of these areas as segregated spaces, because they cannot afford to move outside of them. Therefore, racism is portrayed as being particularly exercised in these low-to-no-income areas. Interestingly, the informant quoted previously claimed that if one could "identify a piece of land" that has not suffered under apartheid, an integrated society would be possible on these neutral grounds. Furthermore, this option would only pertain to Coloureds and Black Africans on middle incomes. In this case, middle-income people are imagined as those most capable of living the ideal of the rainbow nation; accordingly, the idea of the new South Africa is one "not for the Blacks and not for the Coloureds, but for middle income persons" (fieldnote, ward councillor from Mitchells Plain, 10.11.2005). The URP's overall vision of creating a new sense of place was thus ultimately undermined by the politicisation of increasing economic and social inequalities, and heightening mistrust among respective neighbourhoods.

Having investigated the various ways and sites where racism can play into the hands of urban politics in relation to violence, the ANC provincial and local governments subsequently started to organise a series of events, with the goal of opening up a

[...] debate to say to people that it's okay to speak about race relations [in relation to Black Africans and Coloureds] and that it's okay to go beyond 'rainbowism' to deal with the hard things that make it difficult for people to find each other and to live together.

This is a statement from the former ANC Premier of the Western Cape Province, made during a symposium about racism in March 2005 (Adams 2005: 1–2). It supports the viewpoint that the dream of the "rainbow nation" has not helped overcome the realities of unequal power relations and related conflicts on the ground. Moreover, it also hints at two countertendencies; on the one hand, there are local and provincial politicians who talk overtly about the racialised cleavages in South African society and want to open up a dialogue on racism; and on the other hand, especially among urban politicians such as ward councillors, there are those who have built up their political power based on these divides, and thus would rather shift the conversation from that of the rainbow nation to "re-racialisation". These dynamics of divergence characterise political action and representation within the spheres of local government, thereby polarising council and sub-municipal institutions (e.g. sub-councils) along racialised lines.

While ward councillors typically draw these racialised boundaries in political terms around their geographical place, there is also a specific type of ward resident who challenges the ward councillors' place making strategies, namely those activists involved with NGOs and new social movements. Having investigated how ward councillors make use of racialised categories in the Cape Flats, the next step is to elaborate upon the various types of activists and their othering processes.

3.4 Activists: stepping beyond boundaries

Many activists, despite being involved with different NGOs and social movements, shared the view that elected ward councillors do not truly represent their communities in the Cape Flats, as detailed in the previous chapter (see also Jensen 2004; Millstein 2010). By contrast, ward councillors in Mitchells Plain portray the activists within their wards as obstacles to politics, largely because

> NGOs, civil body structures and ward committees as well, are all co-opted by the ruling government, the ANC, because they basically control, they control all these organisations [...] it's a black thing.
> (Fieldnote, ward councillor from Mitchells Plain, 13.02.2006)

In the former Coloured townships, many inhabitants who are locally known as community activists were actively engaged in the anti-apartheid struggle. Generally speaking, at the time of my fieldwork, many of these activists were still allied with the ANC, and after 1994, either continued their work in community-based organisations (CBO), or built up new NGOs. Nonetheless, the ANC has been, and still is, a comparatively weak local force in former Coloured townships, a fact represented by the amount of electoral support in these areas in local and national elections for the opposition parties since 1994.

The most striking difference between ward councillors and activists lies in their way of constituting their everyday lives through "diverse constellations of belonging" (Pfaff-Czarnecka 2011b: 8, 2013), in relation to their place of residence, party-political positioning, and engagement in urban politics.

In accordance with Wimmer (2008a), it can be argued that in this case boundaries are deemphasised through activists' practices and actions, and that they thereby challenge the formal properties of the boundary strategies discussed in Wimmer (ibid.: 1042–1043). For instance, NGO and social movement activists who observed the ID rally in Mitchells Plain, criticised the ID as election campaign for its racialised rhetoric:

> The message that Patricia de Lille [ID leader] was bringing through at that meeting was that 'Coloured must stand together' and 'Whites had a chance and Blacks had a chance', 'The ID is the only party that will take care of the Coloureds' and so on – and I didn't like that.
>
> (Activist for the NGO "Community Correction Care" from Mitchells Plain, 28.02.2006)

Because of the tendency for political parties to politicise the other in racialised terminology, activists in the Cape Flats rebel against the existence of race and ethnicity as categories. The use of these two terms being virtually taboo has seen the use of "class" as the category used to explain inequalities in South Africa and forms the basis of political programmes used to address these inequalities (see Adam 1995). Irrespective of their party-political loyalties or fields of work in NGOs or new social movements, most political activists encountered during fieldwork shared a post-apartheid ideal of an integrative South African society. The following quotation is typical of the views of such activists in that it describes this post-colonial perspective, reflecting attempts to forge new ground:

> [...] the culture is the culture that we create. There is new cultures being created on a daily basis and we need to look at that because many times the Blacks and Coloureds and Whites have the same culture especially when it comes to the youth. They mix a little freer than it was at the beginning. And the culture is also more Westernised, and it cuts across, it cuts across religion and it cuts across your skin colour, right, and those are issues that must be addressed and we need to be doing it every day. It's just that people will tell you 'ach that's an old song'. But the more it's done it becomes a habit, the more you talk about it, the more you listen to it, everyday it's something new and then it becomes a habit. But it needs to be a habit of pro-activeness, a positiveness, not a negative degrading kind of attitude that we must instil in our children. Then I also

learn to children 'Black is beautiful and independent' so even if I wasn't Black we are not better than you.

(Activist from the NGO "Network Opposing Women
Abuse", 07.03.2006)

This quote exemplifies how both the aforementioned positive and negative readings on racialised categories exist in the Cape Flats, sometimes simultaneously. The NGO activist highlights processes of social change by implying that new cultures are being produced on a daily basis, spanning Westernised, racial, and religious boundaries, and that such attitudes should be instilled in younger people as educational principles.

While dismissing the logic of a racialised hierarchy and accentuating the positives of cultural heterogeneity as part of an integrated society, most activists in the Cape Flats still assert historically-rooted attachments to their respective localities. These activists maintain "old" senses of belonging based upon expressions of solidarity within their formerly segregated Coloured or Black African townships. Intermarriages between Coloureds and Black Africans are seldom practiced among activists; and in the home they also maintain the typical cultural institutions of their respective groupings.

Because of these practices, residents and activists in Mitchells Plain subsequently acquire certain labels: "because you are a Coloured you are a racist" (unemployed PhD psychologist and ANC member from Mitchells Plain). Because urban politicians in their everyday interactions build their political logic and arguments upon the significance of being a Coloured, the conception of "Coloureds being racists" is sustained in the public sphere, and reaffirm the boundaries separating a deeply divided society.

Working as an activist permits one to acquire a type of belonging whereby one's *racialised* sense of belonging becomes "blurred". Indeed, there are many empirical examples from my research in which activists create social spaces where race and ethnicity are not the main characteristics used to formulate common goals or grievances against (local) governments. In this respect, it is evident that activism at the interfaces with local government has not been institutionalised, as is the case with the ward committee system;[27] rather this activism can be seen as a response to increasing social inequalities in the Cape Flats. For example, issues with housing such as evictions and water being cut off led to the formation of a new social movement, the "Anti-Eviction Campaign" (AEC) in Mitchells Plain in 2000.[28] The AEC networks across townships in the Cape Flats, including Khayelitsha, and partakes in campaigns with other movements that represent both Coloureds and Blacks. Furthermore, given that many female activists concerned themselves particularly with issues such as crime, HIV and AIDS, and malnutrition, new female political spaces have emerged that enhance, and are themselves enhanced by, communication lines and networking between CBOs and NGOs across the Cape Flats. In the next chapter, the Building Women's Activism Forum is investigated as an example of a distinct social space where women, from different social and economic backgrounds, including those from Mitchells Plain and Khayelitsha, regularly meet. In this specific gendered configuration of actors, racialised boundaries dissolve. Here, activism rejects racism as a "principle of categorisation and social organisation", through coordinated actions that blur boundaries (Wimmer 2008b: 989),[29] and through other pronounced spatial, political, and gendered modes of positioning. It is through shifts between diverse constellations of belonging that (old) boundaries can become blurred, modified, and transformed. The dynamics of convergence characterise these different forms of activism, which all adhere to the idea of a rainbow nation. In these spaces, "future oriented possibilities in forging belonging by incorporating new elements into the existing parameters of togetherness" (Pfaff-Czarnecka 2011a: 204) are shaped by the overall purpose of becoming a democratic rainbow nation. Hence, the politics of belonging within the civil society arena define new common ground for belonging and extend beyond identity politics.

3.5 From segregation to forced integration?

Taking the experiences and spatial dynamics of the inhabitants of Mitchells Plain and Khayelitsha depicted in this chapter into consideration, it can be said that residents have internalised the attachments and divisions of belonging over generations. The place-making strategies of urban politicians and activists, on the other hand, are significantly shaped by either the remaking or the challenging of the racialised differences inherent in former and present-day spatial ordering.

Marcuse (2001; 1997) conceptualises segregation as an involuntary process by which people are forced to cluster within a specific area. In contrast to forced segregation, the author proposes the concept of an enclave, "an area of spatial concentration in which members of a particular population group, self-defined by ethnicity or religion or otherwise, congregate as a means of protecting and enhancing their economic, social, political and/or cultural development" (ibid. 2001: 2; 1997: 235). Following this line of thinking, one might characterise "enclave" and "ghetto" as being different expressions for similar concepts. While enclave is used here to denote spaces with predominantly positive implications for residents, ghetto refers to spaces with largely negative connotations. Additionally, it is important to think along lines where "all spaces of concentrated activity share some characteristics of a ghetto and some of an enclave [...] [p]ure types do not exist" (ibid. 1997: 235). In this sense, despite the economic and social marginalisation of townships, as well as the stigmatisation that they are subjected to in South African society, to a certain extent they can be understood as enclave societies. In this context, criminality and violence emanate from both forms of marginalisation and undercut social cohesions between former Coloured and Black African neighbourhoods.

This chapter highlighted how ways and understandings of belonging, whether it be to a political party or new social movement, grouping, or place or urban neighbourhood, have emerged over time, with the addition of new and sometimes controversial boundary-making dimensions. These metaphors of belonging compliment simplistic narratives on the nature of South African racism, which are perpetuated in the post-apartheid era by both urban politicians and township residents. In effect, we are dealing with two sides of the same coin; on one hand, the historical imposition of racialised categories, and on the other, their continuing repercussions, and manifestations in present, everyday life-worlds. The self-ascriptions of Coloureds and Black Africans, which involve both an active "we" and "they" (Cornell/Hartmann 2007: 77) must be interpreted as active responses to historically rooted circumstances, i.e. "situational transformations" (ibid.: 79). This chapter has brought a significant aspect into the broader picture, relating racism to issues of unemployment and the marginalised economic situation of residents. Urban politicians emphasise the limited social and geographical mobility of the residents of their ward and hence the lack of possibilities to escape from these areas as historically segregated spaces, mostly because of the simple fact that they cannot afford to move to another district.

Two recurring shifts in the urban arena were elaborated upon in this chapter, namely the turn "from race to ethnicity", and "from race to culture", on both a local and a national scale, during the apartheid and post-apartheid era. Both acted as (strategic) attempts to replace the signifier race, burdened as it is by biological determinism, and to connotate the new alternative "positively", i.e. in terms of human equality and justice. However, old classifications still function both as articulations of belonging as spatial and social positioning, as well as modes of exclusion and inclusion. Discourses around the terms ethnicity and culture are influential, supporting claims to entitlements as well as serving as symbolic ends. The category of Coloured is also consciously deployed, especially by politicians, in order to mobilise urban actors around a particular construction of political, geographical, and social belonging in the Cape Flats. In this respect, belonging functions as "a vehicle for diverse political projects, and is the essential building block of racism" (Anthias 1992: 436). Racism emanates not only from party politics but also from: 1) the interface between policies and politics, and everyday societal and cultural practices; 2) categories and ways of talking about racialised ascriptions; and 3) economic inequalities (Wilson 2002: 226). Moreover, it is urban state representatives who are engaged in activating feelings, mostly of fear and anxiety, relating to residents' historically precarious positions within the racialised hierarchy. Former racial segregation practices continue to buttress present-day logics of action, which fosters historical cleavages between groupings, i.e. "the speech has not changed" (Ward councillor from Mitchells Plain). Feelings of commonality among neighbourhoods relies on "categorisation, mental checkpoints, everyday life distinctions and public representations" (Pfaff-Czarnecka 2011b: 3), all of which are supported by identity politics. The dynamics of divergence shape political action and representation within spheres of local government, and reflect societal divisions.

The post-apartheid state continues to maintain the concept of race in the Cape Flats, despite it being increasingly ignored by activists. The ward councillors' perspective of racism, which is based on exclusion and superiority, does not find resonance with the activism discussed in this chapter. Hence, racialised markers are less salient in spheres of activism, where instead, other mechanisms of boundary-making are at work; for instance, those targeting the neoliberal or patriarchal nature of the state. Thus, this kind of activism subsequently functions as a form of counter-racism against the (local) state, by contesting categorisation, and denying the very existence of race and ethnicity. These social spheres are constituted by interactions across boundaries of "colour", i.e. by promoting other modes of spatial, cultural, and gendered positioning represented in diverse constellations of belonging. Accordingly, dynamics of convergence with respect to boundary-crossing shape activism, and ironically, it is here that the contested concepts of diversity and its importance for the "rainbow nation" turns into a lived reality, albeit one that state actors themselves abandoned long ago.

Notes

1 In this respect, Yuval-Davis references Michael Ignatieff (2001), who highlights that belonging is about feeling "safe" (Yuval-Davis 2006: 197).
2 The Ministry of Native Affairs was renamed the Ministry of Bantu Affairs in 1960, and subsequently the Ministry of Plural Relations and Development post-1994 (Wilson 2002: 232). This shows that even though officially this institution became somewhat more politically correct, it still maintained the apartheid philosophy of the NP.
3 Anthropologists in South Africa could be split into two main fields: "*volkekunde*" (mostly Afrikaans-speaking Whites) and social anthropology (mostly English-speaking, but also some Afrikaans-speaking Whites and Black Africans). The principles dividing these anthropologists on the one hand were based on an emphasis on a primordial ethnic identity underlying social and cultural life that makes separate development necessary. On the other hand, the constructivist perspective emphasised that social aspects are fluid and relational, rejecting the idea of separate development. "*Volkekunde*" was centred upon essentialist concepts of ethnic identity, e.g. tradition, religion, clothing, and so forth, which supported the political ideals of White supremacy in South Africa, and found parallels in similar notions concerning culture and race in German and American anthropology at the time (van der Waal/Ward 2006; Wilson 2002; Hammond-Tooke 1997; Gordon/Spiegel 1993).
4 Max H. Gluckman was a South African-born (British) social anthropologist who influenced the field of political anthropology with his analyses of political systems among African societies. Under his auspices, a school of anthropological thought was established that became known as the Manchester School (Kuper 1988). Leo Kuper was a South African sociologist who, among others, worked on race relations in South Africa and was an active member of South Africa's Liberal Party. In the 1960s, he regarded African states as "plural societies", shaped by the dominance of ethnic, religious, or racialised demarcated groupings. Kuper argued against modernisation theorists, who predicted that modernisation in African societies would link and integrate "tribal particularism" into nation-state building. Instead, he contended that urbanisation and modernisation processes lead to "an

increasing accentuation of plural division based on race and ethnicity" (Kuper 1969: 479, quoted in Lentz 1995: 312).

5 Most English-speaking anthropologists "kept their heads down" and did not actively resist apartheid (Wilson 2002: 213). However, there were some exceptions, such as David Webster of the University of the Witwatersrand, who became active in the anti-apartheid movement. He was particularly engaged in the Detainees' Parents' Support Committee, helping those detained by the apartheid government without trial. In 1989, Webster was gunned down outside his house under the orders of the "Civil Cooperation Bureau", a government agency (Kuper 1986 and Gordon/Spiegel 1993).

6 "*Ubuntu*" is translated as: "We are people through other people" and speaks of "community building", a basic respect for human nature, sharing, empathy, tolerance, the common good, and acts of kindness. Desmond Tutu proclaimed: "Ubuntu is the essence of being human; it is part of the gift that Africa will give the world" (Tutu, quoted in Marks 2000: 183).

7 Wilcocks Commission (1937) "Commission of Inquiry regarding Cape Coloured Population of the Union". UG 54-1937. Pretoria: Union of South Africa. Government Printer; Liquor Commission (1945) "Report of the Cape Coloured Liquor Commission of Inquiry". Pretoria: Union of South Africa. Government Printer; Theron Commission (1976) "Commission of Inquiry into Matters relating to the Coloured Group". Pretoria: Republic of South Africa. Government Printer.

8 "*Kafir*" is an Arabic word meaning non-believer, and was used by both Arabic traders and European settlers to categorise the natives.

9 This quotation was noted after a conversation with this male resident in Khayelitsha on the topic of gangsterism in a "*shebeen*".

10 Novels and narratives are endowed with rich material for understanding the construction of these images; therefore, see February (1981) and Coetzee (1988).

11 Many academic institutions functioned as think-tanks to produce knowledge, combining academic work in sociology with practical efforts to advance the welfare of the Afrikaner Volk and White supremacy (Dubow 1995: 157; Erasmus 2001; Terreblanche 2001). "Commissions of inquiry into the Cape Coloureds" summarised leading intellectual thinking on the most logical and scientific practices for the governing of the subaltern majority (Reddy 2001; Dubow 1995; Jensen 2001).

12 This knowledge was also shared by a German Development Expert, who explained that violence prevention programmes such as the Urban Conflict Management Programme have thus far only been introduced in townships previously classified as Black African. He argued that such programmes would not work in the formerly classified Coloured townships, due to the grade of organisation and gang structure which characterises organised crime in these areas.

13 For instance, in 1936 it was estimated that 38 per cent of the categorised Whites in the Cape Province were apparently of "mixed-descent", i.e. Coloured, a figure that was also circulated in scientific discourses (Findlay 1936: 44).

14 During apartheid, the Native (later Bantu) Education Department was responsible for African (later Bantu) education, and with the Indian and Coloured Education Departments came under the control of the central government. During the era of the Tricameral parliament (1982–1994), education for the different groups were managed separately under the different parliaments, i.e. for classified Whites, Coloureds, and Indians, whereas so-called Bantu education was still under the control of the central government (Kallaway 1997: 49).

15 Many teachers who were classified as Coloured are known for fighting long and hard to sustain "standards and traditions of learning in township schools in the apartheid era" (Kallaway 1997: 47). In this regard, there were protests against the government's attempts to close schools in townships in the Cape Flats in 2012. Concerned residents, activists, teachers, and NGOs continue to protest against "the discriminatory two stream system of education: the better one for the 20% elite

rich (ex-)model C type schools, and the other for the 80% inferior public schools of the poor" (ILRIG-Newsletter sent by Email, 02.01.2013).

16 Here I am referring to the local market in "town centre" in Mitchells Plain and the local stands in "Site C" in Khayelitsha. In this context it is important to note that from the point of view of the state local markets and stands form part of the informal economy. The impracticalities of integration are further highlighted by references to protecting these areas against migrants. During fieldwork, fear of strangers escalated due to local newspaper articles which often framed incidents as xenophobic attacks. (See for example: "Somali offer lessons, but we prefer violence", 01.09.2006, in: Cape Argues, p.16; and Rapiti, Dr. E.V., "Somali killings – shocking", 30.08.2006, in: Plainsman, p. 22). In 2008, similar violent actions against immigrants occurred in Khayelitsha, based upon the view that foreigners had taken over specific local trading sectors, such as the selling of airtime (township slang for prepaid mobile credit). Xenophobic attacks are still prevalent in all parts of the country (see Rémy, 27.02.2017, in: Le Monde, p. 3)

17 In 2003, the ANC government launched the "Broad-Based Black Economic Empowerment Strategy", which was signed into law in 2004. The BEE pursues policy objectives such as an increase in the number of people known as Black Africans in executive and senior management positions (Seekings/Nattrass 2005: 343–345; South Africa Yearbook 2004/2005: 181–182). It is important to note that a study conducted in 1997 had already stressed specifically the economic frustration of self-defined Coloureds in the Western Cape Region. It stated that many consider themselves excluded from both practical implementations of socio-economic programmes, mainly the "Reconstruction and Development Programme" and the BEE, and related affirmative action which favours Black Africans (Pickel 1997).

18 "*Imbeleko*" is a ceremony conducted to introduce a child to the elders and ancestors of the family, and is a compulsory step for further rituals, e.g. for boys' circumcisions. For both girls and boys, "*imbeleko*" is imperative for the "*lobola*", the (symbolic) wedding price paid when getting married. "*Umqombothi*" is a ritual held in a shack with family and other residents, who beg the ancestors to bring luck to a person, and involves all present drinking home-brewed beer out of a communal bucket.

19 The research was particularly focused on picking up specialised jargon and township slang, i.e. emic/urban categories and concepts in Afrikaans and isiXhosa, with examples including expressions such as a "Model C", which means a "Black speaking fluent English", or a "township chick", describing a "rough girl". These illustrations indicate the extent to which everyday language categorises people and things in racialised or gendered terms (Gukelberger 2013).

20 For important contributions on politics and culture, see Moore (2000) and Gilroy (1993), who discuss how the "cultural has become a crucial ground for political struggle" (Gilroy 1993: 57) in different regional contexts.

21 http://library.iol.co.za:4321/view/article, accessed on 02.02.2006.

22 The political nexus of the urban governance arena has been thoroughly explained in Chapter 2.

23 According to Statistics South Africa (2006), Mitchells Plain includes the following majorities among its 26 categories of religious groupings: "Islam" with ca. 70,300 people, 39,000 people with "No religion", "Other Christian churches" with ca. 37,000 people, "Pentecostal/Charismatic Churches" with ca. 4,900 people, and "Other Apostolic Churches" with ca. 4,400 people; in Khayelitsha: 67,000 with "No religion", "Methodist Church" with 49,500 people, "Other Christian Churches" with 32,000 people, "Other Apostolic Churches" with 31,000 people, and "Zion Christian Churches" with ca. 25,500 people.

24 For religious belonging to Christian churches in former Black African townships in Cape Town see Burchardt (2013).

25 Provincial and Local Government Department, Republic of South Africa (2007) "Nodal Economic Profiling Project Business Trust, Mitchells Plain".

26 Donaldson and Du Plessis (2011) are of the opinion that once the then-mayor, Helen Zille from the Democratic Alliance, changed her approach towards the URP in 2006, "the working relations eased and the unit could facilitate its projects without political animosity or distrust" (ibid. vii).

27 Chapter 4 situates and analyses the ward committee as a participatory institution within the urban governance arena.

28 The AEC has been discussed in the context of Mr Jeferson's political trajectory in Chapter 2.

29 This quote refers to ethnicity as a principle of categorisation and social organisation, yet in this case it can also be equated with racism.

References

Adam, H. (1995). The Politics of Ethnic Identity: Comparing South Africa. *Ethnic and Racial Studies* 18(3), pp. 457–475.

Adhikari, M. (2005). *Not White Enough, Not Black Enough. Racial Identity in the South African Coloured Community*. Athens: Ohio University Press.

Aké, C. (1993). What Is the Problem of Ethnicity in Africa? *Transformation: Critical Perspectives on Southern Africa* 22, pp. 1–22.

Anthias, F. (1992). Connecting 'Race' and Ethnic Phenomena. *Sociology* 26(3), pp. 421–438.

Anthias, F. (2002). Where Do I Belong? Narrating Collective Identity and Translocational Positionality. *Ethnicities* 2(4), pp. 491–514.

Anthias, F. (2006). Belonging in a Globalising and Unequal World: Rethinking Translocations. In: N. Yuval-Davis, K. Kannabirān and U. Vieten, eds. *The Situated Politics of Belonging*. London: Sage, pp. 17–31.

Ashforth, A. (1990). *The Politics of Official Discourse in Twentieth-Century South Africa*. Oxford: Clarendon Press.

Bekker, S. (1993). *Ethnicity and South Africa*. Centre for Social and Development Studies, University of Natal.

Burchardt, M. (2013). Belonging and Success: Religious Vitality and the Politics of Urban Space in Cape Town. In: I. Becci, M. Burchardt, and J. Casanova, eds. *Topographies of Faith. Religion in Urban Spaces*. Leiden: Brill, pp. 167–188.

Clark, J. (2015): The Demographics of Schooling in the Township. Khayelitsha. Briefing Document 2. School Improvement Initiative, University of Cape Town.

Chipkin, I. (2002). A Developmental Role for Local Government. In: S. Parnell, E. Pieterse, M. Swilling and D. Wooldridge, eds. *Democratising Local Government. The South African Experiment*. Landsdowne: University of Cape Town, pp. 57–78.

Coetzee, J. M. (1988). *White Writing. On the Culture of Letters in South Africa*. New Haven, CT: Yale University Press.

Cornell, S. and Hartmann, D. (2007). *Ethnicity and Race: Making Identities in a Changing World*. Thousand Oaks, CA: Pine Forge Press.

Donaldson, R. and Du Plessis, D. (2011). *Analysis and Highlighting of Lessons Learnt from and Best Practices in the Urban Renewal Programme*. Report prepared for URP, City of Cape Town.

Donaldson, R., Du Plessis, D., Spocter, M. and Massey, R. (2013). The South African Area-based Urban Renewal Programme: Experiences from Cape Town. *Journal of*

Housing and the Built Environment 28(4), Special Issue Title: More than Twenty Years After the Repeal of the Group Areas Act: Housing, Spatial Planning and Urban Development in Post-Apartheid South Africa, pp. 629–638.

Dubow, S. (1995). *Scientific Racism in Modern South Africa*. Cambridge: Cambridge University Press.

Erasmus, Z. (2000). Hair Politics. In: S. Nuttall and C. A. Michael, eds. *Senses of Culture. South African Culture Studies.* Oxford: Oxford University Press, pp. 1–14.

Erasmus, Z. (2001). Re-imaging Coloured Identities in Post-Apartheid South Africa. In: Z. Erasmus, ed. *Coloured by History, Shaped by Place. New Perspectives on Coloured Identities in the Cape.* Cape Town: Kwela Books, pp. 3–28.

Erasmus, Z. and Pieterse, E. (1998). Conceptualising Coloured Identities in the Western Cape Province of South Africa. In: M. Palmberg, ed. *National Identity and Democracy.* Cape Town: Mayibuye Centre, the Nordic Africa Institute and the Human Sciences Research Council in South Africa, pp. 1–20.

February, V. A. (1981). *Mind Your Colour. The "Colored" Stereotype in South African Literature.* London: Kegan Paul.

Findlay, G. (1936). *Micegenation.* Pretoria: Pretoria News and Printing Works.

Gilroy, P. (1993). *Small Acts: Thoughts on the Politics of Black Culture.* London: Serpent's Tail.

Gluckmann, M. (1975). Anthropology and Apartheid. The Work of South African Anthropologists. In: M. Fortes, S. Patterson and I. Schapera, eds. *Studies in African Social Anthropology.* London: Academic Press, pp. 21–39.

Goldin, I. (1987). *Making Race.* London: Longman.

Goldin, I. (1989). Coloured Identity and Coloured Politics in the Western Cape Region of South Africa. In: L. Vail, ed. *The Creation of Tribalism in Southern Africa.* London: James Currey, pp. 241–254.

Gordon, R. and Spiegel, A. (1993). South Africa Revisited. *Annual Review of Anthropology* 22, pp. 83–105.

Gukelberger, S. (2013). Whose Rainbow Nation? Local Politics and Belonging in Cape Town, South Africa. Dissertation. Faculty of Sociology. Bielefeld University.

Hammond-Tooke, W. D. (1997). *Imperfect Interpreters: South Africa's Anthropologists 1920–1990.* Johannesburg: Witwatersrand University Press.

Hall, S. (1994). 'Rasse', Artikulation und Gesellschaften mit struktureller Dominante. In: S. Hall, ed. *Rassismus und kulturelle Identität.* Ausgewählte Schriften 2. Hamburg: Argument Verlag, pp. 89–136.

Horrell, M. (1958). *Race Classification in South Africa, Its Effects on Human Beings.* Johannesburg: South African Institute of Race Relations.

Ignatieff, M. (2001). *Human Rights as Politics and Idolatry.* Princeton, NJ: Princeton University Press.

Jensen, S. (2001). Claiming Community, Negotiating Crime: State Formation, Neighborhood and Gangs in a Capetonian Township. PhD dissertation. Roskilde University, International Development Studies.

Jensen, S. (2004). Claiming Community: Local Politics in the Cape Flats, South Africa. *Critique of Anthropology* 24(2), pp. 179–207.

Jensen, S. (2008). *Gangs, Politics & Dignity in Cape Town.* Chicago, IL: University of Chicago Press.

Kallaway, P. (1997). Reconstruction, Reconciliation and Rationalization in South African Politics of Education. In: P. Kallaway, G. Kruss, A. Fataar and G. Donn, eds. *Education After Apartheid. South African Education in Transition.* Cape Town: University of Cape Town Press, pp. 34–49.

Kallaway, P., Kruss, G., Donn, G. and Fataar, A. (1997). Introduction. In: P. Kallaway, G. Kruss, A. Fataar and G. Donn, eds. *Education After Apartheid. South African Education in Transition.* Cape Town: University of Cape Town Press, pp. 1–5.

Kuper, L. (1965). *An African Bourgeoisie. Race, Class, and Politics in South Africa.* New Haven, CT: Yale University Press.

Kuper, A. (1986). Anthropology and Apartheid. In: J. Lonsdale, ed. *South Africa in Question.* Cambridge: University of Cambridge, pp. 33–51.

Kuper, A. (1988). *The Invention of Primitive Society. Transformations of an Illusion.* London: Routledge.

Lachenmann, G. (2009). Renegotiating and Overcoming Frontiers and Constituting Crosscutting Social Spaces and Institutions: Conceptual and Methodological Issues in Development. *Working Paper* 360. Bielefeld University, Faculty of Sociology.

Lamont, M. and Molnár, V. (2002). The Study of Boundaries across the Social Sciences. *Annual Review of Sociology* 28, pp. 167–195.

Lentz, C. (1995). 'Tribalismus' und Ethnizität in Afrika: ein Forschungsüberblick – 'Tribalism' and Ethnicity in Africa: An Overview of Research. *Leviathan: Zeitschrift für Sozialwissenschaft* 23(1), pp. 115–155.

Lewis, G. (1987). *Between the Wire and the Wall. A History of South African "Coloured" Politics.* Cape Town: David Philipp.

Lijphart, A. (1989). The Ethnic Factor and Democratic Constitution-Making in South Africa. In: E. J. Keller and L. A. Picard, eds. *South Africa in Southern Africa: Domestic Change and International Conflict.* Boulder, CO: Lynne Rienner, pp. 13–24.

Marcuse, P. (1997). The Enclave, the Citadel, and the Ghetto. What Has Changed in the Post Fordist U.S. City. *Urban Affairs Review* 33(2), 228–264.

Marcuse, P. (2001). *Enclaves Yes, Ghettos, No: Segregation and the State.* Paper presented at the Lincoln Institute of Land Policy Course titled "International Seminar on Segregation in the City", 26–28 June.

Marks, S. C. (2000). *Watching the Wind. Conflict Resolution during South Africa's Transition to Democracy.* Washington, DC: United States Institute of Peace Press.

Mecheril, P. and Melter, C. (2009). Rassismustheorie und – forschung in Deutschland. Kontur eines wissenschaftlichen Feldes. In: C. Melter and P. Mecheril, eds. *Rassismuskritik.* Schwalbach: Wochenschau Verlag, pp. 13–21.

Millstein, M. (2010). Limits to Local Democracy: The Politics of Urban Governance Transformations in Cape Town. *Working Paper* 2. Stockholm: Swedish International Centre for Local Democracy.

Moore, D. S. (2000). The Crucible of Cultural Politics: Reworking "Development" in Zimbabwe's Eastern Highlands. *American Ethnologist* 26(31), pp. 654–689.

Seekings, J. and Nattras, N. (2006). *Class, Race, and Inequality in South Africa.* Scottsville: University Press of KwaZulu-Natal Press.

Pfaff-Czarnecka, J. (2011a). From 'Identity' to 'Belonging' in Social Research: Plurality, Social Boundaries, and the Politics of the Self. In: S. Albiez, N. Castro, L. Jüssen and E. Youkhana, eds. *Ethnicity, Citizenship and Belonging. Practices, Theory and Spatial Dimensions.* Frankfurt am Main: Iberoamericana-Vervuert, pp. 199–219.

Pfaff-Czarnecka, J. (2011b). From 'Identity' to 'Belonging' in Social Research: Ethnicity, Plurality, and Social Boundary-Making. *Working Paper* 368. Bielefeld University, Faculty of Sociology.

Pfaff-Czarnecka, J. (2013). Multiple Belonging and the Challenges to Biographic Navigation. *MMG Working Paper* 13–05. Göttingen: Max-Planck-Institut zur Erforschung multireligiöser und multiethnischer Gesellschaften.

Pickel, B. (1997). *Coloured Ethnicity and Identity. A Case Study in the Former Coloured Areas in the Western Cape/South Africa*. Berlin: LIT Verlag.

Reddy, T. (2001). The Politics of Naming: The Constitution of Coloured Subjects in South Africa. In: Z. Erasmus, ed. *Coloured by History, Shaped by Place. New Perspectives on Coloured Identities in the Cape*. Cape Town: Kwela Books, pp. 64–79.

Rodman, M. C. (1992). Empowering Place: Multilocality and Multivocality. *American Anthropologist* 94(3), pp. 640–656.

Salo, E. (2004). *Respectable Mothers, Tough Men and Good Daughters: Producing Persons in Manenberg Township, South Africa*. PhD Thesis, Emory University.

Salo, E. (2003). Negotiating Gender and Personhood in the New South Africa: Adolescent Women and Gangsters in Manenberg Township on the Cape Flats. In: *European Journal of Cultural Studies*, pp. 345–365.

Sherman, R. and Steyn, M. E. (2009). E-race-ing the Line: South African Interracial Relationships Yesterday and Today. In: M. E. Steyn and M. van Zyl, eds. *The Prize and the Price. Shaping Sexualities in South Africa*. Cape Town: HSRC Press, pp. 55–81.

Solomos, J. (2015). Stuart Hall: Articulations of Race, Class and Identity. In: *Ethic and Racial Studies* 37(10), pp. 1667–1675.

Terreblanche, S. (2001). *A History of Inequality in South Africa 1652–2002*. Scottsville: University of Natal Press.

van der Waal, K. and Ward, V. (2006). Shifting Paradigms in the New South Africa. Anthropology after the Merger of Two Disciplinary Associations. *Anthropology Today* 22(1), pp. 17–20.

Van Kessel, I. (2009). South Africa. In: A. Mehler, H. Melber and K. van Walraven, eds. *Africa Yearbook. Politics, Economy and Society Southern of the Sahara, Volume 5*. Leiden and Boston: Brill, pp. 473–489.

Werbner, P. (2000). Essentialising Essentialism, Essentialising Silence: Ambivalence and Multiplicity in the Construction of Racism and Ethnicity. In: P. Werbner and T. Modood, eds. *Debating Cultural Hybridity. Multi-Cultural Identities and the Politics of Anti-Racism*. London: Zed Books, pp. 226–254.

Wilson, R. A. (2002). The Politics of Culture in Post-Apartheid South Africa. In: R. G. Fox and B. J. King, eds. *Anthropology beyond Culture*. Oxford: Berg, pp. 209–232.

Wimmer, A. (2008a). Elementary Strategies of Ethnic Boundary Making. *Ethnic and Racial Studies* 31(6), pp. 1025–1055.

Wimmer, A. (2008b). The Making and Unmaking of Ethnic Boundaries: A Multilevel Process Theory. *American Journal of Science* 113(4), pp. 970–1022.

Yuval-Davis, N. (2006). Belonging and the Politics of Belonging. *Patterns of Prejudice* 40(3), pp. 197–214.

State and non-state sources

Government Communications (2004). *South Africa Yearbook 2004/2005*. Pretoria: Government Communications (GCIS).

Ministry of LocalGovernment (2009). White Paper on Local Government. Draft. Pretoria: Government Printer.

Statistics South Africa (2006). *Religion (Grouped) by Geography, Cape Flats.* Pretoria: Statistics South Africa.

Newspaper articles

Adams, S. (2005). Racism. 'We`re All in Trouble'. In: *Weekend Argus*, 26.03.2005, p. 1–2.
ILRIG-Newsletter, 02.01.2013.
Rapiti, E. V. (2006). Somali Killings – Shocking. In: *Plainsman, Independent Community Newspaper*, 30.08.2006, p. 22.
Rémy, Jean-Philippe (2017). Violences contre les "étrangers" en Afrique du Sud. Les ravages de la drogue "nyaope" et la criminalité, attributes aux immigrés, justifient une xénophobie aveugle. In: *Le Monde*, p. 3.
Staff Reporter (2006). Somali Offer Lessons, but We Prefer Violence. In: *Cape Argus*, 01.09.2006, p. 16.

Websites

ANC Cape Town mayoral media advisor. Available at: http://library.iol.co.za:4321/view/article [02.02.2006].
Author unknown. (26.09.1997). Winnie Mandela: Victims' Families Accuse Winnie of Killings, Assault and Abduction. [online] *Independent*. Available at: www.independent.co.uk/news/winnie-mandela-victims-families-accuse-winnie-of-killings-assault-and-abduction-1241212.html [12.01.2017].
Imibizos. Available at: www.info.gov.za/issues/imbizo/index.html [24.09.2012].
Mandrax. Available at: www.drugaware.co.za/mandrax.html [08.11.2017].
Municipal System Act 32/2000 (Section 16, 17). Available at: www.gov.za/documents/local-government-municipal-systems-act [05.06.2017].

4 Urban governance and parallel spaces

A considerable body of work within academia deals with relationships between democracy and development, with a focus on the "developmental state". The classical theory of the developmental state refers to the model of a centralised state, one ascribed to many East Asian nations after the Second World War. This model purports the state as the main actor directing developmental process in the country, which also co-operates with the private sector albeit from a position of supremacy (Wade 1990). In the last two decades, the debate on whether a developmental state could be thought of as democratic has moved in two significant directions. One sees researchers argue that democratic developmental states are incapable of directing development. The main argument behind this school of thought centres around the objectives of democratic developmental states being "autonomy and accountability; growth and redistribution; consensus and inclusiveness", which are too ambivalent and therefore hard or impossible to achieve (Löwenthal 1963; White 1988). The second school of thought is represented by a rising number of scholars who are in favour of the model of democratic developmental states (Sen 1999; Rodrik 2004). In the 1990s, they reversed the assumption of classic theory of development first – democracy later by proposing democracy as a precondition for development.[1]

Similarly, since 1994, politicians and policy-makers in South Africa have inextricably linked development and democracy, emphasising participatory democratic rule as the vehicle through which development should best proceed according to the interests of the formerly oppressed residents. This view is clearly linked to one of modern South Africa's key documents, the visionary clause "The People Shall Govern!" in the ANC's Freedom Charter (1955), which championed "democratic organs of self-government". Almost half a century after this clause was penned, the ANC, now the ruling government party, has stuck to this rhetoric of self-government in its policy making and has begun to establish new channels for public participation. This chapter looks at how developmental local government is conceptualised and put into practice by the state on the one hand, and activists on the other.

The establishment of developmental local government in South Africa can be divided into three phases between 1993 and 2005, and is considered fundamental to the South African Government's plan for establishing participatory democracy, being

> [...] committed to working with citizens and groups within the community to find sustainable ways to meet their social, economic and material needs and improve the quality of their lives.
>
> (White Paper on Local Government 1998: Section B1)

Hence, the South African Government's vision for participatory democracy is that it be achieved, among other means, through the direct involvement of citizens and community activists in local government matters, including development planning and the delivery of basic services. In this context, government policy further stated:

> Socio-economic development and community empowerment is mainly directed at poverty eradication. The majority of the poor are women, and empowerment strategies which focus on women are likely to prove the most effective and inclusive. Municipalities need to develop their capacity to understand the diverse needs of women in the community, and address these needs in planning and delivery processes to enhance their impact on poverty eradication.
>
> (White Paper on Local Government, 1998: Section B1)

Here, participation becomes more differentiated by emphasising the unequal situation of women, and thus the particular need to empower them. Furthermore, it is legally required that ward councillors and officials foster public participation and support local communities, particularly women, in engaging in municipal affairs (Local Government Municipal System Act 2000: Section 17; Department Provincial and Local Government and German Agency for Technical Cooperation 2005). Similarly, state policies prescribe a holistic concept of participation by concentrating on women's vulnerability, as well as children's and people with handicap's insecure positions within society. However, these policies fail to mention other societal groups who share similar statuses of vulnerability and social insecurity, such as unemployed men, intersex people, undocumented migrants, and so forth. The point here is that the empowerment of women can only be successful and sustainable when men and in fact the whole of society challenge the dominant binary construction of gender based upon heteronormativity. This gender construction implies certain conventions (in the areas of reproductive work, housework, and child-raising) to female-ascribed private and reproductive spheres and male-ascribed public spheres.

Overall, the state addresses, and therefore includes, the community as a single social actor in the developmental practices of local government. In reality, however, communities are represented by various social actors with diverse interests, resources, and logics of action, as exemplified in the milieus in the Cape Flats. At least three prominent actors negotiate the meaning of decentralisation at the state-civil society interface; namely the elected ward councillors, the officials, and the activists engaged in the different development sectors, such as health, safety and security, sports, etc.

In what follows, I focus my attention on the municipal structure, where the sub-council represents an institution that enhances urban governance. While sub-council meetings are open to the public and are supposed to contribute to the creation of an informed citizenry, this chapter details how activists in Mitchells Plain oppose this formalised institution of urban governance. In this respect, I argue that while their participation in formalised institutions is limited, other everyday modes of political action demonstrate how residents and activists actively engage with the local state. Indeed, through these practises, parallel political spaces are being constituted that challenge local government's policies and decision-making processes. The trajectories detailed in Chapter 2 illustrated that single individuals can be active in multiple political spaces, which emerge and are maintained through processes of interaction. A variety of political spaces in the Cape Flats are connected to themes of evictions, water or electricity being "cut off", or women's participation. Activists consider such topics and issues as important in moving towards opening up debates where they might be able to voice their demands and strengthen self-organisation. In this respect, while state policies emphasise improving areas related to women's vulnerability, many female activists strive for empowerment in parallel social spaces, rather than using official, formalised participation channels.

This chapter is divided into three parts. The first provides an overview of the academic debate on decentralisation and public participation in South Africa, contextualising the developmental role of local government. Based upon a particular event that centres on a sub-council meeting and protest actions against water cut-offs in Mitchells Plain, the second part examines and analyses these interactions in and beyond the (sub-)council. The analysis utilises and discusses the categories of "culture of non-payment", "dignity", and (lack of) "trust" and "confidence". The analysis then moves to distinct, parallel public spaces such as the "Building Women's Activism" forum, where people create new ways of coordinating and organising social life with the intention of shaping policy. This approach allows us to form a deeper understanding of the structuration of the urban governance arena and parallel social spaces, first alluded to in the discussion of the ward councillors' and activists' trajectories in Chapter 2. The third and final part compares continuities and discontinuities in urban governance, thereby shedding light on the nature of contemporary relations between local government, civil society, and parallel spaces in South Africa.

4.1 Decentralisation and urban intricacies

The main goal in the developmental role of local government is seen by both state actors and policy makers as poverty eradication. Considering that until the mid-1990s, local government in South Africa functioned as a structural extension of the highly centralised state, the initiative to democratically engage with the citizenry has only been a relatively recent phenomenon, i.e. post-1994. The objective was to build a democracy from below, engaging with the country's citizenry and thereby overcoming a history of racialised social cleavages. To this purpose, the state created institutions for the participation of poor people in the form of sub-councils, ward committees, and "*imbizos*".[2]

Integrating the previously-excluded areas of the Cape Flats into the municipal system of Cape Town has been a complex task for both local government and society. To this day, there remain many informal settlements, both old and new, that are not formally incorporated into the system, and whose size and population are still unknown. In order to facilitate the integration process, city and sub-councils have been required to produce Integrated Development Plans (IDPs), which include spatial, institutional, and financial elements. As part of the push for decentralisation, new institutional arrangements were made in which sub-councils and ward committees are supposed to play a part in the realisation of the IDPs' goals. Sub-councils and ward committees are tasked with bringing local governments and their communities together, providing decentralised political spaces where the actors meet and interact. With the participation of the so-called poor communities, IDPs are supposed to support municipalities in establishing holistic plans for poverty alleviation (Cashdan 2002: 163).

Public participation in South Africa is inevitably linked to decentralisation and vice versa. While decentralisation is linked to the concept of devolution, i.e. the transmission of power to locally constituted entities of government (see Chapter 1), special institutions are to be established which aim to bring local units of government together with "citizens and groups" (White Paper on Local Government 1998: Section B1). Despite their varying focus, analyses of decentralisation processes all point to an ambitious

> [...] commanding, complex, forward-looking and optimistic manifesto to systematically realise a participatory local governance system that is at the heart of an intergovernmental effort to achieve democratic citizenship, integrate development and reconciliation between the divided communities of South Africa.
>
> (Pieterse 2002: 3)

Aside from this rather optimistic observation, scholars have further critically examined at least two simultaneous and interrelated objectives of such decentralisation processes: first, local government's strategic requirement to raise revenue among poor residents; and second, the establishment of instruments for the participation of poor people. While Cape Town's local government is itself responsible for the redistribution of approximately 90 percent of its revenues (Wooldridge 2002: 127), which it earns primarily from local rates and trading accounts such as water and electricity,[3] it is simultaneously confronted with a high rate of unemployment, and residents who cannot pay for basic services. In fact, services such as water, sanitation, waste, and electricity are not only the main revenue sources of municipalities but are also usually provided only to those who can afford to pay for them. Thus, local government often has to address the needs of poor people – who cannot afford to pay for basic services – in a manner that does not exceed the overall capacity for provision or challenge the sustainability of the financial or natural resource base (Parnell 2005: 36). Flights of capital and the prevalence of cases of corruption further aggravate the issue of insecure revenue streams at the urban level.

All South Africans are granted basic socio-economic and environmental rights, i.e. to basic services and a healthy and sustainable environment, as part of the constitution (Liebenberg et al. 2000). In 2000, the Cape Town City Council proposed what is known as the indigent policy, in order to meet and safeguard a similar notion of the public good.[4] The indigent policy is a strategy paper for local governments on how to organise social cash transfers (grants) to residents who cannot afford to pay for basic services. The objective of this policy is to translate the rights proclaimed in the constitution through concrete practices of local government in tackling high levels of so-called "chronic poverty" in Cape Town (van Ryneveld et al. 2003: 5). The differentiation between "paying citizens" and "indigent citizens" in the policy defines who is entitled to receive a grant, and therefore regulates access to resources for those people with low-to-no income. There is no provision in the indigent policy for those unemployed who rely on the State Old Age Pension, Disability Grant, Child Support Grant, Foster Child Grant, or Care Dependency Grant (Samson/MacQuene/van Niekerk 2005: 2).[5] Moreover, the category "indigent" was not used during apartheid, when particularly poor Whites were described as "dependant" and thereby in need of care.[6] Policy makers noted in 2003 that the category indigent is a "legitimate term to refer to that section of the population who are unable to meet their basic needs and pay for their basic services" (ibid: 5). The indigent policy therefore inherently defines an ideal of what a normal citizen should be, i.e. a paying citizen. However, the implementation of the indigent policy and the term indigent itself is contested and disputed by various actors at the urban level. As discussed in this chapter, such conflicts demonstrate how individuals contend with, measure up to, subvert, manipulate, or simply internalise types (Wedel et al. 2005: 37–38) such as "paying citizen" or "indigent citizen" as part of their own identity.

Examining such policies, some studies (Jensen 2004; Millstein 2010) have argued that the ANC government's approach towards participation and development echoes former top-down approaches of the apartheid government:

> As had the old, so did the new government evoke notions of community, and as had the old, so did the new government objectify communities as sites of governmental intervention.
>
> (Jensen 2004: 187)

In similar findings, other research (Mathekga/Buccus 2006; Williams 2006) considers the post-apartheid government's approach to governance as one based on technocratic rationales, suggesting that local government's primary task is restricted to that of a provider of goods and services. Citizens are perceived as customers or clients of social services, and thus the local government system treats community participation as less important and secondary to service delivery (Mathekga/Buccus 2006: 11, 12). Such studies claim that the state's new participatory institutions have not effectively catered to the "dormant participatory culture" persistent among citizens (ibid.: 11), with the authors contending that South Africa entered the new political era "armed with a culture of participation", i.e. one based on the anti-apartheid movement, and one which has subsequently remained dormant since 1994. According to them, the new democratic system is "chiefly characterised by lack of community participation, corruption and poor service delivery" (ibid.: 12).

Alternatively, I contend that the point is not that the national government has simply followed a top-down approach and implemented policy to help

> [...] the state in shaping, controlling, and regulating heterogeneous populations through classificatory schemes that homogenise diversity, render the subject transparent to the state, and implement legal and spatial boundaries between different categories of subjects
>
> (Wedel et al. 2005: 35)

but rather that the focus of analysis should be shifted towards aspects of how public policy is adapted, interpreted, and negotiated at the urban level in unforeseen ways and with unexpected consequences (ibid.: 35). This perspective somewhat mitigates the approaches of Williams (2006: 211) and Mathekga/ Buccuss (2006: 11, 12) in highlighting the role that the apparent total absence of community organisations has in undermining participation in council politics. Rather than acclaiming that there is an absence of participation, I contend that poor residents use different voice options (Hirschman 1970: 4, 17), including non-formalised options, to participate and articulate their demands and rights. Therefore, it is not so much about the omnipresence of state discourses and obedience of subject-citizens, who are treated in such approaches as passive victims of an all-encompassing modern state apparatus under the auspices of neo-liberalism, but rather about the dynamics of how the (local) state addresses the marginalised and how they themselves are able to respond to the state's treatment of them. In other words, it relates to the agency of poor people, including both non-politicised residents and activists in the Cape Flats, and their ways of interacting with local government representatives.

I analyse these processes of interaction in the next section, using the example of an incident where residents protested in front of a sub-council against the pink letters, which were sent to remind households to pay outstanding debts for electricity and water services.

4.2 Negotiating pink letters in (and in front of) the sub-council

A manageable number of neighbouring wards are grouped together into one sub-council, with Cape Town having 24 such sub-councils. The personnel of a sub-council consists of all the ward councillors of the included wards, from whom one is elected chairperson. A non-elect official "sub-council manager" is responsible for organising monthly meetings, where the councillors are expected to discuss issues relevant to their wards. Despite meetings being open to the public, they are not allowed to actively participate. The city council has delegated around 100 specific powers and functions to the sub-councils,[7] encouraging their input into the IDP as well as budgeting, legislation, and policy. Sub-councils also have responsibilities and powers in matters affecting their wards in areas such as the planning and funding of service delivery, and the licensing of selling food or liquor to the public (South Peninsula Administration 2001: 192).

Most of the ward councillors whose trajectories have been discussed in Chapter 2 had their offices in the Mitchells Plain sub-council building. From 2001 until 2005, Mitchells Plain's sub-council was made up of members from different political parties, whereas from 2006 onwards it has been dominated by members from the DA.

The agendas of sub-council meetings[8] were shaped by the precarious socio-economic and marginalised situation of the townships encompassed within the metropolitan region, with issues relating to crime, low-subsidy housing schemes, drug trafficking, HIV and TB infections, illegal dumping, and water cut-offs dominating. Most of the time, the meetings proceeded without notable conflicts, apart from two specific occasions when formal procedures were disrupted owing to strong disagreements. Indeed, one of the conflicts, pertaining to allegations of racism, has been alluded to in the previous chapter. In the following section, the second witnessed conflict is described and analysed in order to show the way in which sub-council meetings are used as spaces for public participation.

The case: the sub-council meeting in Mitchells Plain, 12.10.2006

The sub-council meeting took place during a period when the city council was no longer lead by the ANC, but by the DA. In 2006, the newly-elected local government annulled the moratorium against the introduction of pre-paid water meters in the City of Cape Town, which had been ordered by the previous ANC mayor Nomaindia Mfeketo. Prepaid meters are hooked up to a water supply system and require the user to pay prior to retrieving water.[9] The moratorium was the result of a successful campaign against pre-paid water meters in 2004 and 2005, coordinated along with others by the NGO ILRIG (see Chapter 2). However, there were already mounting financial pressures when the ANC-led council signed the moratorium, owing to the accumulation of unpaid accounts.

In May 2006, the newly-elected DA-government adopted a city-wide credit control and debt collection policy, which re-started the installation of pre-paid water meters and saw the sending out of so-called pink letters to remind households of their obligations in paying outstanding debts for electricity and water services.

In this sub-council meeting, officials of the Department of Revenue gave a presentation on "Indigent Relief, Rates and Debt Management's Actions", announcing the installation of the pre-paid water meters.

Furthermore, the officials introduced a new and comprehensive indigent policy, where the aim was to enhance a culture of personal responsibility among citizens and therefore reduce the rate of failed payments for services. The chairperson of the newly-elected sub-council highlighted:

> I think we must explain to people that the city is going after residents who can pay, but don't, and not residents who cannot afford to pay. Let us show that we care and that we respect people's dignity. They may be poor but they are still human at the end of the day.

Later in the meeting, a mayoral executive member and former ward councillor of Mitchells Plain criticised the officials of the Department of Revenue for not staffing the rates offices with "competent people who know to treat the people of Mitchells Plain with care, dignity and respect, they are maybe poor but they have to be treated with care". Furthermore, he criticised the indigent policy by stating that water had been even cut off to a school in Beacon Valley, Mitchells Plain, due to arrears in paying water fees. In response, an official from the Department of Revenue made it clear that he was convinced that not everyone in Mitchells Plain is poor and unemployed. He recommended that the state should establish a reliable database to identify who is "the really unemployed". The official subsequently addressed Mitchells Plain's ward councillors to "educate and inform" residents properly on the new indigent policy, and urged them not to resort to the "playing [of] the race card". As the debate inside the sub-council building became increasingly heated, the meeting was also disrupted by noise from an outside protest action organised by "Concerned Residents of Mitchells Plain" (CRM). The CRM is a network of different types of organisations such as NGOs, CBOs and private residents who are opposed to the policies of housing evictions, water cut-offs, and the installation of pre-paid water meters. Interestingly, these types of networks also exist in neighbouring townships in the Cape Flats, where the term "concerned" is used in connection with the proper name of the township, namely the "Concerned Residents of Delft" (Millstein 2010: 11). Another current example is the "Concerned Residents of Bonteheuwel", who campaign against the closing of schools in their area. Through the actions of these movements, parallel spaces are generated and constituted. The movements are all engaged in ways that aim to influence the state's decision-making processes. Public resistance against the commodification of basic services and the disconnection of water and electricity supply has been a politically explosive issue, generating boycotts, resistance, and revolts in a number of South African townships (Mottiar/Bond 2012).

Almost all protestors present at the CRM rally were ANC members, like the NGO activist Ms Roosevelt (see trajectory, Chapter 2) who held a poster with the slogan "We say NO! to DA prepaid water meters!". Another held up the flag of the ANC. In her neighbourhood, Ms Roosevelt had experienced disruptions to the water supply in cases where people had defaulted on their municipal payments and then had to cope without a water service for prolonged periods. She referred to the health risks when people are forced to use alternative and often unsafe sources of water in situations of prolonged disconnection.[10] Studies suggest that, since the end of apartheid, as many as 10 million South Africans have had their supply to water cut off and a further 10 million have had their electricity cut off, while some 2 million residents have been evicted from their homes for the non-payment of service bills. In the case of the latter, the Municipal Systems Act grants local authorities the power to seize property in cases of non-payment for services (McDonald 2002: 22). In many cases, residents responded by re-connecting services "illegally",[11] a practice that can be observed particularly in informal settlements, including parts of Mitchells Plain and Khayelitsha, where electricity service is provided through informal and often unsafe installations.

When the sub-council meeting was interrupted, one of the ward councillors went outside to meet with the protestors and discussed the question of allowing public participation in sub-council meetings and the need to provide communication channels for residents at this level. When the sub-council meeting resumed, the matter of public participation was discussed by the ward councillors present, who criticised the fact that citizens are not permitted to speak during meetings, and therefore have little incentive to attend them.[12]

Sixteen people participated in the protest action, which when one considers the high number of Mitchells Plain's inhabitants negatively affected by the pink letters, one might say shows a low level of interest. The CRM subsequently attempted to reach and mobilise more people by networking with other activists. Ms Roosevelt, for example, liaised with Lilly's NGO ILRIG (see trajectory, Chapter 2) and together they organised many events protesting against water cut-offs and pink letters, including meetings, a demonstration in front of the City of Cape Town's customer care and cash office in Mitchells Plain, where water-supply and electricity fees are collected (de Bruin 2006: 1) in Mitchell Plans, and a protest march through the streets of Mitchells Plain. These events were mainly attended by people with either an activist background or ANC membership. The Anti-Eviction Campaign (a new social movement, see Chapter 2), distanced itself from these events, which they perceived as being too influenced by the ANC. Moreover, many so-called ordinary residents of Mitchells Plain, i.e. those directly affected by the pink letters, did not participate in this process.

4.3 Interactions in and around the sub-council

The protest in front of the sub-council demonstrates several aspects that shape public participation, which are examined further in this section. First, while policies and legislation foresee public participation, in practice the sub-council meetings were poorly attended by residents, not only in this particular sub-council meeting but in all seven attended meetings. Second, residents created their own, alternative spaces for participation, i.e. outside the sub-council meetings, in order to negotiate with the state their rights to basic services. Third, in these negotiation processes, residents contested the state's view in relation to how it addressed the public in policy, specifically in the indigent policy.

Low attendance of sub-council meetings

Some scholars working on public participation in Cape Town explain the low attendance of sub-council meetings with poor residents' lack of knowledge of how the political system works (Williams 2006; Esau 2007). Williams (2006: 210) argues that communities are unaware that they have to be present at sub-council meetings, or that they do not know about the existence of sub-council meetings as participatory instruments. In this respect, Williams (2006: 210) questions whether council members, i.e. ward councillors and officials, are sufficiently interacting with their residents (Chapter 2). When questioned, Mitchells Plain's ward councillors rejected the accusation, one also widely circulated in public discourses, of being out of touch with their electorate or not representing them effectively. Instead, they blamed the sub-council as not being an appropriate institution for giving a voice to residents. Indeed, according to my field observations there were many occasions outside the sub-council meetings when a vibrant interaction existed between ward councillors and residents. A compelling example was given by the ward councillor Mr Kal-El Check (see trajectory, Chapter 2), who alluded to well-attended meetings that he occasionally organised for residents in his ward. In contrast to sub-council meetings, on the one hand, this type of community meeting offers a space for ward residents to voice their concerns; while on the other, they allow a ward councillor to inform residents and instigate debate around specific development projects and other issues. Furthermore, many situations occurred during fieldwork when ward councillors were called personally by residents to assist them in occasions of water cut-offs or evictions. These examples at the very least provide evidence that some residents are aware of how to contact their ward councillor and that there is not a total absence of communication lines between ward councillors and their electorate in general, and residents in need in particular. However, these examples could also be interpreted as residents only being interested in issues that directly affect their ward but not in the sub-council's agenda, which includes all wards in Mitchells Plain.

Among other factors, Esau (2007: 21) attributes the lack of interest of for-malised public participation to poverty, which sees people in conditions of poverty restrict their focus to immediate situations that affect them or their close family. This is attributed to being direct consequence of the forced removals, which eroded social networks in the neighbourhoods. Although it is undisputable that forced removals had detrimental effects on the social orga-nisations of families, the trajectories discussed in the previous chapters sug-gest that it was exactly during these times that people began to build up social networks, support networks, street committees, community-based organisa-tions, etc. In the case outlined previously, Ms Roosevelt experienced water cutoffs in her neighbourhood where people were without water service for prolonged periods. Consequently, this prompted her to become involved and engaged with her historically-rooted network of activists to form the CRM, in order to improve the livelihoods of those neighbours. This demonstrates how networking and mobilisation by and among activists constitutes active resistance against local government policies.

Non-payment and dignity: shaping public participation

In the sub-council meeting mentioned previously, the official from the Department of Revenue used the issue of non-payment as an argument for introducing the new indigent policy. According to scholars such as Johnson (1999) and Ajam (2001) (quoted in Fjeldstad 2005: 86) as well as the City of Cape Town itself (van Reyneveld et al. 2005: 41), many poor people can afford to pay something for their services, and therefore contribute to the tax and tariff structure, yet because of a culture of non-payment they do not do so. This culture is said to have its roots in payment boycotts during the apartheid era. Boycotts of rents and user charges became one of the few instruments residents could use to fight against the illegitimate political system during apartheid. Consequently, in the late 1980s, many townships and rural areas in the homelands were entirely ungovernable. While such payment boycotts were expected to stop with the dispensation, the contrary has been the case, and non-payment of service charges appears to have developed as a norm in many places (Fjeldstad 2005: 85).

The protest culture of non-payment of services has created huge obstacles in terms of establishing a new developmental local government system, par-ticularly with respect to institutionalising relations with residents who cannot pay for basic services. Tapscott (2005) and Fjeldstad (2005) argue that the poor have retained a distrust of local government authorities, due to con-tinuing political and administrative shortcomings, and therefore maintain an unwillingness to pay taxes or tariffs or participate in processes of local gov-ernance. Altogether, this results in a perception among many inhabitants in the Cape Flats that there is no need to contribute to revenues which should ultimately finance the state budget.

The concept of non-payment in Mitchells Plain and Khayelitsha is one which is volatile and multifaceted, varying both from ward-to-ward and within them, where it is shaped by various income structures. The notion of unwillingness is contested by representatives of the CRM, who argue that poor people simply cannot afford to pay for services. This argument of non-payment showed itself to be one which agreed most closely with my observations during fieldwork. This is echoed by some researchers who contend that the primary reason for non-payment is de-facto the inability to pay for services, due to insufficient wages and precarious income structures (Oldfield/ Peters 2005: 317–318).[13]

Researchers also hint at a further issue complicating matters, the absence of a reliable database system on either unemployment or housing (van Ryneveld et al. 2003). In the sub-council meeting, the official pointed to this problem by raising the question: "who are the really unemployed?"[14] Only persons who are registered on local government database systems have access to social welfare services, while those who are not are excluded. The database system is administrated by provincial and local governments, and according to urban politicians urgently needs to be updated, consolidated, and made available to the municipality. This line of argumentation is followed by scholars (Oldfield, Summer School Lecture at UCT) who state that the annual arrival of thousands of people migrating to the townships in search of jobs further aggravates the issue. Quite apart from the separate issue of employment insecurity in the townships, there are also many informal settlements about which the City of Cape Town has almost no data. The request to create a reliable database system reminds us of understanding statecraft as a process of rendering populations legible, as argued by Scott (1998) in his book "Seeing Like a State". Scott contends that this is realised through a set of different practices, overseen by the state, such as surveillance and control, including for instance cadastral surveys and population registers, which work as "attempts at legibility and simplification" (1998: 56–76). However, he eventually concludes that these state interventions tend to fail because they are designed and introduced as top-down, standardised methods that ignore the complexity of other social processes that are not visible to the state. This is exactly the problem with the formation of a reliable database system that attempts to reflect the complex social reality of the Cape Flats. In Khayelitsha, for instance, there was the opinion circulated among ward councillors that citizens who received a council house there preferred to rent it in order to gain revenue, themselves returning to live in their former settlement in Site C. These population dynamics, often not formally recognised, make it difficult to bureaucratise the social life in the Cape Flats with the aim of making the urban level more transparent and aiding state interventions. As suggested earlier, it is also an unrealistic demand to ask local governments to uncover such dynamics in order to identify a culture of non-payment among its citizens. The problem of dealing with these dynamics becomes particularly more pronounced in areas prone to violence, where there continuously exists a potential for the collapse of provision in services such as libraries, child care, health, and housing,[15] i.e. where the state is more or less absent. In such areas, which exist in parts of Mitchells Plain and Khayelitsha, everyday life draws attention to the limits of state power and control in terms of interventions and governance.

Furthermore, while research up to this point has only identified mistrust on the side of residents towards urban authorities, the official's question "who is the really unemployed" indicates that both sides mistrust each other to some degree. A constellation of mistrust is co-produced along vertical lines based upon social and economic inequalities that inherently shape power relations. This phenomenon can be described as "relational distrust"; a point to which I will return later.

As argued in the previous chapter, in practice urban politicians tend to equate racialised inequality as being synonymous with spatial, social, and economic inequality. During the sub-council meeting, the official urged ward councillors to "educate and inform" residents about the reasons why the indigent policy would be an acceptable solution for the municipality and its residents. The official wanted to thereby avoid the oversimplified reasoning of racialised inequality being the key driver of social polarisation, which might therefore hinder establishing the indigent policy. This shows how local actors are aware of how easily racism is used in order to explain social inequalities or realities. Furthermore, another notion of inequality became apparent in the sub-council meeting, when ward councillor Mr Beauty asked the officials to treat poor people with dignity, because "at the end of the day they are still human". Jensen (2008: 9–8) differentiates between two interdependent readings of dignity: on the one hand, dignity is a fixed feeling that powerless people retain when all else fails; while on the other hand, dignity only becomes an issue in a moment of humiliation or maltreatment – it can't exist independently of power. "In a way dignity and domination (offence and humiliation) are co-produced; they are interdependent" (Jensen 2008: 9). This interdependency became obvious in a separate meeting (30.10.2006), where officials, a member of parliament, and residents from Mitchells Plain discussed the issue of pre-paid water meters. One resident claimed:

> We are the indigenous people of this country but the previous [apartheid] government has made us indigent and you are fulfilling their plans [...] please give us back our dignity.
>
> (Fieldnote, 16.10.2006)

The audience affirmed the man's comment with accompanying shouts. In other words, residents came to feel that their dignity was under threat when they experienced humiliation under the apartheid system of domination. The post-apartheid government's classification of indigent poses a further threat to their dignity, as they continue to feel humiliated. In this case, the continuity and preservation of dignity in struggles during apartheid past to post-apartheid present is spatially located in the Cape Flats, an area that traces its origins to apartheid's racialised segregation policies. During that time, residents in the Cape Flats became labelled as indigent, in opposition to residents in wealthier suburbs who are predominantly represented by White population groups. Therefore, the government's identification processes of indigents are spatially restricted to the Cape Flats, and at the same time carry the projection of a racialised other.

4.4 Parallel public spaces for claiming ownership

The importance of citizens owning the responsibility for the management of their community affairs and participation in political processes has been gaining currency in the international development community (Donais 2008: 8). The idea of ownership from below has also been identified by national political elites and policy-makers as an important component in drafting strategic plans towards betterment, sustainability, and stability. The afore-mentioned protest actions by the NGO CRM highlight a case where reforms based on the indigent policy did not succeed in penetrating into society at large. In contrast, the CRM pursued their own activities with the goal of reconciling the indigent policy with urban realities in order to actually benefit poor residents who cannot afford to pay for basic services.

The CRM mobilised mainly unemployed citizens active in party political branches of the ANC, CBOs and other networks, and NGO employees. This shows that these actors have alternative knowledge with regard to institutional change, how to network, and organise demonstrations, marches, and boycotts as ways to articulate their will to participate in policy-making processes (see Fischer 2000). This also indicates that the CRM's protest outside the sub-council meeting can be construed as an act that signals non-compliance with the rules and codes of the municipality as well as a lack of confidence in and communication with local government and its constituency. The CRM did not feel part of official structures and therefore employed an old attitude of protest and self-organisation. They gave voice to their concerns in a forum outside formal sub-council meetings, thereby shaping "legal participatory spaces as sites of resistance" (Williams 2006: 205). The fact that the CRM chose the front of the sub-council meeting as the particular space to demonstrate rather than participate inside reflects relations of power connected to local places and spaces as well as broader political processes. Through networking with other organisations, the CRM seeks to alter the indigent policy, with the further aim of shifting dominant power relations. In this sense, networking also infers the shifting of influence beyond a particular place, i.e. a geographically confined jurisdiction, as well the shifting of power relations beyond a particular institution to other institutions in the same place – e.g. to the ward councillor, the sub-council, the City of Cape Town's Customer Care and Cash Office, the City Council, etc. In summary, the CRM structured parallel public spaces for non-formalised participation in opposition to the sub-council meeting.

(Lack of) trust and confidence

Much of the literature treats South Africa as "a low trust society" (Askvik/ Bak 2005: 1) due to its history of racialised subjugation and the resulting tensions between different racialised groupings. Many scholars argue that shared identities and social bonds strengthen confidence, and that this is something critical to understanding social interactions in South Africa. Hence, membership to a constructed identity of Coloured or Black African may provide a basis for defining trust relationships, in the sense of "those who are part of the group can be trusted, those who are not, cannot" (ibid.: 14; see also Yuval-Davis 2006: 4). Of course, it is not that simple, as the case of the CRM movement demonstrates. Even though the local government representatives and the activists all ascribe themselves as belonging with the Coloured collectivity, this does not automatically produce trust among the apparently homogenous community and its members. In fact, it is the CRM activists' ANC membership that allows them to bridge the trust deficit commonly assumed to prevail between the inhabitants of the former Coloured and Black African townships. Furthermore, based on the presumption of a culture of non-payment, officials perceive residents in the townships as not trustworthy, which strengthens relational distrust between both sides. While trust is important for maintaining interpersonal relations (Luhmann 1990: 102), public participation goes beyond interpersonal relations and requires an underlying confidence in the political system. Following Luhmann (1990), in contrast to trust, confidence does not require a previous engagement on the part of the individual.[16] In this sense, without being personally engaged in politics, citizens' confidence relies on politicians' will to do the right thing, avoid being corrupt, evade violent conflicts, etc. For public participation, understood in terms of cooperative interactions, to be possible, I argue that both trusting relationships between ward councillors and the engaged citizenry as well as an overall confidence in the political system are necessary. The aspect of citizens lacking trust in sub-councils and local governments in general is often used as an explanation for low public participation and the inability of political institutions to work, in a sustainable manner, in the interests of the poor (Tapscott 2005: 80; Fjeldstad 2005: 97; Williams 2006: 210; Esau 2007: 22; Ruiters 2002: 41). With respect to the case of the CRM, I contend that the disappointing experiences of residents in the townships with local government in terms of trust have also translated into a decrease in confidence in the political system (see Luhmann 1990: 99), which led to the demonstrations and marches against the indigent policy.

One branch of research literature argues that the commodification of basic services and introduction of cost recovery have encouraged urban authorities and politicians to work against the community that they represent (Ruiters 2002). This has damaged the relationship between communities and local governments and induced a lack of trust between them. Following this line of argumentation, ward councillors have been accused of "policing neoliberal austerity at local level" (ibid.: 42), consequently putting their mandate at risk. Hence, local government is attempting to connect with residents and enhance public participation and at the same time augment the tariff system for basic services and disconnect services in cases where people don't pay. It could be argued that these attempts effectively work against each other and produce public distrust in regulatory spaces. However, Ruiters' analysis does not extend beyond the assertion that the ANC leadership has sold out by embracing neo-liberalism and privatisation. This has led the ANC elite in their approach to distance themselves from the grassroots level and hence, the people. This perspective has certain shortcomings. While it has been shown in previous chapters that the ANC lost members during the second decade following the end of apartheid and is no longer an "unchallengeable movement", there are nonetheless still a considerable number of members loyal to the party at an urban level. To an extent, the CRM actually functioned as a party political extension of the ANC, which suggests that the ANC maintains networks that reach down to the grassroots level and take the form of interactions with ward councillors. Furthermore, it may be the case that the problem of local government not being able to deliver basic services may be largely ascribed to unrealistic demands being placed upon the local government system.

In cases where residents experienced disappointment with respect to trust towards ward councillors, those residents sought out and took advantage of new ways of interacting with local government. There are many examples where squatters first occupy land and then, assisted by advocacy groups, enter into a negotiation process with provincial and local governments, in order to claim land rights and the delivery of services. This newly-emerging interaction between residents, NGO activists, and the (local) government re-structures (public) participation in irregular and non-formalised spaces.

In Tafelsig, the poorest area of Mitchells Plain, there was one case where a group of people who were formally dwelling in the backyards of other houses moved to occupy a vacant school site. From the beginning, this squatter area, called Freedom Park, had no state provision of sanitation facilities, such as water stand pipes or toilets, and squatters instead dug holes in the soil that they used as toilets. Furthermore, they were dependant on water from neighbouring serviced sites, which caused occasional resource conflicts. In conversations, the squatters of Freedom Park constructed the government as corrupt and not capable of delivering solutions for residential infrastructure. After disappointing experiences relating to trust with their specific ward councillor, who failed to assist them in finding solutions for their precarious housing situation, these township residents then addressed their concerns to advocacy NGOs. The NGO "Legal Resources Centre" assisted the people in their struggle to avoid eviction by the City of Cape Town, while another NGO, the "Development Action Group", supported the squatters in their negotiation process with the city in 2000 (Smit 2006: 105). The city subsequently agreed to develop the site and reclassify it as a legal housing space with administrative recognition, including aspects such as postal addresses, a process observed during fieldwork when a housing project was launched on the site. In this case, residents received support from NGO activists who assisted them in claiming ownership of their rights to basic services, and helped residents position themselves along the interface with the state. Precisely because squatters perceive these NGOs as not being allied to local government, and thus more trustworthy, NGOs are able to function as brokers, mediating between local government and citizens. Therefore, although these residents might not attend formal sub-council meetings, they instead create new paths that help them to act in their own interests and manage precarious life situations. This case further illustrates how the indigent policy did not succeed in practice. But what it demonstrates above all is how the idea of taking up ownership and becoming engaged in community matters has penetrated into society at large, and has developed as a *leitmotiv* for activists and residents for making demands with respect to the state.

Building women's activism

The same holds true for the *leitmotiv* of women's vulnerability and the almost obvious observation that women represent an unequal and disadvantaged group in South African society, a view maintained in legislation from the original White Paper of Local Government (1998) to more recent policies on governance, participation, and development. This disadvantage is further compounded by certain geographical factors, e.g. women who find themselves in a poor neighbourhood in the Cape Flats. As a specific category, men are neither mentioned by policy-makers, urban politicians, nor activists, despite their equally low educational level and sharing of disadvantaged positions with women in township society. Even within their own ranks, however, female activists were confronted with the same perception of women being weak, poor, and disadvantaged.

These contradictory perceptions are characterised by exclusionary practices of participation, entitlements, and representations in civil society and party politics (see Chapter 2), leaving the urban poor (or those communities who are supposed to be informed and represented) out of formal politics, decision-making process, and participatory processes in urban planning.

To analyse exclusionary practices within civil society, it is useful to look at the example of the forum "Building Women's Activism".[17] It had its beginnings during a meeting of the NGO ILRIG in 2005, when female staff felt sidelined by their male colleagues, who used "patriarchal cultural and religious arguments to preserve mainstream oppressive institutions, structures and women's subordinate positions" (Report, ILRIG Public Forum 2006: 1). As a consequence of these events, and with the support of the wider female activist community, female activists and scholars decided to establish a parallel space, a forum for women only, called "Building Women's Activism". Benjamin (2004: 87) states that a commonly-held view has emerged in South Africa that men generally dominate leadership structures in the new social movements.

Indeed, during one of the Building Women's Activism's public forums, the organisers discussed the agenda of the ANCWL[18] as being co-opted by the political system, and as a result leading to a fragmentation of the women's movement. At that time, the ANCWL was being criticised by other female activists in South Africa for its strong support of the disputed presidential mandate of the ANC's Jacob Zuma,[19] who had been charged with rape, as well as being known for his discriminatory remarks against women and his practice of polygyny (see Nord 2012: 6). The ANCWL was thereby accused of practicing "state feminism". The forum's organisers thereby position themselves as critical feminists by distancing themselves from state feminists. Additionally, they criticise the women's movement in South Africa for following a "fairly liberal tradition" in their ideas on democracy and equal rights for women. As an alternative position, the forum's organisers recognise "patriarchy as a system of male oppression and domination [...] equal rights within the existing system is not an end in itself" (Essof 2006: 1). They do, however, consider the women's movement with its diverse constituencies as a necessary stage for a structural transformation of society, consequently explaining why they see the importance of integrating it in their emerging parallel space of women's activism. In this way, the forum makes a similar distinction to that of Marx-Ferree and McClurg (2006: 41) where they see women's movements as constituencies with their corresponding organisational strategies, and feminism as a goal and a set of beliefs. In this regard women's movements are able to speak to their constituents as mothers, sisters, and daughters in order to strategically strengthen women's ability to contest existing forms of discrimination and oppression. Feminism, then, embraces not only the need to empower women but also other long-term goals, such as challenging male-dominated institutions and societal structures. Significant not only in this case but also for activists in general is their practice of cross party collaboration, albeit mainly including those belonging to left wing parties such as the ANC, SACP, and other non-party-allied activists. The end-of-apartheid transition period in 1991 was shaped considerably by the WNC's[20] demand to include and enhance women's representation in political office, and to foster the women's agenda and gendered consciousness within the realms of parliament, government, and civil society. The WNC brought together women from different economic, social, and racialised backgrounds, including those from different political parties, as well as various women's organisations including the church, welfare, and health sectors to debate "the need for a coalition of women's interests" (Meintjes 1996: 49). Britton (2006) states that cross-party collaboration of women is possible in civil society, yet within parliament it is severely constrained, because "if women consistently worked against their party ideologies, their seats would be jeopardised" (ibid.: 71). This is also true for the cases discussed earlier in this chapter; where activists practice cross party collaboration, but these cooperation lines are severely constrained in the arena of Cape Town's local governments due to their polarisation between left and conservative political parties.

The forum's founders collaborated with the international donor community for financial support, so that they could act autonomously and independently of the state and political parties. The founders were addressing women as women, which, following Marx-Ferree and McClurg Mueller (2006: 40), can take the form of focusing attention on problems that "women alone face or experience to a greater degree than men do", or as a response to gendered political opportunity structures in order to address community-wide problems.[21] The founders' strategies were an opposition to male exclusionary practices within civil society, local government, and party politics. Hence, this action can be interpreted as a response to gendered structures of exclusion, while at same time accessing international donor community resources in order to promote the organisers' idea of female political spaces.

The forum was initially launched to enhance women's participation and leadership skills, in particular, by creating exchanges of information on organisational issues, funding, and networking, but also by critically engaging with national and municipal politics in respect to issues such as social cash transfers, water cut-offs, evictions, and so forth. Participants who regularly engage with the forum have all either worked in a state-financed NGO, were engaged in other social movements campaigning against water cut-offs or evictions, or ran for election in local government. All of them had some sort of an activist background.

The establishment of the forum was significantly shaped by various alliances between urban poor and urban non-poor. Using the terminology of Das and Randeria (2015: 6), the alliances demonstrate that poorer residents are "enmeshed within networks that include the non-poor who help them marshal information and resources, provide contacts, and mobilise themselves for action".

The public forums took place on the premises of ILRIG and were chaired by its founders, all of whom had some degree of an academic, middle-income background. The participants, from various outlying areas of the townships, were provided with transport and snacks – thereby sustaining women's ability to participate.

The case further shows how various levels of activism are interconnected with each other and that female activists are not positioned at a single sociopolitical level, but rather at multiple levels. Female activists, ward councillors, and those who run for elections usually have links to more than just one organisation and/or campaign, sphere of government, or civil society organisation. The public forums included women with diverse political, social, and economic backgrounds. To speak in the terms given by Marx-Ferree and McClurg Mueller (2006: 40), these forums therefore highlight the current intersectionality of social movements and NGOs. "Intersectionality means that organisations as well as individuals are multiply positioned in regard to social relations of power and in justice" (ibid.: 41, 42). In this sense, acknowledging intersectionality helps us to explore the heterogeneously structured women's movement, and experience how intersectional movements relate to each other.

4.5 Gendering political representation and participation

This chapter emphasised that in cases where participation in formalised institutions is limited, everyday modes of political action reveal other ways in which people actively engage with the local state.

In order to analyse the reasons for the public's absence at sub-council meetings, I elaborated upon two significant lines of interaction beyond sub-council meetings. First, I considered the CRM's protest actions in front of the sub-council as a way of articulating non-compliance with local governments' rules and orders. Their grievances can be related to the indigent policy, which was introduced as a state strategy to cope with the so-called culture of non-payment in the townships. Township residents and activists felt offended by this policy, consequently dismantling it as a continuation of apartheid policies, which saw subsequent decreases in confidence in (local) government. This chapter further highlighted that the tense communication between local government officials and township residents is based on relational distrust, i.e. one where officials also do not trust township inhabitants. Second, although people might not attend formal sub-council meetings, they create new paths towards acting and managing their precarious situations. Even if the policies and legislation concerning public participation did not effectively translate into practices, their *leitmotiv* of taking up ownership and becoming engaged in community matters is still practised in some ways by both female and male township residents and activists.

Up to this point, I have identified two types of actors inhabitants can approach when they need support or want to challenge a state of inequality: either ward councillors, or all sorts of activists including civic, youth, and squatter associations, women's organisations, trade unions, and NGOs. As shown by the case of the sub-council meeting and the other empirical examples, non-participation in "community representative spaces" (Williams 2006: 206) does not mean apathy towards the democratic process. On the contrary, poor residents have developed an agency to act even if their actions resemble (mere) resistance or are as passive as they seemed during apartheid. The notion of passivity should to be seen in light of the former restricted room for manoeuvre and lack of opportunities for participation in formalised political institutions which the apartheid government provided for those living on the margins. For residents in the townships, there was no practical knowledge or memories of democratic local self-government to draw upon, and hence, disruptions and discontinuities in social life based on "discrepancies in values, interests, knowledge and power" (Long 1996: 55) shape encounters at the interface between residents and representatives of democratically elected local governments.

At the beginning of this chapter, local governance and its developmental role was introduced as something radically new, an invention caused by the change in the political system. The invocation of something completely new is a common feature within discourses relating to political transformations; in the South African case, however, despite post-apartheid governments differing markedly in certain aspects from their apartheid counterparts, there were some continuities. These continuities in public participation were structured by individuals who had fought for independence and who carried their political visions into the democratic era. As discussed in Chapter 2, the fact that street committees continued to work, community workers continued their social engagement, (new) social movements emerged, etc. demonstrates how historically developed movements and activism continue to shape democratic public spheres.

The fact that a majority of the population had no political rights before 1994 forced people to adapt strategies to organise everyday life on their own behalf during apartheid. This was expressed either in the formation of civic associations, community-based or faith-based organisations to deal with everyday issues, or in forms of violent participation against exclusive state practices, e.g. boycotts, protest actions, and mass rallies. Enduring attitudes favouring protest is grounded in peoples' lack of confidence in current government institutions, which results partly from these historical encounters. In contrast to democratic local government in modern South Africa, civil society and corresponding parallel spaces are historically grounded and shaped by peoples' specific knowledge and strategies for participating and organising social and political life.

In this respect, the women's movement in South Africa, a movement that includes many different grassroots organisations, constitutes important knowledge spaces for self-empowerment and networking. The empirical insights, both in Chapter 2 and in this chapter, have demonstrated that women use assimilative strategies, for example in cases where activists built up their own NGO, and constructively engage with the state, or develop confrontational strategies, such as the cases with the CRM movement and the "Building Women's Activism" forum. This provides evidence that women use and expand their multilayered social and economic networks to cope with socially precarious situations, such as insecurity. Through "dual" positioning, i.e. between civil society and government, women enlarge decisively their room for manoeuvre, in which they apply a range of strategies and tactics. In this vein, this chapter analysed the current women's movement not as an autonomous movement, but rather as one historically connected to the broader, male-dominated, liberation movement that allegedly seeks an inclusive nation-building project. In fact, women's participation in the liberation movement allowed for a more inclusive egalitarian vision of democracy with respect to human equality and gender justice. After 1994, the liberation movement facilitated women's entry into the public spheres, albeit resting on a profoundly gendered model of the political and social system (Anthias/ Yuval Davis 1989, cited in Hassim 2004: 5). It has become evident that the political arena is not a "gender neutral space" (Strulik 2004: 6), but rather one which abides by the dominant discourse where gender is conceptualised in such a way that women are perceived as weak and ignorant.

Now, with quota interventions enhancing women's representation in formalised political institutions, and (emerging) female political spaces,

> [...] the different political actors are compelled to negotiate and attribute new meanings to 'politics' and 'how one does politics'. In the long run both women and men will have to accept, that the local political arena, if not the meaning of politics, i.e. the way politics is constructed and structured by institutionalised expectations has to transform.
>
> (ibid.: 6; similar line of argumentation in Marx-Ferree/
> McClurg Mueller 2006: 44)

Strulik's analysis of local politics focuses on Indian society being primarily structured along the dominant male discourse, which can also be easily applied in the South African case. From a global perspective this also shows the worldwide construction of feminised systems of "ignorance".

Authors such as Palmieri (2013) and Cisse (2008) state that

> [...] the more women create autonomous groups, in parallel with, yet removed from power systems, the more they distance themselves from decision making forums [...] their work feeds political rhetoric, but no action is taken; they support the government and receive nothing in return.
>
> (Palmieri 2013)

In contrast, as introduced in Chapter 1, Thompson and Tapscott (2010), in reference to Kabeer (2005), state that in the Global South in general, collective action by both women and mixed-gender persons has to be viewed in terms of two axes of participation, horizontal and vertical. Women's forums correspond to horizontal spaces of participation. The authors analyse these as "self-created" or "invented" spaces "where citizens themselves define their modes of engagement with the state and with other interest groups and resort to different forms of collective action" (Thompson and Tapscott 2010: 3, 4). The ways in which collective action, mobilisation, and social movements manifest themselves in these spaces are key to understanding their expression of the "right to have rights" (Gaventa 2010: xii). The formation of these spaces can be interpreted as their response to the institutionalised channels of engagement that have proved weak, or unresponsive and exclusionary, in this case for women, at the vertical level. These vertical spaces are what have been outlined at the beginning of this chapter as the institutionalised participatory structures introduced by the state. The need for creating social spaces to empower and articulate women's rights demonstrates the difficulty that women have to enter the institutionalised governance arena. Hence, the dual positioning of women's activists occurs, on one hand, in their self-created spaces at the horizontal level. On the other hand, they position themselves as NGO activists or ward councillors at the vertical level of urban governance, engendering an interface between civil society and state.

Like Palmieri's (2013) and Cisse's (2008) reading of parallel spaces developing as toothless tigers, social movement theories in their early guises understood institutionalisation as a combination of the depoliticisation of activism, deradicalisation of goals, bureaucratisation and formalisation of movements, and the increasing use of cooperative insider strategies (Banaszak 2006: 28). I consider activism in urban South Africa occurs within organised institutions as well as in parallel to them, in social spaces, and in opposition to institutions (e.g. protest movements); crucial here is the recognition that urban activism exists at different "geopolitical levels" (ibid.: 5), i.e. between local, national, and transnational scales, between civil society and state, and between autonomy and cooptation by the state.

Notes

1 Amartya Sen summarises the debates on democratisation over the last two centuries by stating that "[t]hroughout the nineteenth century, theorists of democracy found it quite natural to discuss whether one country or another was 'fit for democracy'. This thinking changed only in the twentieth century, with the recognition that the question itself was wrong: A country does not have to be deemed fit for democracy, rather, it has to become fit through democracy" (1999: 1).

2 "*Imbizo*" is a Zulu word that means gathering. In a political context, "*imbizo*" signifies a government initiative on public participation, which takes the form of face-to-face interactions and engagements between the public and senior government officials from all spheres of government. On the one hand, it provides the government with an occasion to inform the public about its programmes of action, while on the other, it offers the opportunity for the public to voice their needs, concerns, and grievances (www.info.gov.za/issues/imbizo/index.html, accessed 24.09.2012). During fieldwork, only one "*imbizo*" session was attended.

3 For example, the operating income budget of 72.9 billion Rand for 2003–2004 was funded from the following metro revenue sources: user charges (mainly electricity and water) 42.5 per cent; property rates 19.6 per cent; other (tariffs, fines, subsidies, etc.) 19.6 per cent; intergovernmental grants 11.1 per cent; business payroll and turnover levies 7.1 per cent. The operating income budget comprised 82.4 per cent of the total budget (Stytler 2005: 200).

4 The notion of the public good in South Africa is critically discussed among scholars and activists who argue that privatisation limits the access to goods such as water, electricity, street cleaning, etc. to those citizens that have the financial means (Samson 2007: 121). The following discussion takes up this line of argumentation, albeit not in relation to the debate surrounding public and private goods.

5 The State Old Age Pension provides R 780 (around 66 Euro) per month to men over the age of 65 and women over 60. The Disability Grant provides R 780 per month to adults with disabilities. The Child Support Grant provides R 180 (around 15 Euro) per child per month to families with children under the age of 14. The Foster Child Grant provides R 560 (around 50 Euro) per child per month to families with foster care children below the age of 18. The Care Dependency Grant provides an additional R 780 per child per month to families with children, below the age of 18, with disabilities (Samson/MacQuene/van Niekerk 2005: 2).

6 In 1922, the Union of South Africa, at that time governed by the British, laid the foundation of South Africa's welfare state. At first White soldiers, civil servants, and employees of the state-owned railway and docks were provided with state-financed pensions and insurance. In 1926–1927, classified Coloureds who belonged

to these working classes also received old age pensions (Seekings 2007: 258). Black Africans, making up the majority of the population, were excluded from these welfare schemes. In 1942, according to a report by the Department of Social Welfare, the "very poor" were considered to belong to a "socially-depressed group" among which many "will never develop into useful citizen and may require segregation" (1943: 23). According to this report, it was debated among the authors whether the very poor should be assisted with "pronounced social welfare implications" (Department of Social Welfare 1943: 24). When the NP assumed power in 1945, the question of the "very poor" remained, yet focused predominantly on "poor Whites".

7 www.capetown.gov.za/en/CouncilOnline/Pages/AboutCouncil.aspx, accessed 14.11.2011.

8 Seven meetings were attended in the period from November 2005 to March 2007. Due to local government elections, the sub-council was suspended from January to May 2006.

9 The Department of Water Affairs and Forestry introduced a Free Basic Water (FBW) policy in 2000, in response to evidence of the denial of sufficient access to water for numerous low-income and poor households. FBW guarantees households a basic allowance of 6,000 litres of free potable water every month, to be accessible within a 200-metre radius of that household (Oldfield/Peters 2005: 313). This policy was subsequently adopted by the City Council in 2004. The FBW policy is hotly debated among scholars; "In larger households, FBW may not meet even the minimum definition of access of sufficient water of 25 litres per day. In this manner, using "the household as a unit of measurement for [receiving] free water [...] automatically disadvantages large low-income households" (McDonald 2002: 29, quoted in ibid.: 314). It should be noted that 25 litres per person per day is still half the amount recommended by the World Health Organisation, and that while the first 6,000 litres per month of water is free, high tariffs for subsequent usage often lead to low-income households paying more monthly for water than they did before the introduction of FBW (ibid.: 316). Prepaid water meters are currently in use in Brazil, Curacao, Egypt, Malawi, Namibia, Nigeria, Sudan, Swaziland, Tanzania, the Philippines, Uganda, and the United States. See http://waterfortheages.org/2008/09/20/one-gallon-of-water-prepay-only-please/, accessed on 26.09.2017.

10 See Deedat/Cottle (2002: 82) for a case study in Madlebe, Kwazulu Natal on cost recovery, water cut-offs, and the outbreak of cholera.

11 See Xali (2002: 107) for a case study in Khayelitsha on cost recovery of service provision.

12 As of 2009, citizens are now allowed to participate in sub-council meetings, but they have to register their items on the meeting agenda two weeks in advance.

13 Oldfield/Peters (2005: 218) quote, for example, the studies of Ruiters (2001); Dor/Himlin/Ruiters (2002); McDonald/Pape (2002), all of which criticize the ways in which post-apartheid water policies exacerbate and extend apartheid inequalities.

14 The question of "who is the really unemployed?", also implicitly refers to those who generate income outside the formal economy. Based on my empirical data, quite a number of unemployed people supplement their sources of income by maintaining a small "tuck shop" in their backyard, an illegal liquor shop or *shebeen*, or a stand in the so-called informal market, etc. without declaring it. All such activities are considered illegal as they are not officially registered by state departments and thus not subject to tax.

15 See Report of the Executive Committee/Manenberg Crisis, quoted in Robins (2002: 679).

16 Similarly, Berggren/Jordahl (2006: 143) distinguish between particularised and generalised trust. The former refers to trusting individuals you know or know

something about. By contrast, generalised trust indicates trusting most people you do not know or know nothing about.

17 The analysis of the forum "Building Women Activism" is based upon participant observation of six public forums of "Building Women's Activism", in Woodstock, Cape Town, on 19.04.2006, 24.05.2006, 28.06.2006, 26.08.2006, 06.12.2006 and 15.03.2007 as well as many conversations with activists participating in this forum.

18 ANCWL is further explained in note 8 Chapter 2.

19 Jacob Zuma was president of the Republic of South Africa from 2009 to 2018.

20 WNC is further explained in note 27 Chapter 2.

21 The next chapter introduces two further categories of actors that township residents can approach for support or help, namely sector representatives of ward committees and Community Development Workers.

References

Ajam, T. (2001). Intergovernmental Fiscal Relations in South Africa. In: N. Levy and N. Tapscott, eds. *Intergovernmental Relations in South Africa: The Challenges of Co-operative Government*. Cape Town: IDASA/School of Government, University of the Western Cape.

Anthias, F. and Yuval Davis, N. (1989). *Women-Nation-State*. London: MacMillan.

Askvik, S. and Bak, N. (2005). *Trust in Public Institutions in South Africa*. Aldershot: Ashgate.

Banaszak, L. A. (2006). Women's Movements and Women in Movements: Influencing American Democracy from the "Outside"? Lecture presented at the Midwest Political Science Association Annual Meeting, Chicago, IL, April.

Benjamin, N. (2004). Organisation Building and Mass Mobilisation. *Development Update* 5(2), pp. 73–94.

Berggren, N. and Jordahl, H. (2006). Free to Trust: Economic Freedom and Social Capital. *Kyklos* 59(2), pp. 141–169.

Britton, H. E. (2006). South Africa Mainstreaming Gender in a New Democracy. In: G. Bauer and H. E. Britton, eds. *Women in African Parliament*. London: Lynne Rienner Publishers, pp. 59–84.

Cashdan, B. (2002). Local Government and Poverty in South Africa. In: S. Parnell, E. Pieterse, M. Swilling and D. Wooldridge, eds. *Democratising Local Government. The South African Experiment*. Landsdowne: University of Cape Town, pp. 159–180.

Cissé, K. (2008). *La revendication politique et citoyenne comme réponse à la marginalisation des femmes dans le développement: le cas du Sénégal*. Dakar: CODESRIA.

Cottle, E. and Deedat, H. (2002). Cost Recovery and Prepaid Water Meters and the Outbreak of Cholera in KwaZulu Natal. In: D. A. McDonald and J. Pape, eds. *Cost Recovery and the Crisis of Service Delivery in South Africa*. London: Zed Books, pp. 81–97.

Das, V. and Randeria, S. (2015). Politics of the Urban Poor: Aesthetics, Ethics, Volatility, Precarity. An Introduction to Supplement 11. *Current Anthropology* 56(11), pp. 3–14.

Donais, T. (2008). *Local Ownership and Security Sector Reform*. Berlin: LIT Verlag.

Dor, G., Himlin, B. and Ruiters, G. (2002). Eco-Social Injustice for Working Class Communities: The Making and Unmaking of Neoliberal Infrastructure Policy. In: P. Bond, ed. *Unsustainable South Africa*. Pietermaritzburg: University of Natal Press, pp. 185–242.

Esau, M. (2007). *Deepening Democracy through Local Participation. Examining the Ward Committee System as a Form of Local Participation in Bonteheuwel in the*

Western Cape. Project: Policy Management, Governance and Poverty Alleviation in the Western Cape. Cape Town: University of the Western Cape.

Fjeldstad, O. (2005). Entitlement, Affordability or a Matter of Trust? Reflections on the Non-Payment of Services Charges in Local Authorities. In: S. Askvik and N. Bak, eds. *Trust in Public Institutions in South Africa.* Aldershot: Ashgate, pp. 85–102.

Fischer, F. (2000). *Citizens, Experts and the Environment: The Politics of Local Knowledge.* Durham, NC: Duke University Press.

Gaventa, J. (2010). Foreword. In: L. Thompson and C. Tapscott, eds. *Citizenship and Social Movements. Perspectives from the Global South.* London: Zed Books, p. xii.

Hassim, S. (2004). *Voices, Hierarchies and Spaces: Reconfiguring the Women's Movement in Democratic South Africa. A case study for the UKZN project. Political Studies.* Johannesburg: University of Witwatersrand.

Hirschman, A. O. (1970). *Exit, Voice, and Loyalty. Responses to Decline in Firms, Organisations, and States.* Cambridge, MA: Harvard University Press.

Jensen, S. (2004). Claiming Community: Local Politics in the Cape Flats, South Africa. *Critique of Anthropology* 24(2), pp. 179–207.

Jensen, S. (2008). *Gangs, Politics & Dignity in Cape Town.* Chicago, IL: University of Chicago Press.

Johnson, R.W. (1999). *Not so Close to Their Hearts: An Investigation into the Non-payment of Rents, Rates and Service Charges in South Africa's Towns and Cities.* Parklands: Helen Suzman Foundation.

Kabeer, N. (2005). *Inclusive Citizenship: Meanings and Expressions.* London: Zed Books.

Liebenberg, S. and Pillay, K. (2000). *Socio-Economic Rights in South Africa. A Resource Book.* Bellville: Socio-Economic Rights Project, Community Law Centre, University of the Western Cape.

Long, N. (1996). Globalisation and Localisation: New Challenges to Rural Research. In: H. L. Moore, ed. *The Future of Anthropological Knowledge.* London: Routledge, pp. 37–59.

Löwenthal, R. (1963). Staatsfunktion und Staatsform in Entwicklungsländern. In: F. Nuscheler, ed. *Politikwissenschaftliche Entwicklungsländerforschung.* Darmstadt: Wissenschaftliche Buchgesellschaft, pp. 241–275.

Luhmann, N. (1990). Familiarity, Confidence, Trust: Problems and Alternatives. In: D. Gambetta, ed. *Trust. Making and Breaking Cooperative Relations.* Oxford: Blackwell, pp. 94–107.

Mathekga, R. and Buccus, I. (2006). The Challenge of Local Government Structures in South Africa: Securing Community Participation. *Critical Dialogue – Public Participation in Review: IDASA*, pp. 11–17.

Marx-Ferree, M. and McClurg Mueller, C. (2006). Gendering Social Movement Theory: Opportunities, Organisations and Discourses in Women's Movements Worldwide. In: A. Weckert and U. Wischermann, eds. *Das Jahrhundert des Feminismus. Streifzüge durch nationale und international Bewegungen und Theorien.* Frankfurt am Main: Helmer, pp. 39–60.

McDonald, D. A. and Pape, J. (2002). *Cost Recovery and the Crisis of Service Delivery in South Africa.* London: Zed Books.

Meintjes, S. (1996). The Women's Struggle for Equality During South Africa's Transition to Democracy. *Transformation* 30, pp. 47–64.

Millstein, M. (2010). Limits to Local Democracy: The Politics of Urban Governance Transformations in Cape Town. *Working Paper* 2. Stockholm: Swedish International Centre for Local Democracy.

Mottiar, S. and Bond, P. (2012). The Politics of Discontent and Social Protest in Durban. *Politikon: South African Journal of Political Studies* 39(3), pp. 309–330.

Nord, A. K. (2012). Mehr Geschlechtergerechtigkeit? Zur Frauenquote in Afrika. *GIGA Focus Afrika 5*. Hamburg: GIGA, pp. 2–7.

Oldfield, S. and Peters, K. (2005). The Paradox of 'Free Basic Water' and Cost Recovery in Grabouw: Increasing Household Debt and Municipal Financial Loss. *Urban Forum* 16(4), pp. 313–335.

Parnell, S. (2005). Constructing a Developmental Nation – the Challenge of Including the Poor in the Post-apartheid City. *Transformation* 58, pp. 20–44.

Pieterse, E. (2002). Participatory Local Governance in the Making: Opportunities, Constraints and Prospects. In: S. Parnell, E. Pieterse, M. Swilling and D. Wooldridge, eds. *Democratising Local Government. The South African Experiment*. Cape Town: University of Cape Town, pp. 1–17.

Robins, S. (2002). At the Limits of Spatial Governmentality: A Message from the Tip of Africa. *Third World Quarterly* 23(4), pp. 665–690.

Rodrik, D. (2004). *Industrial Policy for the Twenty-First Century*. A paper prepared for the United Nations Industrial Development Organisation (UNIDO). Faculty Research Working Papers Series, RWP04–047. Cambridge, MA: Harvard University, John F. Kennedy School of Government.

Ruiters, G. (2002). Debt, Disconnection, and Privatisation. The case of Fort Beaufort, Queenstown and Sutterheim. In: D. A. McDonald and J. Pape, eds. *Cost Recovery and the Crisis of Service Delivery in South Africa*. London: Zed Books, pp. 41–57.

Samson, M. (2007). Privatizing Collective Public Goods: A Case Study of Street Cleaning in Johannesburg, South Africa. *Studies in Political Economy* 79, Spring, pp. 119–143.

Samson, M., MacQuene, K. and van Niekerk, I. (2006). *Social Grant, South Africa. Inter-Regional Inequality Facility sharing ideas and policies across Africa, Asia and Latin America*. Policy Brief 1. Overseas Development Institute.

Seekings, J. (2007). Workers and the Beginnings of Welfare State-Building in Argentina and South Africa. *African Studies* 66(2–3), pp. 253–272.

Sen, A. (1999). Democracy as a Universal Value. *Journal of Democracy* 10(3), pp. 3–17.

Sieveking, N. (2008). Women's Organisations Creating Social Space in Senegal. In: G. Lachenmann and P. Dannecker, eds. *Negotiating Development in Muslim Societies. Gendered Spaces and Transnational Connections*. Lanham, MD: Lexington Books, pp. 37–65.

Smit, W. (2006). Understanding the Complexities of Informal Settlements: Insights from Cape Town. In: M. Huchzermeyer, and A. Karam, eds. *Informal Settlements, A Perpetual Challenge?* Cape Town: University of Cape Town Press, pp. 103–125.

Strulik, S. (2004). *Engendering Local Democracy Research. Panchayati Raj and Changing Gender Relations in India*. Unpublished Paper presented at the International Workshop on Local Democracy, organised by the EU-Asia Link Programme "The Micro Politics of Democratisation: European-South Asian Exchanges on Governance, Conflict and Civic Action". Tribhuvan University, Kathmandu.

Stytler, N. (2005). Local Government in South Africa. Entrenching Decentralized Government. In: N. Stytler, ed. *The Place and Role of Local Government in Federal Systems*. Johannesburg: Konrad-Adenauer-Stiftung, pp. 183–220.

Tapscott, C. (2005). Democracy and Trust in Local Government. In: S. Askvik and N. Bak, eds. *Trust in Public Institutions in South Africa*. Aldershot: Ashgate, pp. 73–84.

Thompson, L. and Tapscott, C. (2010). Mobilisation and Social Movements in the South: The Challenges of Inclusive Governance. In: L. Thompson and C. Tapscott, eds. *Citizenship and Social Movements. Perspectives from the Global South*. London: Zed Books, pp. 1–34.

van Ryneveld, P., Parnell, S. and Muller, D. (2003). *Indigent Policy: Including the Poor in the City of Cape Town's Income Strategy*. Cape Town: City of Cape Town.

Wade, R. (1990). *Governing the Market: Economic Theory and the Role of Government in East Asian Industrialisation*. Princeton, NJ: Princeton University Press.

Wedel, J., Shore, C., Feldman, G. and Lathrop, S. (2005). Toward an Anthropology of Public Policy. *Annals of the American Academy of Political and Social Science* 600, pp. 30–51.

White, G. (1988). *Developmental States in East Asia*. New York: St Martin's Press.

Williams, J. J. (2006). Community Participation. Lessons from Post-Apartheid South Africa. *Policy Studies* 27(3), pp. 197–217.

Wooldridge, D. (2002). Introducing Metropolitan Local Government in South Africa. In: S. Parnell, E. Pieterse, M. Swilling and D. Wooldridge, eds. *Democratising Local Government. The South African Experiment*. Cape Town: University of Cape Town, pp. 127–140.

Xali, M. (2002). "They Are Killing Us Alive": A Case Study of the Impact of Cost Recovery on Service Provision in Makhasa Section, Khayelitsha. In: D. A. McDonald and J. Pape, eds. *Cost Recovery and the Crisis of Service Delivery in South Africa*. London: Zed Books, pp. 101–119.

Yuval-Davis, N. (2006). Belonging and the Politics of Belonging. *Patterns of Prejudice* 40(3), pp. 197–214.

State and non-state sources

Department Provincial and Local Government and German Agency for Technical Cooperation (2005). *Ward Committee Resource Book. Best Practices and Lessons Learnt for Municipal Officials, Councillors and Local Governance Practitioners*. Pretoria: Communication Directorate.

Department of Social Welfare (1942 [1943]) Report of a Committee of Enquiry Appointed to Enquire Into Conditions Existing on the Cape Flats and Similarly-Affected Areas in the Cape Divisions, Cape Town.

Essof, S. (2006). Reflections on the Women's Movement. *International Labour Resource and Information Group. Building up Women's Activism*.

ILRIG (2006). ILRIG Report: Public Forum: Building Women's Activism. Cape Town.

Ministry of Local Government. (2009). White Paper on Local Government. Draft. Pretoria: Government Printer.

Union of South Africa (1943). Report of a Committee of Enquiry Appointed to Enquire into Conditions Existing on the Cape Flats and Similarly-Affected Areas in the Cape Division in 1942. Pretoria: Government Printer.

Newspaper article

De Bruin, S. (2006). ANC Members Protest Electricity and Water Cuts. In: *Plainsman Independent Community Newspaper*, 18.10.2006, pp. 10–11.

Websites

Municipal System Act 32/2000 (Section 16, 17). Available at: http://extwprlegs1.fao. org/docs/pdf/saf93030.pdf [26.09.2017].
Palmieri, J. (2013). Mouvements de femmes en Afrique: de l'institutionnalisation à la démocratie directe – les exemples du Sénégal et de l'Afrique du Sud. https://joellepa lmieri.wordpress.com/2013/09/27/mouvements-de-femmes-en-afrique-de-linstitution nalisation-a-la-democratie-directe-les-exemples-du-senegal-et-de-lafrique-du-sud-joe lle-palmieri/ [25.05.2015].
Pre Paid Water Meters. Available at: http://waterfortheages.org/2008/09/20/one-gallo n-of-water-prepay-only-please [26.09.2017].

5 Institutionalising activism at the interface with government

The preceding chapter conceived the sub-council as an institution of public participation where the public's role is reduced to that of an audience. In this chapter, a focus is adopted on different institutionalised gatherings that are depicted in policies as means to strengthen community-state relations by integrating civil society actors from the respective communities into the governance system. These participatory structures foresee the inclusion of civil society organisations that speak and act on behalf of the community. The chapter considers three state-induced ways of enhancing community-state relations and public participation, namely the ward committee system, established by local government and supported by the GTZ; the Community Development Worker Programme (CDWP), monitored by provincial government; and the African Peer Review Mechanism (APRM), a transnational programme facilitated by provincial government. In a way, these transnational public participation programmes highlight how societies, cities, and the global (donor) community have become progressively more interconnected in the course of globalisation. Gupta et al. (2015: 5) highlight how modern globalisation is characterised by "hyper capitalism and technological revolutions [...] leading to increasing interdependence and homogenisation of ideologies [of governance, for example], production and consumption patterns and lifestyles". In this manner, one way that globalisation structures the internationalisation of politics is the worldwide shift from "government" to "governance". As a consequence, new institutional arrangements have become established with the aim of advancing citizen and grassroots involvement in organising, improving, and developing cities. In South Africa, and indeed in many other post-colonial societies, the participatory approach has evolved as "the" tool for use in (transnational) policies and politics, designed to transform former colonised cities into inclusive ones (Parnell 2016). In this context, Gupta et al. describe the relationship between globalisation processes and the establishment of local governance arrangements "as self-reinforcing ways" (ibid.: 5). The emphasis on self-reinforcement puts the central focus on the relational perspective between global and local forces and dynamics.

Hence, the main interest here lies in how global ideas of participatory governance in policies and programmes are translated, interpreted, and practiced at the local level by different actors. Informed by perspectives of policy anthropology, this chapter looks at how local governance is conceptualised and put into practice – by the state on the one hand and by activists on the other. Following Benz and Dose (2010), who point to the importance of embedding governance arrangements into the local economic and societal context, the specific histories of the places in which these governance arrangements have become established rely on material introduced in the previous chapters of this book. In this sense, the urban governance perspectives developed in this chapter give insights into "patterns of interventions linked to specific actors" (Haferburg/Huchzermeyer 2015: 4) and places. The analysis thereby pays attention to all three spheres of governance arrangements, i.e. at local, provincial, and national government levels, as well as supranational institutions, e.g. the African Union (AU). Accordingly, it can be argued that the ANC, as the national governing party, created and institutionalised activism at the interface with local government after 1994. The interesting point is to demonstrate how all three of the previously mentioned state-induced mechanisms for public participation intersect and have become interwoven at the urban level. In this respect, these arranged encounters at the interface, which are conceived in order "to integrate and co-ordinate 'civil society' in local governance" (Oldfield 2002: 98) become entangled in urban agendas and interests that are geographically specific and entrenched in old apartheid divisions.

The chapter is organised as follows. The first section disentangles the different notions of community in policies and politics in order to clarify our understanding of the concept of community-state relations that have developed as the key feature of the internationally-financed urban governance agendas. The subsequent sections shed light on how state actors went about establishing various links with the communities. These links manifest as institutionalised encounters at the interface between the local, provincial and national governments and civil society. In the second section, we focus on ward committees, which are supposed to create a working relationship between ward councillors and representatives from civil society (including CBOs, self-help groups, and NGOs) from different policy sectors, such as health, safety and security, electricity and water management, transport, and sports. These sector representatives act as (unpaid) volunteers within the ward committee system. The third section introduces the Community Development Workers (CDWs) as individuals with an activism background who are recruited, trained, and employed by the state. The CDWs are expected to facilitate communication between communities and the state on policy sectors, and to improve the living conditions among the poor. The fourth section discusses the APRM, an institution under the auspice of the AU, which is supposed to engender a political process at the urban level, one with the aim of evaluating political, social, and economic governance in South Africa.

Conferences that have been organised as part of the APRM-process also took place in Cape Town. While the overall focus lies on how these different concepts are translated and interpreted at the urban level, this chapter also elaborates on the links among these institutional arrangements, and concludes with a summary of how they structure and engender urban governance.

5.1 Community-state relations

The empirical material presented in this book shows that the concept of community is rhetorically invoked in different contexts and situations. While ward councillors describe themselves as "community leaders", activists criticise them for not doing enough "for the community". Both actors pretend, at least vis à vis the state and international partners, to represent community interests and act as legitimate spokespersons for the members of their communities. However, they differ in how they invoke the community in their political work and with references to power in negotiations over the allocation of resources. Ward councillors, for example, predominantly speak of the community as being synonymous with the ward, a clearly delimited political entity, particularly addressing ward residents in their day-to-day practices. This is related to the ward councillors' power being built around their control over some of the budget and state-financed projects executed in their wards. Conversely, many activists follow a looser understanding of community, not just limited to the ward level. For instance, while an NGO might be located in a particular ward, generally its work is dedicated to a broader public, perhaps even including neighbouring townships. Moreover, social movements such as the AEC are based upon cross-boundary activities, and their campaigning is not restricted to a specific ward. In this sense, community is not spatially delimited to a single political entity or specific membership, but is rather constituted by residents who live at the margins of urban society.

Additionally, both government and international actors assume that community interests can be communicated from a local to a national level through representatives such as ward councillors or civil society actors. Thereby, (local) governments "include" the community and its different representatives who are supposed to act for the benefit of the poor, aiming to manifest community-state relations at the urban level. In this way, in policies based on public participation the community is not understood as a loose, flexible entity, but rather as a geographically fixed body, i.e. synonymous with wards. The Municipal System Act specifies its understanding of community participation by stating that a municipality should establish appropriate mechanisms, processes, and procedures in wards to enable the participation of communities in the municipality's affairs, and that the municipal council and other political structures should thus hold public meetings and hearings (Municipal System Act No. 32, 2000). In implementing this act, the state has created institutions for the participation of poor people in the form of sub-councils, ward committees, and *"imbizos"*.

As the key feature of developmental local governance, provisions for community-state relations have become common-place in many departmental policies, such as safety and security, transport, and the delivery of services. However, it is evident that civil society and state actors' varying conceptions of community also hint at different understandings of inclusion and representation. At the same time, both perspectives share the common view that the community is "weak", in terms of being economically deprived and politically immature. Their image of a community is that of a grouping in a disadvantaged and unstable position, which needs to be empowered by state and/or civil society actors.

Studies on community-state relations in South Africa (Jensen 2004; Mathekga/Buccus 2006; Williams 2006; Esau 2007, 2008) often fail to sufficiently take into account translocal and transnational dimensions of state interventions. These studies neglect the fact that international partners and experts were highly committed to the idea of community participation, attaching conditions on development aid to its implementation – in both policy and practice. The concept of involving people in decision-making processes that affect their lives had already become part of development discourse in the 1980s, subsequently being discussed during the World Social Summit in Copenhagen in 1995, and then further in the G7 leaders' initiative in Cologne in 1999, in which "Heavily Indebted Poor Countries" would receive broader and faster debt relief in return for firm commitments that they would use the benefits to improve the lives of all their people. The Cologne initiative therefore calls for the development of a new framework linking debt relief with poverty reduction, whose specific goals among others centre on greater transparency in government budgeting and much wider consultation with civil society in the development and introduction of economic programmes. These goals resulted in development programmes that increased focus on "interaction" structures between government and civil society, and the integration of "target populations" within the development process. This so-called participatory approach was developed and discussed in the social sciences, decisively influencing development policy (Lachenmann 2001: 186), and is also reflected in the World Bank's Poverty Reduction Strategy Papers:

> [...] create administrative structures, procedures and mechanisms that will facilitate the institutionalisation of policy participation. Participation works best, when it is built into ongoing public institutions and decision-making procedures [...] the most successful cases are those where participation becomes institutionalised [...].
>
> (Brinkerhoff/Goldsmith 2001: 9)

Therefore, participation was not only considered an important aspect on the project level, but also on the institutional level. Indeed, it was conceived to foster democratic development and institutions at the urban level by providing democratic institutions greater power, particularly the authority to decide upon and participate in decision-making processes. These developmental policies were also implemented in South African programmes. For example, in 2000 the South African Department of Provincial and Local Government (DPLG) developed the ward committee system with the assistance of the German Agency for Technical Cooperation (GTZ) and the Australia-South Africa Local Governance Partnership (ASALPG).[1] The ward committees were supposed to give substance and practical meaning to the political commitment "the people shall govern". The view that participatory democracy is a precondition for development became part of international discourses on development and democracy, and has subsequently been appropriated and translated as a leitmotiv into many diverse contexts and settings. To cite a few examples, there now exist such programmes as participatory budgeting in Brazil, the district councils in Uganda (Pieterse 2001: 412), *"Panchayat"* reforms in India (Strulik 2004: 3–4), and CDWPs in South Africa, India, and Cuba (Conversation with CDWs, 15.05.2006). In all such cases, the state's overall intention to create systems of participatory governance through top-down reforms appears to be contradictory; on the one hand, potentially more radical forms of participatory democracy emerge from ideas at the grass-roots bottom, and on the other, attempting reforms on entrenched, existing structures from the top-down. The point of this chapter, however, is not to dwell on such contradictions, but rather to focus on how public policy is adapted, interpreted, and negotiated in different ways at the urban level, often with unforeseen consequences.

5.2 Ward committees in Mitchells Plain and Khayelitsha

The basic goal of the ward committee system was to support historically disadvantaged communities through addressing underdevelopment, unemployment, and poverty. A ward is a clearly-defined electoral entity with electoral boundaries, and a ward committee is a sub-municipal structure, which comprises the ward councillor as its chairperson and several members, who are supposed to represent particular interest groups within the ward community and thus understand the varying needs of that community.[2] In order to include the diversity of interests within a ward, the original policy-makers facilitated participation through sectors (Esau 2008: 374), which in the case of Cape Town's Council were identified as follows: youth, women, religious groups, sports and culture, health and welfare, senior citizens, the disabled, education, community safety forums, non-political community-based organisations, ratepayers' associations, agricultural associations, informal traders' associations, and employment (Esau 2007: 14). In this case, it is important to note that all the member representatives of these sectors share a so-called background in community work, i.e. they are engaged in self-help groups, CBOs, NGOs, faith-based groups, among others. The members are nominated by the community, with the nomination procedure supervised by the Speakers Office of the city council.

The ward committee system theoretically functions by informing sub-councils and municipalities about people's aspirations, potentials, and problems. Ward committees are conceived as advisory bodies, assisting the elected ward councillor and city sub-councils (executive committees) in managing service delivery and development. Consequently, ward committees form a bridge by facilitating better communication between a council, sub-councils, and citizens. Former ward committee members summarised their role as acting as a mouthpiece for urban communities.

Ward committee meetings are chaired by the ward councillor, take place once a month, and are open for the public to actively participate. The committee is meant to have the power to influence IDP, municipal budgeting, and municipal performance management processes.[3] Besides the allocation of R 200,000 (around 16,940 Euro) to each ward, a further R 40,000 (around 3,400 Euro) was provided for community projects.[4] Ward committees are supposed to organise budget hearings within their respective wards and provide specific feedback to the (sub-)council on ward submissions (City Council meeting, Civic Centre, Cape Town, 31.05.2006). Accordingly, suitable projects should be identified and initiated through the creation of (development) cooperations. The extent to which ward committee meetings function as a mechanism to enable citizens to de-facto influence budget spending is discussed in this chapter.

In Cape Town, the ward committee system only existed as a forum from November 2004 until 2006, when the city council was governed by the ANC. During the DA-governed city council (2006–2008), no ward committees existed in Cape Town. It is worth noting that city councils are not legally obliged to implement ward committees, and the DA opposed the ward committee system during their election campaign as ineffective and "a waste of money". Its advocates, on the other hand, have criticised the new DA mayor for not having introduced any alternatives to enhance public participation. The disbanding of the committees sparked public controversy, and the system was re-introduced by the DA leadership in 2008, albeit as a new ward-forum mechanism under the direction of the larger sub-councils (Millstein 2010: 15).[5]

There are few existing empirical studies on the ward committee system in the Cape Flats. Esau (2007, 2008) examines them in the former Coloured township of Bonteheuwel, an area established in 1965 as a result of the forced removals. Meanwhile, Millstein (2010) discusses the committee structure in the mixed township of Delft, an area constructed between 1994 and 2002 where the new government explicitly used housing development as a tool for "racial integration" (ibid.: 5). More influenced by the history of apartheid segregation policies, and therefore in contrast to new projects such as Delft, Bonteheuwel and Mitchells Plain are still inhabited predominantly by self-defined Coloured populations, and the township of Khayelitsha is predominated by Black African populations. Esau concludes that the ward committee system in Bonteheuwel did not function owing to the inability of the poor to participate, rather than because of party politics. By contrast, Millstein defines the ward committee system in Delft as a highly-politicised and racialised institution. Taking these studies as points of departure, it can be said that both Mitchells Plain's and Khayelitsha's ward committee systems could be classed as politicised, while a lack of resources also limits public participation.

The ward committees in Mitchells Plain and Khayelitsha cannot be said to operate in the same way, and their experiences also differ from those in Bonteheuwel and Delft. In Mitchells Plain the ward committee did not live up to urban politicians' and activists' expectations, owing to imbalances of political and economic power by member representatives, the affordability of participation, and the limited ownership and influence on decision-making, especially in regard to budget spending at the ward level.

Questions of representation

The quality of representation on ward committees was problematised by ward committee members with regards to: a) the nomination and election processes, and b) sectors that were not nominated at all, or considered to have weak representation.

All the ward councillors and ward committee members in Khayelitsha shared an allegiance to the national ruling party, the ANC. The ward councillors in Mitchells Plain, by contrast, were from oppositional parties, whereas the ward committee sector representatives were well-known members of the ANC. Therefore, I argue that while party-political factionalism in Mitchells Plain shaped their committee, in Khayelitsha it worked as a party-political extension of the ANC government. Interestingly, when speaking about other areas not restricted to the Cape Flats, Piper and Deacon (2008: 44) highlight that there is a close relationship between ward committees and the branches of political parties. Indeed, this was also the case in Khayelitsha and Mitchells Plain, where many sector representatives were also active in the ANC party-political branches. In this respect, one might adopt a historicising perspective with respect to the place where a ward committee began to be established. In Chapter 2, the trajectory of the ANC ward councillor in Khayelitsha, Ms Parrow, revealed how she remained an activist throughout her dual position between associations and organisations related to both her activism and to the state. This positioning decisively shaped her manner of co-operating and networking with the sector representatives in her ward. In this case, it is their common ANC past that links ward councillors and sector representatives, and simplifies their working relationships. In contrast, the ward councillors in Mitchells Plain did not share the same party-political background as activists and sector representatives.

Additionally, unlike in Khayelitsha, a primary concern in Mitchells Plain was related to the make-up of sector representation on ward committees. Ward councillors in Mitchells Plain questioned the nomination processes of sector representatives to the committees, accusing the ANC-governed city council of election fraud and complaining about the lack of transparency in the committee member election procedures. They pointed to the fact that all sector representatives in the ward committees in Mitchells Plain were aligned with the ANC, and in this regard, racialised the concept of the ward committee system as a "Black thing" that the ANC "created in order to manage public voice instead of listening to it" (DA ward councillor from Mitchells Plain). Millstein (2010: 16) highlighted a case in the mixed area of Delft, where DA ward councillors were accused of fraud and racism during the nomination process when they allegedly refused nominations for sector representatives from some ANC activists, including Black Africans. The ANC activists claimed that the DA ward councillors gave nomination application forms to their friends and also ensured that they were then nominated as sector representatives in order to support their own political agendas. As a result, the nomination process in general can be interpreted as being driven by different party-political interests and agendas, and becoming racialised in this particular case.

While the nomination process in both Mitchells Plain and Khayelitsha was predominantly influenced by different party-political interests, it cannot be said that references to racialised problems occurred among members. On both ward committees, ANC activists highlighted the fact that they directed their campaigns towards different interest groups in order to gain support for their candidates. Consequently, in Mitchells Plain, suspicion and lack of trust prevented cooperation between the DA ward councillors and the ANC sector representatives in some cases, i.e. between political actors from differing parties. The sector representatives criticised tense lines of communication with their ward councillors, who were perceived to be boycotting the committees. This manifested itself through the non-attendance of ward councillors as chairpersons at meetings, which led to many cases in which it was impossible to form a quorum.[6] A quorum is necessary to make binding decisions on issues or proposals which are then forwarded to the sub-council and city council.

However, these experiences stand in stark contrast to the situation in Khayelitsha, where according to the sector members there, the organisation and preparation of meetings functioned well. The sector members and their sub-council manager could put pressing items on the agenda within the bounds of the allowed time periods, referring to such examples as issues concerning development – such as the repairing of potholes, the installation of street lights, road upgrades, youth development, etc. They reported being able to form a quorum in their meetings most of the time, and were therefore able to take committee issues to higher levels of council. Moreover, communication between councillors, sector representatives, and council officials were described as efficient and co-operative.

Hence, in both cases the committee system and its operation were affected by the political alliances of their members and became highly politicised. In Mitchells Plain, this politicisation led to racialising the institution as an ANC initiative and a "Black thing", which restricted its ability to operate effectively.

In both Mitchells Plain and Khayelitsha, representatives on the ward committees constituted 10 different sectors, although significantly the sector for people with disabilities was not represented in either case. People with disabilities were effectively excluded from the ward committee system, as no supplementary assistance was provided to help them participate in the nomination process, for example by organising appropriate transport, etc. This point is also addressed by Esau (2008: 375) in her case study in the neighbouring township of Bontheheuwel, where similarly no sector for people with disabilities exists.

Moreover, the youth sector and the informal trader's sector were not represented in Mitchells Plain, although both of them were represented on the ward committee in Khayelitsha. In Mitchells Plain, ward committee members explained the lack of representation of the youth sector by saying that the majority of youth are either not politicised or more into drugs and gangsterism than politics. In Khayelitsha by contrast, there is an active presence of the ANC Youth League, and there was no problem in establishing a representative from the youth sector on the committee. According to Mitchells Plain's committee members, the informal trader's sector was not represented due to local traders being too suspicious of participating in a formalised political process.

Furthermore, with respect to the women's sector, the quality of representation was questioned by other sector representatives from the ward committees in Mitchells Plain, but not in Khayelitsha. In some ward committees in Mitchells Plain no women's sector existed as no one applied for the position of representative. In others, where a women's sector was represented, the quality of such representation with respect to the interests of women within the ward was criticised by other ward committee members, who perceived the representatives as not being active enough in providing substantial contributions to proposals, or even in putting items on the meetings' agendas. Nevertheless, on the committees in both areas the majority of all sectors' representatives were women. Here it is important to note that in women's cases in particular, their participation, specifically its activeness and regularity, was restricted by their ability to access necessary resources.

The affordability of participation

It is worth noting that very few of the sector representatives in Mitchells Plain and Khayelitsha were employed in the formal economy and in addition participated in the ward committees as unpaid volunteers, while ward councillors received a regular salary. The committees' sector representatives in both areas complained about the lack of remuneration for their work, as it was understood to be on a voluntary basis.

In line with Esau's (2007: 22) research on ward committees in a neighbouring township, committee members often found themselves in unsafe environments that made it risky to attend the evening ward committee meetings and other public meetings in general. As previously mentioned, Esau argues that the ward committee system did not work in Bontheuwel due to issues of poverty and violence rather than party politics. Most sector representatives in both the areas researched for this book walked to meetings due to the lack of transport facilities or the lack of resources to be able to pay for transport, which caused them to be more exposed to (gender-related) crime, whereas by contrast, ward councillors had access to their own cars. Despite sector representatives perceiving violence in their area as an obstacle to holding ward committee meetings, they more often than not attended the meetings.

All sector representatives expounded on the problem of acting as a mouthpiece between the community, the ward committee, and local government. An education sector representative, for example, organised a special community meeting in order to inform ward residents on a community project that had been approved by the council. Due to only four ward residents attending the meeting, she argued that non-politicised ward residents had limited time in which to attend community meetings, particularly those single mothers with parental responsibilities and a lack of access to transport, as well as those who had more than one job. In this respect, many female activists argued that the right to basic services, housing, education, freedom from sexual violence, and other rights – necessary to enable full participation in public life – do not extend to the majority of women. This hints at some of the difficulties in truly reaching and including all members of a ward in the process of establishing cooperative relationships. All ward committee members confirmed that many ward residents simply did not participate in their organised community meetings, which also touches upon the difficulties of representing the whole community in policies, and by extension, the quality of community representation in said policies.

According to sector representatives in Mitchells Plain, political cleavages between ward committee members and members of the sub-council made following the official policy-making process difficult. Some of the sector representatives in Mitchells Plain accused the manager of the sub-council of not making resources available (e.g. phone, printer, fax, etc.) and information accessible (e.g. by making themselves available for meetings or other communications). They assumed that these problems occurred due to the oppositional political allegiance of the sub-council manager (to the ANC) and consequently their opposition to the committee system as a whole. By contrast in Khayelitsha, the sector representatives maintained a good relationship with the sub-council manager (and their ward councillors), which made it easier to co-ordinate the agenda of the ward committees.

Limited power in influencing decision-making processes

One of the key issues debated among sector representatives concerned the power that they had to influence council decision-making, especially in regard to budget spending.

According to sector representatives in Mitchells Plain and Khayelitsha, only a handful of proposals on community projects submitted by ward committee members have been approved by the city council over a period of five years. For example, in Khayelitsha, the women's sector gained approval for project to the sum of R 10,000 (around 845 Euro), and in Mitchells Plain, the education sector received R 30,000 (around 2,450 Euro). However, the business and economic development sector representative in Mitchells Plain complained that she had to wait several years to get through her proposal. In Mitchells Plain all sector representatives stated that the ward councillor failed to approve their request to make the ward budget and expenditure more transparent. Furthermore, during the participation of some sector representatives in sub-council meetings, they failed to observe the ward councillor immediately putting forward proposals or items that had been discussed in the ward committee meetings. In contrast, sector representatives in Khayelitsha witnessed their committee items, such as the upgrading of infrastructure, becoming issues in the sub-council meetings.

As an advisory body, the ward committee's influence on budget spending in both Mitchells Plain and Khayelitsha appears rather restricted. Sector representatives in both areas concurred that they had no real power to influence decision-making processes and budget-spending. Specifically, sector representatives in Mitchells Plain expressed their frustration because many of their ideas and project proposals were not forwarded to the sub-council or responded to by the council. The limited influence on decision-making and resource allocation at ward level by ward committees is also confirmed by Himlin's (2005) study in the city of Johannesburg.

In the case of Mitchells Plain, the sector representatives clearly allocated the blame for the lack of influence to party-political factionalism within the committee system. In Khayelitsha, the sector representatives typically depicted the ward committee system as a well-functioning, participatory system, albeit one with a reduced influence due to its advisory status. Again, their overall positive self-representation is due to a certain extent to their party-political allegiance with the ANC, the national ruling party.

Despite the ward committee system being touted as a new institution in former Coloured and Black African townships, the specific histories of these places have shaped how they function there. Consequently, plans for coordination and institutionalisation as outlined in civil society policies of local governance have become entangled in urban agendas and geographically specific interests, which themselves are products of persisting apartheid-era divisions. In fact, even the question of who should be included in formalised spaces of participation is contested by members of the same political party, as illustrated in the next section.

5.3 "Are we duplicating things?": the Community Development Workers

The CDWP is a state programme introduced in 2005, essentially with the same broad aim of the ward committees, i.e. enhancing community-state relations. At the time of writing, I had not come across any research conducted in the Cape Flats focusing on either CDWs themselves or their relationships with other participatory institutions of self-governance, such as the ward committees or sub-councils.[7]

The category of CDW causes confusion among politicians, activists, and inhabitants in the Cape Flats, where it exists as a contested idiom. First of all, this is due to the fact that all urban political actors understand themselves as community workers per se, which leads to feelings that CDWs duplicated or replaced their functions. A well-known ANC activist in Mitchells Plain stated:

> My concern is the differences, or the role of the ward committees which seems to be the same as the Community Development Workers. Then you look at the NGOs, where do they come in? So my concern is, I don't have a problem with change – but are we duplicating things?
>
> (Head of the Women's Sector of Mitchells Plain Urban Renewal Programme for the NGO "Network Opposing Women Abuse", 07.03.2006)

Similar concerns were also voiced by Mitchells Plain's ward councillors and sector representatives, who started to question the state's development mantra filtered by the number of mouthpieces in official policies and planning frameworks indicated earlier.

In his annual State of the Nation address in February 2003, the then-President Thabo Mbeki introduced the establishment of a new "public service echelon of multi-skilled Community Development Workers" to act as the government's direct link to communities in promoting democracy. CDWs are supposed to make the first clause of the Freedom Charter, "The people shall govern", more relevant and meaningful, and to translate *"Batho Pele"* (People First) into practice (Richard Dyantyi, Member of the Executive Council for Local Government and Housing, 2005: 1). *"Batho Pele"* is an initiative launched by the ANC government in 1997 to transform government public services along more people-friendly and developmental lines (ibid.: 9). Integral to *"Batho Pele"*, the roles of the CDWs are explicitly defined as being: 1) engaged in development, service delivery, and poverty alleviation; 2) promoting *"Batho Pele"*, tackling corruption and poor delivery; 3) building partnerships with civil society; 4) building organisation by an informed citizenry; and 5) helping people with their problems. While their work is not limited to a specific ward, they "should have a special relationship and partnership with the ward councillor(s) and ward committees and should have regular discussions with councillors around local development priorities and programmes" (ibid.: 6). The CDW programme was first piloted in four provinces, namely Mpumalanga, Limpopo, North West, and Gauteng. In 2003 and 2004, the process of institutionalising CDWs in the Western Cape was rolled out by the Provincial Government (Interview with the Director of Community Development and Public Participation, Department of Local Government and Housing, 14.02.2006).

While approximately 1,300 people applied to participate in this programme in the Western Cape, there was only space for 400, all of whom were provided with a "donorship" of R 888 (around 75 Euro) per month. In the first year, these CDWs received part-time training at the Western Cape University, and also had to work for a municipality. At the conclusion of this first year, 364 graduates had completed the training, which saw them rewarded with level 4 in the national qualification framework, a qualification officially recognised as being beyond grade 12 (Interview with the Director of Community Development and Public Participation, Department of Local Government and Housing, 14.02.2006).

Therefore, while the CDWs share the same background of community work as the sector representatives, by contrast they are formally trained and receive a qualification certificate as well as an initial donorship and later a salary from the state.

Ten CDWs have been employed by the provincial government in Mitchells Plain and Khayelitsha respectively since February 2005, with the CDWs being "introduced" to ward residents through local newspapers and advertisements (see e.g.. de Bruin 2006: 10). During fieldwork, I observed the different ways in which CDWs were involved in community issues. For instance, a CDW who had to compile a report about service delivery for the provincial government in the informal settlement site C in Khayelitsha, consequently turned his attention to counting lacking water taps.[8] In both Mitchells Plain and Khayelitsha, CDWs recounted having to organise community workshops on topics such as citizen's rights and responsibilities in relation to the pre-paid water meters, as well as talks on social grants and national programmes (interview with two CDWs in Mitchells Plain, 15.05.2006). Like the ward committee members, CDWs are nominally positioned as brokers between residents and the (local) state. In contrast to the sector representatives, however, CDWs have direct links to specialised services of specific government departments, such as the Department of Water Affairs and Forestry. For example, CDWs organised workshops on pre-paid water meters, which were instructed by national government, specifically the Department of Water Affairs and Forestry. According to the CDWs, the department had identified four areas in the Cape Flats, including Mitchells Plain, where they wanted to educate residents through workshops; how to read water meters properly, how to identify leaks in water meters, taking responsibility for fixing taps, and paying accounts on time. The CDWs pointed out that such workshops were well-attended. It is worth noting that according to the ward committee members (both ward councillors and sector representatives), they had not been informed about these workshops and related activities of the CDWs during a time in which protest marches and actions arose opposed to the pre-paid water meter policy in Mitchells Plain. With respect to this issue, CDWs did not participate in ward committee, subcouncil, or city council meetings. This indicates that despite the state providing multiple spaces where the different actors could coordinate politics and participatory governance, there was a lack of establishing real lines of interaction between them.

In a government report focusing on the aforementioned CDWP pilot phase in the province of Gauteng in 2004, a similar problem was identified related to a lack of "information sharing across departments to facilitate project implementation" and a lack of cooperation between "CDWs and ward committees" (SAMDI 2005: 69),[9] without specifying any possible reasons behind these issues.

CDWs in Mitchells Plain argued that the problem lay with the three spheres of government

> [...] work[ing] like islands, everyone doing its own thing. Sometime lots of duplications, and then also what happened a lot of these good pro-grammes that national government has, seems not to come down to the community.
>
> (CDW from Mitchells Plain, 15.05.2006)

Indeed, ward councillors complained that there was never a memorandum of understanding between the local and the provincial government on the exact role of the CDWs. Concerning relationships between CDWs and ward councillors in Mitchells Plain, similar issues existed as those between CDWs and sector representatives of the ward committees. Ward councillors, who were not included in the selection process of CDWs, accused provincial government of not making the nomination process transparent and open for all people, i.e. those from opposition parties, to apply for CDW posts. Hence, like the ward committees, the CDW programme was perceived in Mitchells Plain as an ANC initiative aimed at "controlling" civil society. In his study on CDWs in Worcester, Williams (2006) concluded that "ordinary people contact no longer their ward councillor but their CDWs to attend their daily concerns and problems" (ibid.: 23). Rather than an alternative, my fieldwork showed that the introduction of CDWs in Mitchells Plain and Khayelitsha added an additional official option for township residents to receive some sort of help or assistance. Ward councillors in Mitchells Plain argued that while CDWs are appointed by the provincial government, ward councillors are elected in local elections, where voter turn-out is around 50 per cent (in both areas). According to the ward councillors, whereas their own position is thereby legitimised, CDWs only gain their legitimacy through their appointment by the state. The local government representatives thereby also underplay the value of the CDWs professionalisation and educational qualifications.

Furthermore, CDWs as a form of state-induced participation is evidently a technical, bureaucratically organised process. It is associated with a professionalisation of individuals, many of whom had no formally recognised qualifications, which can be regarded as a typical problem of the non-White population. Many CDWs stated that they wanted to make use of their new qualifications and study further:

> Ja, I'm planning to study further next year because I am, you know my dream was always to help people and to assist in the communities and it

happened, so I think I must study further next year in community development, maybe for diploma or whatever.

(CDW from Mitchells Plain, 10.03.2006)

Many ANC community workers in Mitchells Plain and Khayelitsha who worked on a voluntary basis, including sector representatives on the ward committees, applied for the CDWP, and those who were not accepted into the programme felt rejected in terms of being recognised by the government. Competition for CDW posts was high among activists, given that they offered both a formal qualification and regular income, i.e. both social and economic security. As mentioned previously, the sector representatives in both Mitchells Plain and Khayelitsha complained about the lack of remuneration for their work: "[we] do the same job, but don't get a cent" (Ward committee member, sector education, 15.09.2006). Herein lies the danger of CDWs being seen as a parallel structure to the ward committees in a participatory governance system: while the CDWs experienced a social and economic "upgrade", the "volunteers" felt crowded out and marginalised. I argue that the state's actions to partly professionalise, bureaucratise, and monetarise community-state relations led to cleavages and rivalries between those who are paid and those who are not. This can be seen as a typical problem in Africa, having occurred in many self-help approaches there over the years. In contrast to other African countries, however, where institutions similar to the CDWP have long existed, South Africa represents a special case due to its history and its post-apartheid spaces of activism, which were in place long before democratic state institutions.

5.4 The African Peer Review Mechanism: bringing everything together

The African Peer Review Mechanism (APRM) was established by the APRM Western Cape Province in 2006, a date that coincided with my fieldwork. The APRM is a "political process" which reviews governance systems in African countries with the goal of reducing levels of poverty and dependency (Demé 2005: 14; Grimm/Nawrath 2007: 5). In 2006 I attended three different APRM conferences held in Cape Town as an observer, where the relevant actors – all of them introduced in this study – met in order to debate the state of South Africa's democracy. Besides these conferences, CDWs also held workshops to inform citizens about the APRM. CDWs had been identified by the provincial government as one of the key players in rolling out the APRM programme at the urban level. At the date of writing, I had found no empirical research that had been conducted on the establishment and appropriation of the APRM at the urban level in Cape Town.

The APRM has been developed by the AU for countries to improve their governance systems. Participation in the scheme is voluntary for each member state of the New Partnership for Africa's Development (NEPAD) programme, which is supposed to foster the adoption of NEPAD's principles (Engel 2005: 15;

Déme 2005: 15). NEPAD is a strategic policy framework and socio-economic development programme, in whose formulation South Africa played a major role. It aims "to eradicate poverty and to place their countries, individually and collectively, on a path of sustainable growth and development, and at the same time to participate in the world economy and body politic" (NEPAD 2001: 1).[10] The main focus areas of the APRM, also part of the memorandum of understanding, are based upon NEPAD's main pillars: democracy and good political governance; economic governance and management; socio-economic development; and corporate governance (focusing on economic development). The APRM is monitored by a team from the AU, comprised of a panel of eminent persons who visit the country under review (Grimm/Nawrath 2007: 2). This team consists of independent individuals who are not from the country under review, who subsequently present an expert opinion upon the functioning of government, justice, parliament, and civil society. Therefore, as part of its review, the team participates in consultative conferences organised by the respective provincial governments across the country. Based upon their own findings and the country's self-assessment report, the AU team compiles an independent country report (Kebonang/Fombad 2006: 47).[11] With respect to the country's self-assessment report, national and provincial governments are expected to include government, business, and civil society interests, while academics are to be commissioned to analyse core issues, and to organise information and data collected from CDWs. In South Africa, the CDWs played an important role in the country's self-assessment report, given that it was partly based on findings from their workshops (Mbelle 2010: vii; 5). In the final step, the South African government had to develop a programme of action to address the weaknesses and shortcomings, which were identified from their own findings and the subsequent discussions of the heads of state.

One of the roles of the CDWs was defined as creating awareness of the APRM and NEPAD at the local level, and serving as a conduit for community views on their relevant issues – including democracy, service delivery, equity, economic management, and corruption. In this respect, CDWs organised workshops across the country, where the structure of these workshops was designed on the basis of an APRM questionnaire.[12] Furthermore, the CDWs had to forward reports detailing the findings from the workshops to the provincial government, who were involved in the compilation of the aforementioned self-assessment report.

In Mitchells Plain, the workshops on the APRM were not well attended by ward residents. As a result, CDWs decided to change their strategy and instead employ rather non-conventional methods in order to contact the citizens there. They took to visiting day-clinics in order to distribute information about the APRM and solicit residents' views on democracy – "We decided no, if the people don't want to come to us, we go to them" (CDW from Mitchells Plain, 10.03.2006). Despite this, the self-assessment report saw accusations of being biased and infiltrated by ANC-government ideology, given the CDWs' disputed position within the political arena of Mitchells Plain, as discussed previously. Many NGOs critical of the state, such as the NGO ILRIG or social movements such as the AEC, complained that the report was monitored and written solely by the government and its officials, rather than receiving inputs from independent individuals from civil society.

Furthermore, as indicated previously, three separate consultative conferences took place, organised by the provincial government for actors from both civil society and local and provincial government (including provincial coordinators, NGOs, CBOs, CDWs, ward committee members and other local government representatives, social movements, media representatives, business representatives, faith-based organisations, and academics). All conferences were supposed to interactively identify shortcomings and weaknesses in the various areas of governance and development. However, the team from the AU only participated in the third and final conference.

The first two conferences (on 11.02.2006 and 5.07.2006) were held in the Cape Town Civic Centre, were professionally organised and very well-attended. Both conference programmes were divided into three main parts. In the first part, the provincial co-ordinators introduced the APRM as a national, provincial, and local process. The second part was organised into four "breakaway" sessions according to NEPAD's four pillars: democracy and good political governance; economic governance and management; socio-economic development; and corporate governance. As a participant observer, I joined the sessions on democracy and good political governance on both occasions. The conferences each concluded with a plenary, with each of the breakaway sessions having to report and summarise the main issues discussed. Tea, coffee, and lunch were provided for conference participants, at considerable cost to the South African state.

The second breakaway session on democracy and good political governance was chaired and moderated by Dr. Leon Gilbert Pretorius, a senior lecturer in "Public Finance and State-Civil Society Development Management and Policy" at the School of Government at the University of the Western Cape. He highlighted that

> [...] there is democracy in the country – we had four elections that were free and fair [...] the importance of this session is to provide a platform and to look at the understanding of democracy at urban level, grassroots level [...] and to find solutions for the problems.

The session unfolded in a deliberative way, whereby criticism and pessimism were widespread. Interestingly, not only opponents of the ANC government but also ANC members themselves used it as a public space to articulate their concerns with government policies and politics. It was striking that women particularly were vocal in their criticisms.

A female ward committee member from Mitchells Plain, who is a well-known ANC activist, asked:

What happened to the concept of 'the people shall govern'? As ward committees we should form part of decision-making […] It's the people that have the problems. I don't think that the government has problems. People are unemployed; HIV, abuse […] then the CDWs were sent out to ask questions. But we want answers […] Democracy is much stronger on national level and very fragile at local level.

Mr Jeferson from the Anti-Eviction Campaign, whose trajectory has been discussed in Chapter 2, added:

This democracy has failed our people. Services are not delivered as a benefit to our people. People, CDWs are being co-opted by government. Political freedom means for me economic access. In order for democracy to work, we do not have to allow corrupt officials in parliament.

This was followed by another question from a woman from the grassroots organisation "New Women's Movement" in Mitchells Plain, who wanted to know "why women are not enough addressed". Dr. Pretorius answered that the government's plan is to focus more on the interactions between ward committees and ordinary people, women, and people with disabilities, i.e. concentrating on the people who should be supported and informed by the ward committees. He made no reference to CDWs. Subsequently, a male participant unknown to me expressed his lack of confidence in the government and the APRM reporting process by suggesting:

People from other African countries have to come to monitor service delivery? In order for democracy to work, we do not have to allow corrupt officials in parliament […] Has the APRM process been a neutral one? Why officials are taking over this session? Those APRM reports do not reflect issues expressed by our community. You do have no respect, you do harm.

The discussion continued in this relatively hostile tone.

The third consultative conference, conducted in front of the AU Team, did not differ greatly in the critiques expressed by its participants. In this final conference, Professor Anyang' Nyong'o, a Kenyan member of parliament asked the audience, "in this post-1994 South Africa, do you feel free, do you feel free to ask questions, do you feel this is your political system, do you feel that you have ownership?" A female ANC activist and ward committee member from Mitchells Plain responded thusly: "[W]e can see hardly things done in the community. It just doesn't come through from national level." Furthermore, the female CDW Coordinator of the Western Cape added that "we have very good policies but the practice looks different; the problem is the administration, the bureaucracy and the departments".

In summary, these responses deny feeling any sense of ownership in these political processes, which are instead significantly shaped by the aforementioned cleavages and obstacles. Professor Anyang' Nyong'o's concept of ownership reflects the APRM's core philosophy of African states taking responsibility for their own development, based upon a corporate identification of "being proudly African" (Gruzd 2014: 8). On the one hand, the APRM-initiative has been welcomed by the international (donor) community, while on the other hand, its notion of ownership has been criticised by some South African activists and scholars as a neo-colonial and neo-liberal initiative, which "is essentially the same as that imposed by the International Monetary Fund, State Department and Brussels" (Bond 2010: 3). According to Bond (2000), NEPAD and the APRM are primarily instruments for attracting foreign investment capital and aid-donor programmes under the flag of (improving) good governance. Interestingly, during the launch of the APRM-process in 2005, then-president Thabo Mbeki questioned the problematic nature of the relationship between the government and certain NGOs, particularly "whether these bodies could truly be African if foreign funders set their priorities" (Kebonang/Fombad 2006: 48). While the APRM establishes itself as an African-owned initiative at the AU and national levels, it has failed to establish these identification processes at the urban level. Many civil society activists deconstructed the APRM as another "talkshow" and therefore a waste of time and money, something that became evident in all three consultative conferences, and highlighted the governance system as being one which is more-or-less an exclusive political process that the majority does not feel part of.

In Cape Town, the APRM became a highly-politicised process perceived by many activists and ward councillors from Mitchells Plain as being controlled by the ANC government, although it provided some sort of dialogue between the state and civil society. This dialogue did not include Mitchells Plain's ward councillors, who did not participate as local government representatives and boycotted the APRM consultative conferences. As previously discussed, ward councillors loyal to the opposition parties construe federal initiatives such as the CDWP, the APRM, and ward committees serving under ANC-dominated city councils as party-political extensions of the ANC government and as mechanisms to control the civil society sector. Particularly with reference to the APRM conferences, I argue that CDWs and ward committee members (even including those loyal to the ANC) did not act as uncomplicated conduits through which the ANC government could simply impose its conception of democratic rights. On the contrary, especially female participants voiced their opinions and showed that they have their own understanding of democratic rights, and of what democracy could or should mean in practice. The activists, CDWs, ward committee members, and government employees all held the (local) state accountable for perceived democratic failings during these conferences.

Distrust with the process arose in the Cape Flats because the comments and priorities voiced by different community representatives were not addressed by the (local) state. Therefore, different critical activists (NGOs, social movements, etc.) questioned whether the organisation of all the workshops, conferences, and seminars was either meaningful or efficient. According to critics, there was seldom any advanced information about the reports and questionnaires that were to be conferred at these events, and organisers and delegates apparently only received materials on the same day as the event (Mbelle 2010: 25). Therefore, there remain legitimate doubts as to whether the APRM will continue to develop into little more than a rhetorical exercise on good governance rather than have quantifiable effects in terms of policy and decision-making.

It is striking that the three APRM conferences resembled each other so closely in both their structure and outcomes. Therefore, the amount of time and money spent on organising three separate conferences appears questionable, given that there were no significant plans set in motion after each conference in terms of finding alternatives or implementing possible solutions. Furthermore, it is doubtful that the AU team was able to delve sufficiently into the intrinsic problems of urban governance in Cape Town, having only participated in the final conference for no more than three hours. This shortcoming is reflected in the AU team's final country report, which mainly focused on the widespread issues of violence and racism/xenophobia. The AU team put crime, violence against women, violence against children, etc. at the top of their recommended action-agenda in their report, noting that the distinctive feature of crime in South Africa lies not in its volume, but rather in the brutality of its violence (APRM South Africa Report 2007: 284–286). Significantly, in the section on "Democracy and Political Governance", the cooperative governance system and the "*Batho Pele*" principles were described as best practices (ibid.: 28), with the CDWP and ward committee institutions mentioned as mechanisms that "ensure broader public participation and dissemination of knowledge and information" (ibid.: 88, 89). However, no critical points were raised with respect to the difficulties encountered in realising these participatory institutions at the urban level and linking these failings with the prevalent violence and racism paradigms that are so symptomatic of South Africa. Hence, the report did not show any deeper reflections concerning whether racism, crime, violence, and poverty have any influence on the institutionalisation of "*Batho Pele*" and thus citizen's participation.

Furthermore, the ANC Government's Third Progress Report on the implementation of APRM Program Action in 2013 again highlighted "South Africa's commitment to a people-centred democracy through public participation [which] is cumulative improving" (APRM 2014: 31). The ward committees, alongside other initiatives, are mentioned as the most successful way of interacting with the public (ibid.: 31, 32). In this report, client satisfaction surveys, which have already been used particularly in the Western Cape and Northern Cape, are suggested as another way of collecting inputs from the public, as well as their suggestions for policy improvement. Interestingly, in the AU's "Agenda 2063. The Africa we want", "good governance", "capable institutions", and "transformative leadership" are all highlighted as being of utmost importance for establishing democracy and justice, yet the APRM as a mechanism for guaranteeing efficient and sustainable participation is not referenced (AU Commission 2015: 5, 6).

5.5 Is there room to manoeuvre?

This chapter has considered three concrete state-driven ways of enhancing community-state relations and public participation; the ward committee system, established by local governments; the CDWP, monitored by provincial government; and the APRM, a transnational initiative.

These decentralisation measures offer new avenues for public participation. Policy intent and implementation, however, are often confronted with the realities of party-political organisations, structures, and networks that have their roots in specific histories of place. These differences create conflicts and backlashes "on the ground", but at the same time can also lead to the rearrangement of the post-apartheid political order and open up room to manoeuvre in negotiation, competition, contestation, and also deliberation. These aspects will be briefly specified and summarised here.

Essentially, three different approaches to decentralisation have become articulated in the South African political arena:

- the ANC government arguing for decentralisation as a means of enhancing public participation and development;
- activists (social movements and certain NGOs) criticising the state for enforcing neo-liberalism (i.e. the market-driven provision of basic services) through decentralisation and non-inclusive state practices; and
- opposition party politicians criticising the ANC government for regulating, controlling, and co-opting participation and public opinion through decentralisation.

This chapter showed how policies outlining the integration of civil society in urban governance structures became entangled in historically-rooted urban agendas, perpetuating conflicts that made it difficult to establish meaningful community-state relations. This phenomenon is far from specific to South Africa, and is typical in other African countries regarding interactions between the political system and actors from civil society (Lachenmann 2006). The reasons are many-fold. First of all, the issue of lack of trust between (local) government representatives and activists is difficult to overcome given the continuation of non-cooperative interactions post-1994. At the same time, as shown in Chapter 4, activists who do not feel included in official structures often maintain or regain their old "protest" attitudes and create their own non-formalised spaces for public participation. These attitudes are reinforced by the state including some and excluding others into state-driven institutions for enhancing community-state relations. For example, the state's initiative to recruit activists from civil society and professionalise them to work as state employees is construed by critics as an "appropriation" of civil society.

The state's institutionalisation of "brokers", i.e. spokespeople in the form of ward committees' sector representatives (who are voluntary representatives of civil society) and CDWs (who in contrast are paid professionals) typifies the state's engagement with communities as one which is increasingly procedural and technical. In other words, the institutionalisation of brokers in South Africa took place with a professionalisation of activists entering the urban governance arena. Brokers between the community and state bodies, such as CBOs or NGOs, have always existed in South Africa as in other countries. This chapter showed that these institutionalisation processes work in a highly politicised manner, and that they accordingly structure the urban governance arena. In fact, while some spaces for participation have become more formalised during the last decade, other non-formalised spaces for public participation have emerged, as shown in Chapter 4. Like many of the protests that have arisen against local governments at the community-level since 1994, they show how citizens feel alienated, ignored, and excluded by the formalised system of participatory governance, such as ward committee meetings, sub-council meetings, etc. It is this context that explains why many activists see the new wave of state-induced participation as an instrument to control public opinion.

The policies and programmes studied here show a gender-sensitive approach, with the ward committees including a women's sector, the CDWP employing many female activists, and so forth. However, it is notable that it is in particular women who feel that they must be vocal and voice their critiques in deliberative spaces (e.g. those created during the APRM conferences) due to feeling practically sidelined by male-dominated politics. As discussed in Chapter 2, while female activists represent the majority in civil society, the representation of women in formal politics at the urban level is still considered the exception rather than the rule. In particular, the continued existence of policies that conceptualise the communities and especially women as being "weak" and "vulnerable" hint at an approach which focuses on deficits rather than capacities. In this vein, these policies still fail to fully recognise and acknowledge heterogeneity and pluralism in their conceptualisation of communities.

Policies and programmes embedded in particular social and political practices all show a transnational dimension that is most obvious with respect to the debates surrounding the APRM. Whereas the concept of the ward committee system resulted from a cooperation between German, Australian, and South African governments, the APRM is built upon an officially African initiative. Indeed, the difference between the transnational dimensions of the two initiatives is that the ward committees are based upon a cooperation between the Global North and the Global South, while the APRM is built upon a South-South collaboration. The APRM indeed explicitly proclaims as one of its aims long-term financial and substantive independence from the Global North community. In both cases, conceptions of ownership, i.e. the taking up of responsibilities of development and democratisation, shape the realisation of the political policies and programmes, albeit at different societal levels. While the ward committees identify civil society activists as the key local owners, the APRM encompasses a broader vision of owners, i.e. citizenship, which includes the entire country's citizenry, rather than just local citizens. However, while these concepts are finding heavy promotion transnationally, in particular the APRM and its idea of an "African-owned" initiative has not succeeded in translating these identification processes to the urban level.

In conclusion, this chapter has analysed the room to manoeuvre in terms of interaction, negotiation, competition, and deliberation, which predominantly involved the three categories of ward councillors, sector representatives of the ward committees, and CDWs. Based on empirical research, almost no exchange of information or knowledge between representatives of the three spheres of government took place, which rendered interactions between the spheres largely non-cooperative. Accordingly, despite the state creating additional potential spaces for action, the actors' room for manoeuvre to engage in formal politics, decision making processes, policy making, bargaining, negotiation, and so forth remains confined and contested.

Notes

1 DPLG and GTZ (eds.) (2005) Ward Committee Resource Book. Best Practices and Lessons Learnt for Municipal Officials, Councillors and Local Governance Practitioners, Pretoria: Communication Directorate; DPLG, GTZ and ASALPG (eds.) (2005) Having Your Say. A Handbook for Ward Committees, Pretoria: Communication Directorate.
2 Notice for members of the ward committee for Ward 82 of the city of Cape Town (2005), Rules for the establishment and operation of ward committees in the metropolitan area for the city of Cape Town.
3 Department of Provincial and Local Government, Republic of South Africa and GTZ (2005).
4 Each ward encompasses around 50,000 residents (see SSA Mitchells Plain 2006).
5 The following analysis is of the ward committees at work from 2004 until early 2006. The analysis is based on three focus group discussions conducted with sector representatives from Mitchells Plain and two focus group discussions with sector representatives from Khayelitsha. The focus group discussions were organised and conducted together with two researchers from the NGO International Labour Research and Information Group. Additionally, several interviews and conversations were held with sector representatives from both areas on different occasions; Report of Sub-council 12, Submission of Minutes of Ward Committee Meetings, 12.11.2005.
6 For example, according to the Report of Sub-council 12 (12.11.2005), only two ward committee meetings had a quorum up until November 2005, whereas the other four meetings had to be adjourned due to lack of a quorum.
7 Williams (2006) discusses CDWs as potential advocacy planners in South Africa, basing his analysis on a case study in Worcester, located approximately 90 kilometres north east of Cape Town.
8 In this case I assisted the CDW with his fieldwork at Site C, Khayelitsha, 04.05.2006.

9 South African Management Development Institute, Research Report (2005) "Evaluation of the Community Development Worker (CDW) Programme".
10 A memorandum of understanding of the APRM was endorsed at the inaugural summit of the AU held in Durban in 2002 (Kebonang/Fombad 2006: 45). Some authors have questioned the sincerity of NEPAD's good governance rhetoric: "With very few exceptions (Botswana, Mauritius, Senegal, South Africa) the majority of the heads of state involved in NEPAD are quintessentially leaders of neo-patrimonial regimes and certainly do not regard their rule as temporary, nor that institutional law should constrain their pre-eminence or that their rule be transparent and accountable" (Taylor 2005, quoted in Bond 2010: 2).
11 The AU team's report is subsequently discussed by the heads of the participating states, and is made available to the public. Participating countries are reviewed every two years, in order to assess progress in its programme of action. For a detailed account of the review process, which is carried out in five stages, see Kebonang/Fombad 2006: 46–47; Mbelle 2010: 1–3. Interestingly, almost half of the members of the AU, for example Namibia or Botswana, rejected participation in the APRM (Grimm/Nawrath 2007: 2).
12 The APRM questionnaire was developed by the South African APRM secretariat, which comprised officials from the Department of Public Service and Administration, four researchers, and two members of the South African Chapter of the Economic, Social and Cultural Council, which is an advisory organ of the AU representing civil society. The research unit made up of the four researchers who were part of the secretariat was responsible for conceptualising the questionnaire, translating the original questionnaire from English into the remaining 10 official languages, and working together with CDWs to organise workshops. The research unit also shortened the 88-page master questionnaire into a six-page document, with both made accessible on the South African APRM website (Mbelle 2010: 5, 9).

References

Benz, A. and Dose, N. (2010). Governance-Modebegriff oder nützliches sozialwissenschaftliches Konzept? In: A. Benz and N. Dose, eds. *Governance-Regieren in komplexen Regelsystemen: Eine Einführung.* Wiesbaden: VS Verlag, pp. 13–36.
Bond, P. (2010). Removing Neocolonialism's APRM Mask: A Critique of the African Peer Review Mechanism. *AISA Policybrief* 24, pp. 1–7.
Brinkerhoff, D. W. and Goldsmith, A. A. (2001). *Macroeconomic Policy, PRSPs, and Participation, Action Learning Program on Participatory Processes for Poverty Reduction Strategies.* Washington, DC: World Bank.
Déme, O. (2005). *Between Hope and Scepticism: Civil Society and the African Review Mechanism.* Ottawa: Partnership Africa Canada.
Engel, U. (2005). Deutschland, Afrika und gemeinsame Interessen. *APuZ. Aus Politik und Zeitgeschichte* 4, pp. 11–17.
Esau, M. (2007). *Deepening Democracy through Local Participation. Examining the Ward Committee System as a Form of Local Participation in Bonteheuwel in the Western Cape. Project: Policy Management, Governance and Poverty Alleviation in the Western Cape.* Cape Town: University of the Western Cape.
Esau, M. (2008). Contextualizing Social Capital, Citizen Participation and Poverty through an Examination of the Ward Committee System in Bonteheuwel in the Western Cape, South Africa. *Journal of Developing Societies* 24(3), pp. 355–380.
Grimm, S. and Nwarath, K. (2007). Der African-Peer-Peer-Review-Mechanismus – eine Abkehr vom Krähenprinzip. *GIGA Focus Africa* 3, pp. 2–7.

Gruzd, S. (2014). The African Peer Review Mechanism: Development Lessons from Africa's Remarkable Governance Assessment System. *Research Report* 15. South African Institute of International Affairs.

Gupta, J., Pfeffer, K., Ros-Tonen, M. and Verrest, H. (2015). Setting the Scene: The geographies of Urban Governance. In: J. Gupta, K. Pfeffer, H. Verrest and M. Ros-Tonen, eds. *Geographies of Urban Governance: Advanced Theories, Methods and Practices*. Heidelberg: Springer, pp. 3–26.

Haferburg, C. and Huchzermeyer, M. (2015). *Urban Governance in Post-Apartheid Cities: Modes of Engagement in South Africa's Metropoles*. Stuttgart: Borntraeger Science Publishers.

Himlin, R. (2005). *Johannesburg Ward Committee Assessment*. Johannesburg: Planact.

Jensen, S. (2004). Claiming Community: Local Politics in the Cape Flats, South Africa. *Critique of Anthropology* 24(2), pp. 179–207.

Kebonang, Z. and Fombad, C. M. (2006). The African Peer Review Mechanism: Challenges and Prospects. In: H. Melber, ed. *AU, NEPAD AND THE APRM: Democratisation Efforts Explored*. Uppsala: The Nordic Africa Institute, pp. 39–54.

Lachenmann, G. (2001). Globalisierung der Entwicklungspolitik: Sozialwissenschaftliche Konzepte geschlechtsspezifisch betrachtet – Fallstudien zu Armutsbekämpfung und Dezentralisierung in Afrika. In: H. Schrader, M. Kaiser and R. Korff, eds. *Markt, Kultur und Gesellschaft. Zur Aktualität von 25 Jahren Entwicklungsforschung; Festschrift zum 65. Geburtstag von Hans-Dieter Evers*. Berlin: LIT Verlag, pp. 181–210.

Lachenmann, G. (2006). *Decentralisation and Civil Society: Negotiating Local Development in West Africa*. Working Paper 358. Bielefeld University, Faculty of Sociology.

Mathekga, R. and Buccus, I. (2006). The Challenge of Local Government Structures in South Africa: Securing Community Participation. *Critical Dialogue – Public Participation in Review: IDASA*, pp. 11–17.

Mbelle, N. (2010). *The APRM Process in South Africa*. Johannesburg: Open Society Initiative for Southern Africa (OSISA).

Millstein, M. (2010). Limits to Local Democracy: The Politics of Urban Governance Transformations in Cape Town. *Working Paper* 2. Stockholm: Swedish International Centre for Local Democracy.

Oldfield, S. (2002). 'Embedded' Autonomy and the Challenges of Developmental Local Government. In: S. Parnell, E. Pieterse, M. Swilling and D. Wooldridge, eds. *Democratising Local Government. The South African Experiment*. Cape Town: University of Cape Town, pp. 92–104.

Parnell, S. (2016). Defining a Global Urban Development Agenda. In: *World Development* 78/C, pp. 529–540.

Pieterse, N. J. (2001). Participatory Democratisation Reconceived. *Futures* 33, pp. 407–422.

Piper, L. and Deacon, R. (2008). Partisan Ward Committees, Elite Accountability and Community Participation: The Msunduzi Case. *Critical Dialogue* 4(1), pp. 41–46.

Strulik, S. (2004). *Engendering Local Democracy Research. Panchayati Raj and Changing Gender Relations in India*. Unpublished Paper presented at the International Workshop on Local Democracy, organised by the EU-Asia Link Programme "The Micro Politics of Democratisation: European-South Asian Exchanges on Governance, Conflict and Civic Action". Tribhuvan University, Kathmandu.

Taylor, I. (2005). Can NEPAD Succeed Without Prior Political Reform? *Working Paper* No. 23. Copenhagen: Danish Institute for International Studies.

Williams, J. J. (2006). Community Development Workers as Advocacy Planners in South Africa. A Bourdieu Approach. *Occasional Paper* No. 5. Bellville: University of the Western Cape, Project: Policy Management, Governance and Poverty Alleviation in the Western Cape.

State and non-state sources

AfricanUnion (2001). *New Partnership for Africa's Development. A Programme of the African Union*. Abuja, Nigeria.

African Union Commission (2015). *Agenda 2063. The Africa We Want*. Final Edition, Popular Version.

African Peer Review Report (2007). Midrand: APRM Secretariat.

African Peer Review Mechanism (2014). *Third Report on the Implementation of South Africa's APRM. Broadening of Public Participation*. Republic of South Africa.

Department Provincial and Local Government, German Agency for Technical Cooperation and Australia South Africa Local Governance Partnership (2005). *Having Your Say. A Handbook for Ward Committees*. Pretoria: Communication Directorate.

Department Provincial and Local Government and German Agency for Technical Cooperation (2005). *Ward Committee Resource Book. Best Practices and Lessons Learnt for Municipal Officials, Councillors and Local Governance Practitioners*. Pretoria: Communication Directorate.

Minutes of the Meeting of the Council of the City of Cape Town (07.12.2006). Civic Centre, p.18.

South African Management Development Institute (2005). *Evaluation of the Community Development Worker (CDW) Programme*. Research Report.

Newpaper article

De Bruin, S. (2006). CDWs are Linking Policy to Practice. In: *Plainsman*. 29.03.2006, pp. 10.

6   Urban experiences in politics and activism

This book has made a case for an actor-oriented approach in analysing how urban politics work in Cape Town. Its main contribution to the debate on public participation in urban governance is grounded in the specific approach of constructing political trajectories and events. The trajectories function as an entry-point in the arena of urban governance through the lens of individual pathways from apartheid to democracy. Additionally, the book has dealt with events where people engender, negotiate, and contest, on a daily basis, concepts, policies, and institutions that have been introduced under the banner of democracy. Conceptualising these events as encounters at different knowledge interfaces develops a locus for an anthropology of policy, i.e. an analysis of negotiations in urban politics. The research has shown a variety of social and political actors participating in the negotiation process, which itself involves intricate, varied, and contentious rationalities of action.

This book has paid particular attention to those people who suffer a "lack of emancipation[,] [which] refers to an inadequate access to material (e.g. income) and immaterial (e.g. education) resources" (Schuurman 2007: 50). It has furthered our understanding of how people at urban peripheries manage their everyday lives under harsh circumstances and whom they turn to for support. In doing so it also has taken into account those who have the "defining power" and provide for hegemonial meaning and interpretation at a local, national, and international level in order to solve this lack of emancipation. Hence, an actor-oriented and contextualising approach sheds light upon the structuration of urban society where local, national, and global forces are in constant interplay.

This book's approach offers an alternative perspective to scholars who contend, from a largely state-centred perspective, that the rich culture of participation that has its roots in the anti-apartheid movement has remained inactive since 1994 (Mathekga/Buccus 2006; Muiu 2008; Williams 2006; Mattes 2002). According to their theories, the state's new participatory institutions have not effectively addressed the dormant participatory culture that persists among inhabitants of the former townships. Rather than primarily focusing on the state's failures, my research has captured and elaborated upon the actual process of negotiating the political order, providing insights into how state, supranational, and non-state actors negotiate and contest the vision of a participatory democracy. This approach made it possible to identify a variety of speeches, representations, and actions of state and supranational actors on the one hand, and a variety of modes of political action by non-state actors to challenge top-down interventions on the other. The analysis elaborated on the problems, conflicts, and successes of translating policies on public participation to service delivery at the urban level, i.e. putting urban experiences at the forefront of what people say and do or do not say and do.

Along with the Northern Cape, the Western Cape is introduced as one of the unique provinces in South Africa where a majority of the population are Coloureds. Accordingly, this research adds a new perspective to the debate surrounding the social construction of racialised identities in the Western Cape (Lewis 1987; Erasmus 2001; Salo 2004; Adhikari 2005; Jensen 2008), by relating it to the arena of urban governance with its parallel spaces, i.e. shifting the focus to interactions between ward councillors and activists. This book has highlighted that racialised identifications in the urban periphery of Cape Town became politicised after 1994, presenting occasions for urban politicians to effectively "play the race card" in the public sphere. The research identifies racism as a major continuing conflict that perpetuates the old logic of apartheid, i.e. the racialised classifications of "Coloureds as in-between Black and White". Racism works in the spheres of government as a mechanism that maintains distrust between local politicians and activists, thereby polarising state and civil society activities. I argue that the post-1994 use of the "rainbow nation" as an emblem of unity by politicians and activists is theoretically flawed, given that it conceals historically situated unequal power relations that continue to exist in South African society.

My concluding remarks summarise the empirical complexity of the research and present the findings in relation to the key concepts raised in the chapters, namely the politics of positioning, violence, place-making, and belonging and their consequences for gendering governance arrangements and parallel spaces.

6.1 The politics of positioning

This book has illustrated that a contextualising perspective is vital towards understanding continuities and discontinuities in speeches, representations, and action rationales. Historical slogans such as "*Amandla Awethu*", which have their roots in the apartheid-era liberation movement, are still being used in political settings, and symbolise both the achievement of ending apartheid and the on-going struggle. This book has identified crucial historical events including the Sharpeville Massacre in 1966, the Soweto Uprising in 1976, and the United Democratic Front Movement in 1983, which are still memorialised at the urban level. Indeed, they have emerged as memory landmarks that individuals refer to in order to explain and argue their past and present political actions.

These memories align with those of the segregation politics that shaped the political order during apartheid and the respective collective knowledge reservoirs, based on an ideology of keeping population groupings separated from each other through whichever means. This research has demonstrated that these senses of commonality, attachment, and mutuality even within groupings have become restricted, violated, and destabilised through strategies of cooptation, resulting in rifts within families, between neighbours, and in townships. In this vein, this book has proposed combining two separate concepts, the politics of positioning and the politics of belonging, to theoretically analyse social and political changes as South Africa moves from apartheid to democracy.

The reconstruction of the trajectories of urban politicians and activists offers nuanced accounts through which this study has developed empirically-grounded types of actors, characterised by their modes of positioning. The ward councillors encompass four types: "The defector: from the political right to the political left" (type A); "The founder of a new political party" (type B); "The disillusioned comrade: a former UDF youth turned conservative" (type C); and "The loyal ANC comrade" (type D). All types include individuals who had been forcibly relocated to the outskirts of the Cape Flats and who were racially classified. Furthermore, these types also encompass restrictive forms of belonging, shaped by gendered and racialised discrimination (types A to D), or those who have gone underground and been on the run (type D). However, oppression in these cases led not only to revolt and resistance against the political system; indeed, being classified as Coloured allowed individuals to access restricted resources such as housing, education, jobs, etc. Such privileges, accessible to those classified as Coloureds and not Black Africans, split inhabitants living in the former Coloured townships into factions who either cooperate with (type A) or fight against (type C) the system, or who remain impartial and apolitical (type B). Scholars have tended to focus exclusively on political actors of type A, arguing that individuals who were elected as ward councillors in the former Coloured townships in the elections in 1994 had a significant past history of collaborating with the apartheid regime (Jensen 2004; Cameron 1998). This study furthers understandings of these actors and their motivations by adding types B and C.

The four types of activists stand for a radical rejection of the formally-imposed racialised classification system, and represent the fight for a non-racial and inclusive approach in (post-)apartheid politics. In this vein, their re-positioning in post-apartheid public spheres and the building up of civil society with its parallel spaces encompass: "The founder of an NGO through government linkages" (type E); "The transnational activist: embedding a urban development project in the community" (type F); "The career-changer: from new social movements to local government" (type G); and "The advocacy-worker: activist, student, researcher" (type H). Types E and F illustrate how the social construction of a civil society in South Africa can be linked, albeit in different ways, to the ruling party, the ANC, where this party played a leading role in the liberation movement. In contrast, types G and H represent actors who developed a critical eye towards the ANC after they assumed power in 1994, and took up resistive roles in the forms of new social movements (type G) or internationally financed NGOs (type H).

6.2 The politics of violence, place-making, and belonging

The historicising perspective in this book has described the emergence of townships as places at the margins of society, as a consequence of the apartheid-era forced removals of those classified as non-Whites. From the ashes of the battlefields of hard fought and violent uprisings against the oppressive apartheid state, the townships converted into spaces of democratisation and development intervention after 1994. These areas inherited desperate socio-economic conditions and structural violence (Galtung 1996), which has continued from times of colonialism through to democracy, i.e. the situation in the townships has been tinged with violence since their inception. During apartheid, this structural violence became institutionalised and manifest in the uneven distribution of power and resources, according to the construction and classification of race. Therefore, this study conceptualises violence as intrinsic to the social order, rather than an aspect beyond what is considered "normal".

The analysis of the trajectories has allowed the combining of both the diachronic and synchronic dimensions of violence, and thereby stresses gendered dynamics in violent and non-violent conflict settings. Our understanding of the heritage of structural violence in South Africa was further extended by Moser's categorisation of political, social, and economic violence (2001), which illustrated how these categories structure recent urban politics in the townships. However, despite such categorisations and clarifications, I have shown through the examples of individual pathways that distinguishing between social and economic violence is not always a simple task. It depends on the social context, and they are often interconnected and have an influence on one another.

Apartheid segregation politics treated place as a territorial configuration that divided townships along racialised lines, and in turn these political processes of place-making led inhabitants to develop attachments and senses of belonging to places. This book has analysed and specified how bonds of commonality, sociality, and mutuality are maintained in several cultural practices and institutions that confirm and re-produce, but also challenge and modify social, racialised, and geographical boundaries. This research points to the specific construction of Coloured and Black African senses of belonging, with their respective cultural items that provide crucial platforms for identity politics that local politicians can hark back to in order to strengthen and re-enforce their statements. In this vein, practices of social location of Coloureds and Black Africans vary according to how racialised categories intersect with economic and gender categories. Following these ethnographic insights, one of my findings is that the cultural has developed into a crucial arena in Cape Town micro-politics.

6.3 Social boundary-making and the idea of the rainbow nation

This book has identified dynamics of divergence and convergence both within and outside the urban governance arena that manifest themselves in the different usages and approaches to constructing race in relation to the idea of the rainbow nation. In post-apartheid democracy, a new vocabulary has developed in order to depict the social and political order using notions of nation-building, integration, unity, racial harmony, and reconciliation. Despite racialised phenomena being underplayed or glossed over in order to facilitate a peaceful transition in national politics, it continues to matter at the grassroots local level. There was little real debate concerning how racism continues to influence and shape present identification processes and interactions. The research showed that the second decade after apartheid has been characterised by a return of race in public debates, an acknowledgement of the importance of recognising and addressing race as a stumbling block and recognising discrimination related to race in political and social life. This analysis has provided essential insights into racism as a way of understanding urban politics. However, this study has also stressed the importance of not oversimplifying or reducing the influence of context in how race is constructed.

This book has focused on the turning points when individuals were able to reposition themselves in democratic public spheres as ward councillors or activists. It is also at these points when the politics of belonging came to occupy the political agenda, and reified assumptions about the construction of Coloured identification in relation to place. This analysis shows how the indelible paradigm of positioning as "Coloureds in-between Black and White" evolved as a mechanism to bolster racial divides, maintain boundaries, and explain inequalities within spheres of local government. The politics of belonging work with the "boundaries of the political community of belonging, the boundaries which, sometimes physically, but always symbolically, separate the world population into 'us' and 'them'" (Yuval-Davis 2011: 3). Therefore, the politics of belonging essentially built on, reinforced, and reproduced the values, beliefs, and actions of respective constructions of groupings of Coloureds and Black Africans. In this sense, the politics of belonging within spheres of local government are shaped decisively by identity politics prone to nuance collectiveness, sharp boundary-drawing, and reinforce the social exclusion of the "other". Policies and programmes such as the APRM and URP have become embedded in the realities of urban agendas. In this vein, urban politicians reproduce the cultural legacy of racism in spheres of local government, and polarise political spaces along racialised lines.

At the same time, activists discussed in this book who have been engaged in building up post-apartheid civil society challenged these mechanisms of boundary making and rejected the category of race as a primary mode of political identification. Activism deemphasises racialised boundaries, instead emphasising other boundary markers such as "class and capitalism", "neoliberalism and global economy", or "gender and patriarchy". Furthermore, activists make use of a global language that makes reference to ideas of spatial and social justice. Activists, who share the same attachment to their places of living as ward councillors in the former Coloured townships, forge new grounds for belonging beyond racialised identifications. It is here where the political project of the rainbow nation is based primarily on levels of "social and political citizenship" (Hess/Lebhuhn 2014; Marshall 2006 [1950]), i.e. belonging to South Africa on just and equal terms. Hence, the politics of belonging in civil society or parallel spaces delineate novel shared grounds among people that extend beyond identity politics.

In a way, the rainbow nation concept implies that the predominant conflict in South Africa was, and still is, one of racialised antagonism, which is why it *a fortiori* highlights the message of the need for an integrated society. However, the rainbow allegory is misleading, as it focuses attention away from the socio-economic and political dimensions of inequality. Public perception in the townships on Cape Town's periphery is that the rainbow nation is "not for the Blacks and not for the Coloureds, but for middle income persons" (see Chapter 3). Therefore, the social cohesion of South Africa's diversity is a question of affordability, which renders integration and membership to the rainbow nation as a privilege. The research has highlighted that questions of affordability of basic services, a decent life, and dignity split inhabitants of Cape Town into either paying or indigent citizens in this, the second decade of rainbow democracy, where the indigent is equated with constructions of particular "races", places, and violence. To be classified as an indigent citizen brings with it access to an indigent grant for water and electricity, an initiative of a local government strategy paper on how to organise social cash transfers to residents who cannot afford to pay for basic services. The indigent policy is also meant to serve to counteract the protest culture of non-payment that stems from payment boycotts during the apartheid era. Such protests and boycotts were expected to cease with the inauguration of the rainbow nation, given that post-apartheid, poorer residents were expected to be capable of contributing to the tariff structure; however, in many cases this did not eventuate. Instead, the question of affordability and a protest culture is now associated with the non-payment for basic services by the periphery of society, i.e. the so-called Cape Flats, whose inhabitants are presumed to be non-White, and marked by social disorders such as HIV and AIDS, gendered violence, and the high consumption of drugs and alcohol.

6.4 Institutionalising activism

With the aim of fostering more inclusive and participatory development processes, and guided by the *leitmotiv* of good governance, new governance arrangements, from local initiatives such as the ward committees, to transnational initiatives such as the APRM as part of the New Partnership for Africa's Development, became institutionalised at the urban level. Global concepts of public participation are translated into urban settings, and attribute meaning to the ANC's historical, longstanding commitment that "the people shall govern". For this process of translating global or local concepts, the positioning of brokers within the urban governance arena is critical. A strategy of institutionalising brokers has been championed in policy as one way of engendering and deepening democracy from below. Building on this, I have argued that "knowing" a place, in terms of possessing a detailed internalised map of specific historically rooted political sites, hot-spots and no-go areas, gang territories, township slang, weak infrastructure issues, and cultural practices reflects the key resource when entering an urban governance arena. Accordingly, ward councillors' and activists' possession of this knowledge enables them to act as brokers and relate their work to place, while publicly framing these efforts as attempts to develop and democratise their neighbourhoods.

The research showed that while brokers maintain roots in an urban context, they connect these places to those actors engaged in democratisation on a global level. These translocal and transnational connections in place-based politics revealed themselves in the field in various ways. The analysis centred upon two distinct lines of cooperation: North-South and South-South. For instance, the book has discussed a North-South cooperation on the basis of a global idea of democratic socialism, with a state-critical advocacy NGO linked to the German Rosa Luxemburg Foundation. The book has also touched on a South-South collaboration, highlighting the APRM as a political process of reviewing governance systems in African countries, a process developed by the AU. The APRM is an endorsement of a truly African-owned initiative at a transnational level, one that became essentialised by the-then president Thabo Mbeki's remarks on the problematic nature of relationships between government and state-critical NGOs, whose international funders set their agendas. This analysis looked at the peer reviews taking place in Cape Town's city centre and Khayelitsha, concluding that these particular African-owned identification processes of managing development and democratisation could not ultimately succeed at the local level, due to the dynamics of divergence and reduced confidence in the political system. Hence, the same places become translocally and transnationally connected in different ways and evoke specific dynamics in how they manifest a rainbow nation-building process.

In this respect, the book introduced two further categories of brokers, besides ward councillors and activists, to mediate between needy residents and different institutions of government. These are the ward committee members concerned with the different sectors of health, women, safety and security, etc., and the CDWs. These two new categories of brokers are considered to have a background of activism. They are also now part of the vocabulary of enabling participatory democracy in the world of international development. The state's intention to recruit civil society activists and professionalise them as CDWs is constructed by detractors as an appropriation of civil society. The notional objective to partly professionalise, bureaucratise, and monetarise community-state relations led to cleavages and rivalries between those who are paid for such work and those who are not. Interactions between these different actors are often characterised by friction, with little exchange of knowledge taking place. To sum up, despite the state providing spaces for action, actors' room for manoeuvre at the different interfaces becomes decisively contested and restricted at the urban level due to vertical and horizontal frictions and fractures. As outlined by Swyngedouw (2005) in the context of multi-level governance, these contradictory tendencies are also prevalent in general in the governance system established in South Africa, and are characterised by exclusionary practices of participation, entitlements, and representation, excluding those inhabitants most in need of information and representation from participatory processes in urban planning, as well as from decision-making processes and formal politics in general.

Additionally, urban experiences of activists, including NGO activists in Mitchells Plain and Khayelitsha, who participate in local government, show that they target micro-material issues above all because of time and financial constraints. Schuurman (2009) identifies this tendency in particular in left-wing oriented local governments in the Global South and adds that fundamental political discussions are being replaced by less serious concerns. He argues, "[t]here is nothing inherently wrong with that but the idea of political emancipation does not appear to come any closer", and states that civil society actors de-politise in the process of cooperating with local government (ibid.: 839), i.e. in the process of establishing governance. However, informed by an ethnographic perspective, I disagree with the widespread assumption that unlike popular participation, governance has solely apolitical technical connotations (e.g. Schuurman 2009; Mouffe 2005; Wickramasinghe 2005; Feldman 2003). Neither policies on governance nor the realisation of policies are purely technical processes. As the analyses of the institutionalisation of brokers have demonstrated, these are highly competitive and politicised processes of one who comes in and yet remains outside the urban governance arena. Furthermore, all policies discussed in this book, whether municipal, provincial, national, or international, are part of a global mantra of promoting participation and the integration of civil society actors in governance processes as one decisive factor in achieving sustainable economic growth and thereby eradicating urban poverty. In accordance with Shore and Wright (1997), policies emerge out of particular contexts and in many ways "encapsulate the entire history and culture of the [transnational] society that generated them" (ibid.: 7; Wedel et al. 2005: 33). Most significant to this understanding of policy is that they may be formulated in neutral language. But

> [...] their ostensi[ve] purpose [is] merely to promote efficiency or effectiveness – they are fundamentally political. In fact, "a key feature of modern power", Shore and Wright contended, is the masking of the political under the cloak of neutrality.
>
> (Wedel et al. 2005: 34)

This proves to be the case in both policies that tackle the institutionalisation of brokers as well as the practical institutionalisation process of brokers at the urban level, which as the book has shown, is anything but depoliticised. In this respect, Schuurman (2009) refers to Chantal Mouffe's booklet, "On the Political" (2005), "which has aptly described this process [of depoliticisation] and emphasises that we should turn to 'the political' in the sense of what she calls agonistic confrontations" (ibid.: 839). Although it is clear that the state's engagement with communities, in particular the institutionalisation of brokers, and by extension activism, has increasingly procedural and technical, it has also turned local governance into a more politicised arena. However, Schuurman's reference to Mouffe's concept of "agonistic confrontation" does seem of heuristic relevance when it comes to explaining the increased attempts of counter-action in the spaces parallel to the urban governance arena.

6.5 Parallel spaces

While the integration of activists in urban governance through institutionalised processes has been analysed here as conflictive, this book has also highlighted both old and new modes of political action and agonistic confrontation forging alternative orders: either as continuities from apartheid histories, or as new ways of creating political spaces parallel to formalised political institutions.

This book has analysed continuity using the example of service delivery protests organised by new social movements (although not entirely new, given that they stem from apartheid boycotts and continue to maintain a protest culture of non-payment). The similarities and continuities to apartheid protests lie in the non-racialised approach of these movements and their non-compliance with the rule of order. Scholars depict the urban protests as a response to the state's failures, protests often characterised by violent actions and uprisings. Interestingly, according to the APRM Report in 2014, there has been a dramatic surge of service delivery protests in South Africa since 2009, with the most protests (113) recorded in 2012 (APRM 2014: 34). Within the academic literature (Mathekga/Buccus 2006; Mattes 2002; Ruiters 2002), such protests tend to be constructed as the public's only participation in council and national politics. Conversely, this research stresses that a variety of actors participate in politics employing different strategies, both assimilative and antagonistic.

This book has emphasised new ways of interaction with the post-apartheid state and civil society, focusing on emerging female political spaces as responses to gendered exclusionary practices within spheres of local government and civil society. The analysis has revealed that local government continues to be male dominated, despite the existence of quota policies that are supposed to enhance women's participation in the city council. In contrast, the majority of members of civil society organisations are generally women. This book has identified a variety of forms of women's organisations, highlighting the high number of women in civil society organisations engaged with gender-specific violence-related issues. Some female activists have started to contest the male-dominated leadership of new social movements and NGOs. The analysis has shown that female activists and female ward councillors often have links to more than one organisation, campaign, sphere of government, or branch of civil society. Many female activists and ward councillors maintain dual positionings, which enable them to pursue both assimilative and confrontational strategies of engagement with the (local) state. In one cited example, female activists continue to build up their own NGO through government linkages, whilst at the same time participating in the internationally-financed state-critical forum Building Women's Activism. This forum provides a space, for women only, to reflect upon the patriarchal nature of state institutions, discuss ways of changing decades of state neglect concerning gendered violence, as well as to exchange knowledge of organisational and political experiences. In the tradition of the women's movement, the forum provided evidence that female activists continue to practice cross-party collaborations, albeit among individuals who belong to more left-wing oriented parties. Accordingly, female activists network and cooperate through these party political and organisational linkages. Female activism on the ground re-arranges the oft-touted fragmented nature of the women's movement (e.g. Hassim 2004, 2006; Essof 2006; Albertyn 1995; Meitjes 1995) through their dual positioning, and significantly shapes parallel spaces, promoting alternatively gendered order. The peculiarity, observed in this research, between the formation of new, female (alternative) political spaces and the constitution of spheres of local government and civil society is not an either/or state of development, but is rather a clearly interrelated and intertwined process. The transformation of dominant discourses and consequent institutional change is a slow enterprise and faces many limitations in terms of future shifts in the structuration of the political space and gender relations.

In this vein, Appadurai (2000) states that a number of new social forms have arisen to contest, interrogate, and reverse unequal or unjust developments, and "to create forms of knowledge transfer and social mobilisation that proceed independently of the actions of corporate capital and the nation-state system (and its international affiliates and guarantors)" (ibid.: 3). Appadurai analyses these social forms as relying "on strategies, visions, and horizons for globalisation on behalf of the poor that can be characterised as 'grassroots globalisation' or, to put it a slightly different way, as 'globalisation from below'". These emergent social forms have been discussed in this book using the example of the forum Building up Women's Activism, which is part movement, part network, part organisation (ibid.: 15). Furthermore, the movement Concerned Residents of Mitchells Plain has also emerged as part of a new type of network of movements from other adjacent neighbourhoods on Cape Town's periphery, all actively engaged in influencing the state's decision-making processes against evictions, cut-offs of water and electricity supplies, and the current closing of schools- particularly in former Coloured townships. Significantly, these movements use the term "concerned" in connection with the proper name of the township, namely in such cases as Concerned Residents of Delft (Millstein 2010: 11), or Concerned Residents of Bonteheuwel (ILRIG-Newsletter, 02.01.2013). The "concerned" movements provide alternative schemes for interpreting inequalities and problems in their neighbourhoods, as well as comprising a series of demands or challenges to holders of power from a social category previously lacking an established political position, and thus far by non-violent means. In accordance with Appadurai (2000) "these [social] forms are the crucibles and institutional instruments of most serious efforts to globalise from below" (ibid.: 15). Hardt/Negri (2017: 79) argue that "from below is indeed the standpoint of a wide range of projects for liberation", which are driven by the subordinated. The authors further emphasise that "from below" means that power needs to be seen in a relational way, i.e. from the position of the subordinated, "whose knowledge is transformed through resistance and struggles of liberation from the domination of those 'above'" (ibid.: 83). In accordance with Hardt/Negri, it could be said that this book conceptualises "from below" as the political trajectory from apartheid to democracy with a focus upon institutional and informal projects that not only have the power to subvert instruction "but also the capacity to construct politically an alternative society" (ibid.: 83).

In this vein, the incidents of resistance analysed in this book, with their memories and metaphors of the apartheid era, are being mobilised in urban politics and global discourse against the "government of the liberation movement", i.e. the current ANC government. The Sharpeville Massacre, an apartheid-era memory landmark, has been compared both in South Africa and international media with the Marikana miners' strike in 2012. The latter attracted international attention following a series of violent encounters involving the South African Police Service, security stakeholders, the leadership of the National Union of Mineworkers, and striking workers, which resulted in the deaths of approximately 47 people, the majority of whom were mineworkers. In response to the brutality and violence of the police, both the South African (Mail & Guardian Online, Landau 2012) and international (Le Monde Diplomatique, Cessou 2013: 4) media made comparisons with the Sharpeville Massacre in 1960, in which approximately 70 people were killed, during a demonstration against the pass laws (Frankel 2001: 242–247). This comparison shows how deep apartheid is ingrained in the collective memory, and even in the global collective memory in this case. Furthermore, in 2016, a similar comparison to the Soweto Uprising 40 years earlier was made by users of online media with respect to the #Feesmustfall and #Rhodesmustfall protest movements. The #RhodesMustFall movement, which initially sought to decolonialise the University of Cape Town, mobilised students from universities all over the country. As freelance writer Thapelo Mosuoia reflected upon these movements on the digital platform OkayAfrica:

> Fast forward to 2015, a year of student activism in South Africa in which university students all around the country stood up against the

government's proposed 10.5% increase in tertiary education. From the songs, to the now iconic images to the indomitable faces of the movement South African young people disproved the notion of apathy among today's youth [...] moments that show the spirit of 1976 is still alive in South Africa.

(Mosuoia 2016)

While the rebellious spirit of 1976 is memorised by this modern-day youth activism, continuities with other aspect of the Soweto uprising also lie in the violence police exerted against protesters as well as in the gendered, economic, and racialised dimensions of persisting structural violence that continue to affect young people and society as a whole; such as poverty, unemployment, limited access to social services, poor-quality education, high dropout rates, crime and gangsterism, rape, and unwanted pregnancies (see Gukelberger, forthcoming). While beyond the task of this book, perhaps deeper analysis of this discussion and the associated discourse of resistance might reveal ways in which the public in South Africa sees the ANC government as reproducing similar coercive institutions to those of the pre-democratic political era.

The penetration of social justice into urban society is dependent upon people's participation in the political system and in civil society. Furthermore, such participation must be inclusive of all of society. This book has demonstrated that many actors – scholars, politicians, and activists – emphasise political participation at the various levels of governance as a key to making urban societies work on a more democratic basis. Although, or indeed because the political system is often perceived as exclusive by certain actors, these same actors are actively engaged in transforming old mechanisms of gendered and racialised discrimination and segregation into inclusive ones. While most of the actors discussed in this book demand inclusiveness, it is clear their notions of inclusiveness differ fundamentally; in contrast to local government representatives, activists employ a global vocabulary with a non-racialised basis, instead speaking in terms of social justice, and social and political citizenship. Through analyses of urban politics of positioning and belonging at the interfaces between state and civil society, there emerged divergent claims in equality and justice. Despite these claims being hotly contested, they are still being negotiated in day-to-day interactions and forging social change as South Africa moves into a third post-apartheid decade. In the introduction to this book, I stated that following the inception of democratic rule, "the politics of hope" became entangled with "the politics of democracy". However, there are still important continuities from apartheid to democracy, which naturally require hope. Actors require hope in their engagements in council politics, in their fight for democratic principles, and a decent and better future, but ultimately hope's appeal rests on the possibility of those aims and goals being achievable.

References

Adhikari, M. (2005). *Not White Enough, Not Black Enough. Racial Identity in the South African Coloured Community.* Athens, Cape Town: Double Storey Books.

Albertyn, C. (1995). National Machinery for Ensuring Gender Equality. In: S. Liebenberg, ed. *The Constitution of South Africa from a Gender Perspective,* Cape Town: David Philip, pp. 9–22.

Appadurai, A. (2000). Grassroots Globalisation and the Research Imagination. *Public Culture* 12(1), pp. 1–19.

Cameron, R. (1998). *Democratisation of South African Local Government: A Tale of Three Cities.* Cape Town: J. L. van Schaik Academic.

Erasmus, Z. (2001). Re-Imaging Coloured Identities in Post-Apartheid South Africa. In: Z. Erasmus, ed. *Coloured by History, Shaped by Place. New Perspectives on Coloured Identities in the Cape.* Cape Town: Kwela Books, pp. 3–28.

Feldman, S. (2003). Paradoxes of Institutionalisation: The Depoliticisation of Bangladeshi NGOs. *Development in Practice* 13(1), pp. 5–26.

Frankel, P. (2001). *An Ordinary Atrocity: Sharpeville and Its Massacre.* New Haven, CT: Yale University Press.

Galtung, J. (1996). *Peace by Peaceful Means: Peace and Conflict, Development and Civilisation.* London: Sage.

Gukelberger, S. (forthcoming). Youth, and the Politics of the Generational Memories (Soweto riots, South Africa). In: A.-M. Peatrik and M. Champy, eds. *Pour une anthropologie critique de la jeunesse en Afrique.* Ateliers d'anthropologie.

Hardt, M. and Negri, A. (2017). *Assembly.* Oxford: Oxford University Press.

Hassim, S. (2004). *Voices, Hierarchies and Spaces: Reconfiguring the Women's Movement in Democratic South Africa. A Case Study for the UKZN project.* Johannesburg: University of Witwatersrand. Political Studies.

Hess, S. and Lebuhn, H. (2014). Politiken der Bürgerschaft. Zur Forschungsdebatte um Migration, Stadt und citizenship. In: *sub\urban. Zeitschrift für kritische Stadtforschung* 2(3), pp. 11–34.

Jensen, S. (2004). Claiming Community: Local Politics in the Cape Flats, South Africa. *Critique of Anthropology* 24(2), pp. 179–207.

Jensen, S. (2008). *Gangs, Politics & Dignity in Cape Town.* Chicago, IL: University of Chicago Press.

Lewis, G. (1987). *Between the Wire and the Wall. A History of South African "Coloured" Politics.* Cape Town: David Philipp.

Marshall, T. H. (2006 [1950]). Citizenship and Social Class. In: C. Pierson, ed. *The Welfare State Reader.* Cambridge and Malden, MA: Polity Press, pp. 30–39.

Mathekga, R. and Buccus, I. (2006). The Challenge of Local Government Structures in South Africa: Securing Community Participation. *Critical Dialogue – Public Participation in Review: IDASA,* pp. 11–17.

Mattes, R. (2002). South Africa: Democracy Without the People? *Journal of Democracy* 13(1), pp. 22–36.

Meitjes, S. (1995). The Women's Struggle for Equality During South Africa's Transition to Democracy. *Transformation* 30, pp. 47–64.

Moser, C. O. N. (2001). The Gendered Continuum of Violence and Conflict: An Operational Framework. In: C. O. N. Moser and F. Clark, eds. *Victims, Perpetrators or Actors? Gender, Armed Conflict and Political Violence.* London: Zed Books, pp. 30–51.

Mouffe, C. (2005). *On the Political*. London: Routledge.

Muiu, M. (2008). *The Pitfalls of Liberal Democracy and Late Nationalism in South Africa*. New York: Palgrave Macmillan.

Ruiters, G. (2002). Debt, Disconnection, and Privatisation. The Case of Fort Beaufort, Queenstown and Sutterheim. In: D. A. McDonald and J. Pape, eds. *Cost Recovery and the Crisis of Service Delivery in South Africa*. London; New York: Zed Books, pp. 41–57.

Salo, E. (2004). *Respectable Mothers, Tough Men and Good Daughters: Producing Persons in Manenberg Township, South Africa*. PhD Thesis, Emory University. Department of Social Anthropology.

Schuurman, F. (2007). Development Studies: Work in Progress. *Journal für Entwicklungspolitik XXIII*, pp. 45–63.

Schuurman, F. (2009). Critical Development Theory: Moving Out of the Twilight Zone. *Third World Quarterly* 30(5), pp. 831–848.

Shore, C. and Wright, S. (1997). *Anthropology of Policy: Critical Perspectives on Governance and Power*. London: Routledge.

Swyngedouw, E. (2005). Governance Innovation and the Citizen: The Janus Face of Governance-Beyond-the-State. *Urban Studies* 42(11), pp. 1991–2006.

Wedel, J., Shore, C., Feldman, G. and Lathrop, S. (2005). Toward an Anthropology of Public Policy. *Annals of the American Academy of Political and Social Science* 600, pp. 30–51.

Wickramasinghe, N. (2005). The Idea of Civil Society in the South: Imaginings, Transplants, Designs. The Deep Structure of the Present Moment. *Science & Society* 69(3), pp. 458–486.

Williams, J. J. (2006). Community Participation. Lessons from Post-Apartheid South Africa. *Policy Studies* 27(3), pp. 197–217.

Yuval-Davis, N. (2011). *Power, Intersectionality and the Politics of Belonging*. FREIA Working Paper Series 75. Feminist Research Center, Aalborg University.

State and non-state source

African Peer Review Mechanism (2014). *Third Report on the Implementation of South Africa's APRM. Broadening of Public Participation*. Republic of South Africa.

Essof, S. (2006). *Reflections on the Women's Movement*. Building up Women's Activism International Labour Resource and Information Group.

ILRIG-Newsletter, 02.01.2013.

Newspaper article

Cessou, S. (2013). Le Régime Arc-En Ciel Discredité. Trois émeutes par jour en Afrique du Sud. In: *Le Monde diplomatique*, 03.2013, pp. 4–5.

Websites

Landau, L. (2012). Marikana, Mayfair and "Legitimate Hate". Available at: http://mg.co.za/article/2012-09-04-marikana-mayfair-and-legitimate-hate [accessed 12.11.2012].

Mosiuoa, T. (2015). Rhodes Must Fall (University of Cape Town, March 2015). Available at: www.okayafrica.com/featured/south-africa-spirit-of-1976-youth-day/ [accessed 26.09.2017].

Index

The letter 'n' after a page number indicates the endnote number.

For Product Safety Concerns and Information please contact our EU
representative GPSR@taylorandfrancis.com Taylor & Francis Verlag GmbH,
Kaufingerstraße 24, 80331 München, Germany

Printed and bound by CPI Group (UK) Ltd, Croydon, CR0 4YY
01/05/2025
01858357-0005